Fatal Links

The Curious Deaths of
Beethoven and the two Napoleons

Fatal Links

The Curious Deaths of Beethoven and the two Napoleons

Gail S. Altman

Auguste-Schöne Publishing
Tallahassee, Florida

Fatal Links: the Curious Deaths of Beethoven and the Two Napoleons
Copyright © 1999 by Gail S. Altman

All rights reserved. Printed and Bound in the United States of America. No part of this book may be used or reproduced in any manner whatsoever without written permission except in the case of brief quotations embodied in critical articles or reviews. For information and reprint permission contact
The Anubian Press/Auguste-Schöne Publishing, P.O. Box 12694, Centerville Station, Tallahassee, Florida 32317-2694

**Publisher's Cataloging-in-Publication
(Provided by Quality Books, Inc.)**

Altman, Gail S.
　Fatal links : the curious deaths of Beethoven and the two Napoleons / Gail S. Altman. -- 1st ed.
　　p. cm.
　Includes bibliographical references and index.
　ISBN: 1-888071-02-8

　1. Beethoven, Ludwig van, 1770-1827--Death and burial. 2. Napoleon I, Emperor of the French, 1769-1821--Death and burial. 3. Bonaparte, Francois-Charles-Joseph, Herzog von Reichstadt, 1811-1832--Death and burial. 4. Malfatti, Johann. 5. Poisoning--Europe.　I. Title

HV6555.E87A58 1999　　　　　364.15'23'094
　　　　　　　　　QBI99-576

Acknowledgements

The author extends grateful appreciation to the Florida State Univesity, Tallahassee, Florida, in particular the Allen Music Library and the Paul Dirac Science Library , and the Special Collections Department of Robert Manning Strozier Library which allowed me to review many rare books and materials. My appreciation also goes to the University itself for granting me special borrowing privileges.

Many thanks must also go to Dr. Pál (Paul) Perjési, pharmacist, chemist, and specialist in toxicology, Senior Lecturer, Department of Medical Chemistry, University Medical School, Pécs, Hungary, for his information, advice, and materials on toxicology he so generously provided to me; and to Klara Nagy, friend, colleague, and ever-willing liaison with Dr. Perjési.

I must also extend my appreciation to Dr. Ben Weider for his fascinating book, for his inspiring courage in presenting this theories in the face of criticism, and for his kind letter to me which encouraged me to conduct my research.

And of course, a loving dedication of this book goes to

my Muses
Burt & Eric
Klara & Kate

Table of Contents

Introduction
...xi

Chapter 1
Poisons & Medicines in the 19th Century
...1

Chapter 2
Drugs & Diseases: Symptomatic Similarities
...7

Interlude
Introducing the Motives
...25

Chapter 3
Austrian Politics 1740-1832
...27

Chapter 4
Beethoven & His Politics
...45

Chapter 5
The Sister-in-Law: Johanna Reiss van Beethoven
...69

Chapter 6
Doctor Under Suspicion: Johann Malfatti
...83

Interlude
Beethoven from 1822-1826
...91

Chapter 7
Beethoven's Last Four Months
...95

Chapter 8
Beethoven's Last Treatments
...103

Chapter 9
The Nephew: Karl van Beethoven
...115

Chapter 10
Johanna van Beethoven Revisited
...141

Chapter 11
The Brother: Nicholas Johann van Beethoven
...145

Chapter 12
Another Sister-in-Law: Therese Obermayr van Beethoven
...149

Chapter 13
The Friends: Anton Schindler & Karl Holz
...155

Chapter 14
The Duke of Reichstadt
...165

Table of Contents

Chapter 15
Another Link: Count Moritz von Dietrichstein
...175

Chapter 16
Malfatti Revisited, 1827
...181

Conclusion
...193

Appendices

A: Common Medicines of the 19th Century...207
B. Toxins & Diseases: a Comparison of Symptoms...209
C. Beethoven's Port-Mortem...213
D. Malfatti's Report on the Health of the Duke of Reichstadt...215
E. The Duke of Reichstadt's Post-Mortem...217

Bibliography
...219

Index
...225

❖ Illustrations ❖

Cover:

(left) Napoleon Bonaparte, (center) Ludwig van Beethoven c. 1818, (right) Franz Karl, Duke of Reichstadt, c. 1830

Following page 94:

Ludwig and Johann van Beethoven
Prince Clemens Metternich and Count Joseph Sedlnitsky
Dr. Johann Malfatti and Dr. Andreas Wawruch
Franz Karl, Duke of Reichstadt
Karl van Beethoven as a Cadet and in later years
Anton Schindler and Karl Holz

Page 126:

Sample of Karl van Beethoven's handwriting, 1827

Introduction

A coincidence is defined as a remarkable but likely accidental occurence of events which suggests but lacks a causal relationship. Yet if enough of these coincidences keep colliding and surround and involve certain people time and time again, the applicability of the term is called into question. Such has been the case with these three men: composer Ludwig van Beethoven; Francis Charles, the Duke of Reichstadt and the natural son and heir of Napoleon Bonaparte, and the doctor who treated them both at critical times in their lives, Guiseppi (Johann) Malfatti.

The trigger which set off the investigation that ultimately resulted in this book was a visit in 1995 to Florida State University in Tallahassee, Florida, by Dr. Ben Weider. Dr. Weider was, at the time of this writing, president of the International Napoleonic Society, and came to address the FSU community in conjunction with his latest book, *Assassination on St. Helena Revisited.* This book was, as its title suggests, a revision of one of Weider's earlier books, *Assassination on St. Helena* and incorporated both new research findings and material from another work, *Who Killed Napoleon?* written in 1978 and 1961, respectively. These earlier works, which put forth Weider's controversial theory about the death of Napoleon Bonaparte, had been written in conjunction with the late Sten Forshufvud, a Swedish dentist who was also a brilliant amateur toxicologist. In them, Weider and Forshufvud claimed and offered substantial proof for the fact that Napoleon had not died of stomach cancer, the long-accepted cause of his death, but that he had been systematically poisoned, and by a member of his own staff. More about the Weider-Forshufvud theory on the death of Napoleon will be covered later. It is important at this point only to note that it was Weider's visit to FSU and his book that provided the coincidence central to my own research.

Weider's lecture was so fascinating that I was compelled to read *Assassination Revisited*, and bought a copy that same weekend. As engrossing as any modern murder mystery, it was a quick read, and I soon reached a brief discussion on Napoleon's son, the Duke of Reichstadt, which had not been included in Weider's previous book. The Duke's mother had been Marie-Louise, the daughter of Franz I, Emperor of Austria. Although the Duke had been raised Austrian, and many had tried to shield him from knowledge of his famous father, there had been no way to keep the young man's natural curiosity about his heritage at bay. And the more he learned about his father, the more determined he became to follow in Bonaparte's footsteps, an ambition that the Austrian government had tried desperately to circumvent, but failed to do so. The Duke died young, barely 21, and, as Weider pointed out, had exhibited the same symptoms and pattern of illness as his famous father even though the official causes of their deaths were vastly different: Napoleon's being ascribed to stomach cancer and his son's to tuberculosis. It was Weider's contention that the Duke, obviously a problem to the Austrian government, had been dispatched by poison. Napoleon II following in the dark footsteps of Napoleon I.

In this discussion, one name sprang out at me as if someone had highlighted it on the page: Malfatti. As a long-time scholar of Beethoven, this name was very familiar to me. Beethoven had had a close association with the Malfatti family around 1809-1810, and with Dr. Johann Malfatti in particular from 1809 to 1817, and again at the time of the composer's death in 1827. But was the Malfatti mentioned in the Weider book as Napoleon II's doctor, his surname given only, the same Malfatti as had been known by and served as physician to Beethoven? And if so, was there any significance to the seeming coincidence that a person named Malfatti had been associated with both Beethoven and the Duke of Reichstadt just prior to their deaths?

In Weider appendix was a letter to him from the FBI which gave me an address by which I could contact him. I inquired and Weider responded: Yes, the Malfatti mentioned in his book was indeed Dr. Giovanni (Johann) Malfatti, an acclaimed physician in the Austrian court. Because Weider had not done extensive research specifically on the Duke of Reichstadt, he could not say with absolute certainty that Malfatti had been responsible for the premature death of the duke. Yet he would not dismiss the idea, either. He was convinced that the duke had been poisoned in much the same way as his father, and it made sense to him that the government would use a man like Malfatti to accomplish this end. For my part, I had long harbored an uneasy feeling about Malfatti and his treatment of Beethoven, both in 1817 when Beethoven suffered odd symptoms including mental aberrations, and again ten years later at the time of his death. Malfatti's unexpected connection to another "murder victim" gave me the impetus to research the issue more thoroughly.

One other thing in Weider's book drew my attention. In the appendix was a list of symptoms relating to arsenic intoxication. I copied them and e-mailed them to a friend of mine, asking "Reading these, who do you think of?" Her answer: "That's too easy. Beethoven, of course." Only it was not to Beethoven that this list of symptoms alluded, but Napoleon Bonaparte.

Armed with that information and rising suspicion, it became my quest to determine whether these men had indeed suffered natural deaths or whether opportunists had taken advantage of their already precarious health to dispatch them to their graves earlier than nature had intended. And if there was enough evidence to suspect an unnatural cause of death, I also felt it was important to find links between these three men—Beethoven, Napoleon II and Malfatti—and to ascertain whether the good doctor had, in fact, gotten away with murder. Why has he not been a suspect up until now? Perhaps because the physicians who have studied the medical histories of both Beethoven and Napoleon II, good doctors themselves, could not conceive of a colleague— even one far removed in time—purposefully doing harm to a patient, of violating a sacred professional oath. Of course, it is possible that Dr. Malfatti had simply been in the wrong place at the wrong time and someone else was to blame. As we shall see, there are other suspects who had the means, motives and opportunities to push Beethoven and Napoleon II into early graves. Whatever the case however, I felt that neither credentials nor personal relationships should put a person above suspicion. The century in which these men lived was a politically volatile time and many people were more concerned with their own well-being than with morals and ethics.

In some ways, this book is a historical "who-done-it," but although it would be tempting from the standpoint of selling books to talk about "murder" and foul play, I must note at the outset that this book is not an attempt to prove that either Beethoven or Napoleon II had been murdered outrightly. Admittedly, throughout his life, Beethoven had been a sick man. He suffered endlessly from various physical ailments, including what doctors today have determined was probably a form of irritable bowel syndrome, or chronic gastroenteritis, or even Crohn's disease, as well as other ailments known to us today which were unfamiliar to doctors in the 19th century. Medical reviews of Beethoven's autopsy results show conclusively that he suffered from cirrhosis of the liver which contributed to his death, although even in this I must put forth from the outset that the cause of this disease may not be as apparent as most scholars have thought. Of course, it is possible that even without outside intervention from someone intent on "doing away" with Beethoven, he might not have lived a very long time beyond the 56 years he had. Yet until the autopsy showed graphically his chronic ailments, it is unlikely that even his physicians knew he was mortally ill until he was but a short time away from death. After all, he had a strong constitution, and he had been on the point of death before and recovered. There was little reason to believe that he might not pull through one more time.

Napoleon II, likewise, was not in optimum health during his short lifetime. He was rather frail and prone to illness. Yet shortly prior to his death, he had been ascertained to be in good health, at least acceptable enough to withstand the rigors of army life.

It is my contention, then, that Beethoven's and Napoleon II's deaths had not so much been caused, as they had been insured, and that it had been someone's intention to make certain Beethoven did not recover from his illness in 1826, and then to carry out a similar task in 1832 with Napoleon II. Interestingly, Beethoven had been politically intertwined with the Duke of Reichstadt and those men surrounding him, and the composer's political leanings had become an annoyance, if not an actual threat, to the Austrian government. Likewise, as he became an adult, the presence of Napoleon II became an embarrassment and a concern to the Court. Such people were not readily tolerated and, in those days, eliminating obstacles was not very difficult.

In 1996, during the course of my research, the Center for Beethoven Studies at San Jose State University in California, acquired a lock of Beethoven's hair. At the time, I inquired as to the provenance and testing of the hair, noting that my specific interest was in arsenic or other toxins which might have been present at the time of his death. I was told that, initially, only an evaluation of the opium content of the hair would be made. Shortly thereafter it was determined that Beethoven had not taken any opium or derivative during his final illness. The results were distributed both to the members of the American Beethoven Society and to the media. No further tests were planned at the time but I was assured that we—the members of the American Beethoven Society to which I belong—would be informed if other tests were ordered.

I was thus surprised by an article which appeared November 30, 1998 in the *New York Times Magazine* entitled " Beethoven's Hair Tells All!" by Phillip Weiss, discussing further testing of the hair, specifically for arsenic and mercury. Further, the article noted that the results of these

Introduction

tests would not be revealed until the publication of a book on the subject, to be authored by Russell Martin and issued early in the year 2000. The director of the Beethoven Center, Dr. William Meredith, wrote to the internet discussion list "Ludwig" on December 2, 1998:

> It is indeed true that a writer named Russell Martin is writing a book on the lock of hair for Broadway Books. He has been doing a tremendous amount of research in Europe and the United States. Ira Brilliant and Dr. Guevara [joint owners of the lock] have signed an agreement to keep the work of the three men on the history of the lock of hair and any new test results unpublished until Mr. Martin finished his research and writes his book.

As there seemed to me to be little reason for anyone to do "tremendous research" on the issue of poisoning unless there was a basis for it (i.e. that there had been positive results for one or both of these substances, or other toxins), I felt that my original premise must have been correct: Indeed, shortly thereafter I learned via a correspondent in Norway, that tests for lead had been done on the hair and found to be positive. The implications of these results will be discussed more fully later; for the time being I felt assured that, as I had suspected, Beethoven (and most like Napoleon II, too) had been helped to an early grave.

Because I am not now and will not be privy to the results of these scientific tests, but must rely on various documentation, I must confess that this book is not, nor should it be, the final word on this issue. It is meant to be a prelude to research and test results which may eventually and conclusively determine criminal involvement (or not) in the deaths of Beethoven and Napoleon. Yet to wait for iron-clad evidence to emerge before publishing this book seemed wrong. The evidence at hand already is so compelling, so fascinating, that I felt the general public would find it as interesting as I did. Those who prefer a more scholarly or academically oriented book may wish to consult Mr. Martin's when it comes to press. Since beginning my research, I also have learned that in 1994 Dutch author Harke de Roos had entertained the notion that Beethoven may have been poisoned. I have only a rudimentary understanding of his theory and, as I do not speak Dutch, it is unlikely I will ever be able to delve more deeply into it. Correspondents in the Netherlands have suggested that his "fantastic theory" was based on "twisted facts," but not having studied his work myself, I can neither refute nor confirm that opinion. However, while his evidence and suspects must remain a mystery to me, I do know that I, myself, have found an incredible amount of "straight" facts that have led me to the same conclusion as de Roos. Thus I feel de Roos's instincts and theories deserve recognition. I also recall Dr. Weider noting that when established Napoleonic scholars learned of his and Forshufvud's theory of Napoleon Bonaparte's murder by poison, they had proclaimed it "amusingly far-fetched." Now, of course, those same scholars have had to dine on those words. I suspect that those who have offered me similarly bemused words regarding Beethoven will soon enjoy the same fare.

To my knowledge, no other book, perhaps not even de Roos's, has ever linked Beethoven with Napoleon II and Dr. Malfatti, and it was no doubt only a fortunate happenstance that Malfatti's name caught my eye in a book that had no connection to my primary historical interest, Beethoven. It is my hope that the findings in this book will stimulate others to seek the truth and, perhaps, even allow justice to prevail.

Chapter 1
Poisons and Medicines in the 19th Century

How could Beethoven possibly have been poisoned without anyone—either in his own time or in our medically advanced time—suspecting foul play? Several factors might account for a lack of suspicion. One, Beethoven was plagued with periodic bad health for almost the last three decades of his life. Two, during his life and particularly through his last illness, he was attended by physicians—actually a common ploy of poisoners, as we shall see—and this perhaps averted any doubts about his treatment by their modern-day colleagues. Three, medicines were radically different in Beethoven's day from those we now know. Although a few have come down to us through time, like digitalis—used in the treatment of heart ailments which was derived from the foxglove plant—many fell out of use because of their potential danger to the patients they were designed to cure. The greatest percentage—some experts have estimated it as high as 90%—of a 19th century doctor's medicines were either inks, dyes, or poisons. In addition, there were no regulations on the sale of poisons to the man on the street. With easy availability (one might be surprised to learn what an easy commodity poison was to come by), it is little wonder that poisons were the means of choice for anyone desiring to do away with an unsavory person in his or her life. Fourth, the symptoms exhibited by a person as a result of having ingested a toxic substance are remarkably similar to known diseases. It is often difficult for our 20th century practitioners to recognize symptoms of poisoning in a patient; we can thus well imagine how it was nearly impossible for their 19th century counterparts—without sophisticated testing at their disposal—to do so. Finally, the fifth factor that might have diverted suspicion away from poison as a possible link to Beethoven's death was his occupation. As a skeptical friend of mine noted, he had been "just a composer." In cases where the victim occupied a position of power or potential power, such as in the cases of Napoleon and the Duke of Reichstadt, his son and heir, many might have suspected poison, but either were reluctant to voice their suspicions or did not have the means to prove them. But Beethoven? Who would want to kill Beethoven? Little wonder that no one has assumed anything but natural causes for his death. The reader may be surprised later on to find not only several possible motives for Beethoven's death, but a substantial number of suspects from whom we will have to choose.

First, however, it is important at this point to look at a brief history of drugs and poisons used in Beethoven's time to determine if, indeed, it is logical to suggest that a toxic substance could have been used to bring Beethoven to the brink of his grave.

THE STATUS OF DRUGS IN THE EARLY 19TH CENTURY

The livelihood of the 19th century chemist and druggist depended upon his ability to meet his customers' needs. Fortunately for him, these needs were grounded in the old tradition of family self-medication. Self-diagnosis and treatment of ailments were the standard practice at all levels of society, rich or poor. It was the ordinary person, rather than a trained physician, who regularly dispensed medicines to friends, family members, and servants. Laymen believed, probably with good reason given that a doctor's cure rate in those days was rather poor, that they could understand illness and treat it just as effectively as any medical practitioner. By the late 18th century, middle-class families commonly stocked their larders with drugs and medicines bought from the chemist or druggist who supplied them by concocting family recipes. The regulation of drugs in terms of what was available and to whom did not become the subject of debate until the second half of the 19th century, well after the deaths of Beethoven and the two Napoleons.

In the 1840s, for example, movements such as Medical Botany even opposed the professionalism of medicine itself, claiming that every person had the right to be his own physician. Another movement, called Coffinism after Albert Isaiah Coffin who championed herbal remedies, asserted that

> the licensed to kill enters the house of sickness and, at the bedside, takes in charge, with the authority of law, his exclusive right over the prostrate victim, whose blood he draws, whose frame he tortures, whose bowels he secretly poisons, and whose

disease he cures, or, at his will, prolongs, but kill or cure, hischange is made in amount wholly at his own discretion.[1]

Thousands perish under their hands who would otherwise have survived. Mercury, opium, alcohol, and the use of the lancet (for bloodletting) are of themselves sufficient to account for the speedy depopulation of the world.[2]

Obviously these groups did not have a very positive view of physicians! In many ways, however, they were justified in their criticisms. Drugs we now know to be harmful or even deadly, have dangerous side effects, or cause serious addictions were prescribed as remedies for a variety of, and sometimes even unrelated, illnesses. Opium, for example, was prescribed in numerous preparations not only as an analgesic and narcotic, but also as a diaphoretic and as a remedy against diarrhea, vomiting and cough. In his *Elements of Medicine* John Brown (1735-88) had recommended opium as the strongest and most diffusible stimulant, the powers of which surpassed those of ether, camphor, volatile alkali, musk and alcohol. (Fortunately, we know from the testing of his hair, that Beethoven did not partake of opium, even when he suffered the most excruciating pain at the end of his life.) Products were crudely formulated and dosages were difficult to control, making even those medicines doled out by physicians potentially dangerous. Remedies in a more controllable pill form were available from the early 19th century on, but these consisted mainly of substances such as aloes, powdered ginger and soap. (See Appendix A for commonly used medicinal herbs.) Most medications took the form of powders and tinctures, and if one considers how the difference of one grain or one drop extra can change a medicine from a relatively harmless substance to a deadly poison (such as in the case of tartar emetic which in small doses simply induces vomiting but in larger doses can cause hemorrhage), it is little wonder that prescriptions could be so potentially dangerous. Inadvertent poisoning certainly could have been the case with Beethoven. Schindler reported that if, for example, a doctor prescribed a teaspoon, Beethoven sometimes took it upon himself to increase the dosage to a tablespoon, believing—as even some people do today—that if a little will cure, a little more will cure faster. Such careless attention to a doctor's prescription could have been very serious, even deadly.

The 18th and 19th century saw a great emphasis on the use of drastic remedies such as purgatives and emetics. Factual knowledge about medicines tended to be ignored by most physicians and pharmacists, and

---

[1] Holloway, 83   [2] Holloway, 84

the complications of polypharmacy were still widely accepted and applied. Disputes arose between homeopaths—those who believed a person could be cured by receiving small doses of substances that in large doses would produce symptoms similar to the disease—and allopaths—those who believed a person could be cured by receiving medicines that produced the opposite effects of the disease, actually similar to the way medicine is practiced today.

Before 1841, then—long after Beethoven's death, and even nine years after Napoleon II's—a person was free to buy any drug or poison he wished, in any quantity, without restriction from the chemist or the necessity of a medical prescription. Even when there was an actual prescription issued by the doctor, there was only a minimum of medical control because it belonged to the patient and could be refilled indefinitely. Since the majority of raw materials for the production of these drugs were so cheap, and the competition between vendors was so fierce, they obligingly made the most potent substances obtainable to everyone, with the possible exception of the totally destitute who could not afford them. Pennyworths of poison, observed John Simon in 1854, were handed across the counter as nonchalantly as cakes of soap.

In many countries (France, Norway, Sweden, Denmark, Finland, Russia and Germany) there were strict laws governing the education, qualification, examination, and licensing of chemists and druggists. (England was considerably behind the rest of Europe in the regulation of the profession.) But the sale of poisons, supposedly to be used for the killing of rats, mice, and other vermin, was not regulated anywhere until late in the 19th century. In the 1840s, some prohibitions were set up in the sale of arsenic and prussic (hydrocyanic) acid. The buyer had to be 21 years of age, accompanied by two witnesses to the sale, and the details of the transaction was to be recorded in a book. By the 1850s the seller was required to keep a register, noting the name and address of the buyer, the exact time of the transaction, and the precise quality and quantity of the substance bought. No doubt the authorities finally began to notice that other beings besides common pests were dying somewhat mysteriously. In addition, the pharmacist was to ask the buyer for the reason behind the purchase and record the buyer's response in case later on there was reason to suspect that the substance had been used in the commission of a crime. How effective this law was is difficult to judge, but one has a hard time imagining the buyer confessing to wanting poison to do away with Uncle Harry in order to inherit his fortune. In Beethoven's day, of course, no such restrictions were present. Poison was still sold as nonchalantly as any other grocery item. Thus the means for poisoning an undesirable was open to virtually anyone, although a knowledge of the actions of poisons on one's victim certainly would be helpful if the death was to seem as natural as possible. The sudden collapse of a perfectly healthy person would seem very suspicious. Most poisonings were carried out over a period of time, even years, gradually undermining the victim's health until the final fatal dose was administered. By then, the victim's death would come as no surprise to anyone.

In Beethoven's case, those likely to have the most knowledge about various toxins included his brother, Johann, who was by trade a pharmacist, and by association, his wife, Therese. We could also include Beethoven's other sister-in-law, Johanna who had had an affair with a medical student, and likewise by association, her son Karl. Interestingly, Napoleon II shares one knowledgeable person with Beethoven: the doctor who attended them both, Johann Malfatti. With the ready availability of poisons, however, we would be remiss to discount any of our suspects on the basis of perceived lack of medical knowledge. Only the very young or the very ignorant would fail to realize that poison can be deadly, and besides, detailed accounts of famous poisonings and how they were accomplished were accessible to anyone.

Chapter 2
Drugs and Diseases: Symptomatic Similarities

THE TOXINS

Because arsenic was my primary suspicion in regard to Beethoven, I will present the consequences of arsenical intoxication first, showing how these are related to him. Not being a person with a medical background, I have had to rely on the expertise of physicians to answer my many questions about the effects of arsenic and other metals on a human being, beyond the obvious. Naturally, if the poison is administered in a highly toxic dosage, it will be fatal. But what it is administered in small doses? What then? What effects does it have on the human body? Are any portions of the body more likely to be affected than others? Does how the poison was administered matter? And most important, what symptoms are manifested and are there any that are exclusively associated with a toxin rather than a natural disease? While medical books and articles on toxicology were helpful, many of my questions were fielded by Dr. Paul Perjési at the University Medical Center in Pécs, Hungary, and his assistance was both appreciated and enlightening.

ARSENIC: TOXIC LEVELS

Although I do not presently have the data on Beethoven's hair taken in 1827, when it is finally made available it will be interesting to compare the levels of arsenic found in it (if any) to that which was found in Napoleon. Tests on Napoleon's hair showed 10.38 and 10.58 parts per million (p.p.m.) of arsenic in two separate samples. A normal reading for that time period, because of fewer chemicals being present in the environment, should not have exceeded today's norm of 0.86 p.p.m. and in fact, should have read no higher than 0.65 p.p.m. It is obvious that the amount of arsenic in Napoleon's body drastically exceeded the normal amount present in a human body. Although it is unfortunate that we do not have hair samples from Beethoven from the crucial years of 1815-1817, his symptoms speak loudly enough on their own.

Hair is a useful source of testing because it readily absorbs and retains residuals of various substances that the person might have ingested. The average person's hair grows approximately .35 mm per day, thus the hair samples used for both Beethoven and Napoleon were grown in the last six months to one year of their lives. Human hair contains arsenic naturally, but in such small amounts that it is not detectable by chemical means. There are several ways that arsenic can come to be deposited in the hair: diet, respiration (although Beethoven was not anywhere where the industrial use of arsenic would have been taken in this way), in hair pomades (which Beethoven, whose hair was always allowed to grow *au naturale,* did not use), enemas (which we know Beethoven was administered, at least during his last days), and vesicatories (also among his prescriptions). If Beethoven's hair tests positively for any toxin, it will be possible to cut the remaining hairs into sections and thus determine a timeline—such as was done in Napoleon's case—as to when the toxin(s) had be administered to him. This data can then be placed into a historical context in order to perhaps narrow the list of suspects, i.e. who was with him at the time ingestion took place.

THE IMMUNE SYSTEM

An important initial effect of arsenic on the system is that it can suppress the immune system and leave a person susceptible to natural disease and infection. According to Drs. Burns, Meade and Munson,"As with many other metals, exposure to low concentrations of *As* (arsenic) often leads to enhanced immune response while exposure to higher concentrations results in immuno-suppression."[1] In the late 19th century, it was common for minute amounts of arsenic to be prescribed as "strengthening tonics," however the amounts ingested were not enough to cause the toxic reactions Beethoven suffered. In the case of Beethoven, he may have received just enough arsenic for it to have acted upon him in a way similar to HIV or AIDS, which destroys or severely damages a person's immune system. This is an important consideration in Beethoven's case, because his medical history shows he was already susceptible to illness, and arsenic certainly would have weakened his already low natural defenses. When one compounds the effects of arsenic with small amounts

---

[1] "Toxic Responses of the Immune System," 376

of alcohol—such as Beethoven drank—the results can be disastrous. Neumayr also who pointed out that even raw oysters could be extremely dangerous to persons with adversely affected immune systems. Beethoven's conversation books have several references to him eating and enjoying oysters, both fried and raw. Many restaurants and grocery stores who serve or sell raw oysters today issue disclaimers that persons with damaged natural immunity—such as those with AIDS—should avoid eating raw oysters because they carry bacteria which can cause such illnesses as hepatitis. Naturally, in Beethoven's day, no such connections were made, but one can only imagine the possible contamination levels of the oysters or fish he consumed in a time when raw sewage often was dumped into city water supplies.

DISEASE OF THE LIVER

Interestingly, arsenic and related toxins—although they are deposited in all parts of the body—concentrate in the bowel, the liver, the kidneys, and the stomach. Once ingested, it does not leave the body readily so that the effect of small doses administered over time becomes cumulative. Thus a serious, life-threatening consequence of arsenical intoxication is that it can cause cirrhosis of the liver. Moslen writes in her article "Toxic Responses of the Liver" that

> Many industrial compounds and therapeutic agents are well established as injurious to the liver... Factors are known that determine why the liver, as opposed to other organs, is the dominant target for specific toxins. ... The liver is the first organ to encounter ingested nutrients, vitamins, metals, drugs, and environmental toxicants... All the major functions of the liver can be detrimentally altered by liver injury resulting from acute or chronic exposure to toxicants.[2]

Rice and Cohen corroborate this in "Toxic Responses of the Skin," noting that "The liver appears to be the major site of arsenic biotransformation."[3] as does Goyer in "Toxic Effects of Metals"[4]: "Neurotoxicity usually begins with sensory changes, parethesia (abnormal sensations usually of the skin), and muscle tenderness followed by weakness. More chronic ... exposures producing more gradual, insidious effects may occur over a period of years." The liver attempts to deal with the arsenic's toxicity much

---
[2]Moslen, 403
[3]Rice and Cohen, 543
[4]Goyer, 697

as it attempts to metabolize alcohol, but repeated doses of the poison soon render the liver's ability to do so inadequate to protect the body from its effects.

Repeated dosages of arsenic over a period of time—as short as eighteen months—can damage the liver so that the scarring associated with cirrhosis develops. As Moslen writes

> With repeated chemical insults, destroyed hepatic cells are replaced by fibrotic scars. With continuing fibrosis, the architecture of the liver is disrupted by interconnecting fibrous scars. When the liver becomes subdivided by scar tissue surrounding nodules of regenerating heaptocytes, this is termed cirrhosis. Cirrhosis is not reversible and has a poor prognosis for survival. Cirrhosis is usually a result of repeated exposure to chemical toxins.[5]

Toxins, and in particular arsenic, fall into one of the top three causes of cirrhosis which includes viral hematites and other infections, and chronic alcohol abuse accompanied by malnutrition. There is no doubt that Beethoven suffered from cirrhosis and that it contributed to his death, but how did he develop this condition in the first place? Infection and alcohol have always been put forth as the most likely causes, and, unfortunately, many people still ascribe to the erroneous view that Beet-hoven had been a heavy drinker. Up until now, toxins have not been explored as a probably cause. But what if he had ingested enough arsenic at various points in his life for it to be a viable cause? Although a liver suffering slight damage can regenerate, if it is damaged repeatedly (as happens when arsenic is ingested over time) there comes a point when the liver can no longer generate new cells. Arsenic and related toxins kills off cells and fibrous tissue is deposited around all the small vessels within the organ. The lobes of the liver become scarred, eventually interfering with the flow of blood, with the liver's ability to store nutrients, and, most importantly, with its ability to detoxify chemicals either produced by the body or introduced from outside. Thus the damage inflicted by repeated doses of arsenic would become cumulative to the point where the liver was no longer able to function as a filter for subsequent toxins. The person becomes even more sensitive to substances such as alcohol, even taken in small quantities as was Beethoven's habit. As Goyer noted

> Lifestyle factors such as smoking or alcohol ingestion mayhave indirect influences on toxicity. Cigarette smoke by itself contains

---

[5]Moslen, 409

some toxic metals such as cadmium. ... Alcohol ingestion may influence toxicity indirectly by altering diet and reducing essential mineral intake.[6]

We know that Beethoven was in the habit not only of drinking small quantities of wine, but also of enjoying a pipe on a regular basis. Either or both factors could have contributed to the increasing toxic effects that ingesting arsenic already had on him.

The way that Beethoven's cirrhosis clinically manifested itself was not consistent with the type of cirrhosis caused by alcohol. Externally these signs include redness of the skin on the palms of the hands due to congestion of the capillaries, spider-shaped dilated blood vessels on the skin as a whole but particularly on the chest, enlarged mammary glands in males, shrunken sex organs in males, and significant loss of body hair. Although Beethoven may have had these manifestations, none were noted by any of his doctors nor by the pathologist who performed the autopsy. The latter noted only the condition of the liver itself which, indeed, did show signs of advanced cirrhosis. However, a liver suffering from advanced cirrhosis induced by alcohol shows micronodules; Beethoven's was noted as having macronodules. If the majority of persons suffering from alcohol-induced cirrhosis have these tell-tale signs, perhaps we must look elsewhere for the cause of Beethoven's cirrhosis. Certainly viral hepatitis cannot be ruled out. However, there are times in Beethoven's life when the symptoms he exhibited match rather remarkably those of arsenical intoxication, thus it is my contention that this cause cannot be ruled out either. Interestingly, many of the symptoms of hepatitis and other natural diseases are shared with those induced by toxins, which may have been the primary reason that a toxic cause for Beethoven's disease has been overlooked.

ANTIMONY, MERCURY, AND LEAD

Antimony was discovered in the 17th century and is a member of the arsenic family. It is used legitimately for alloying in the production of metals and is often combined with tin and lead. Because of the hardness it imparts to metals, it was used in the production of type for the printing trade. It was also used in the dyeing of cloth. Medicinally, antimony was an ingredient in the often-prescribed tartar emetic (potassium antimonyl tartrate) which was used in doses of a few hundredths of a grain to induce vomiting. Antimony is very irritating to mucous membranes and tissues,

---

[6]Goyer, 693

thus it is interesting to note that in Beethoven's journal for 1815 he made a notation that read "althea root," which is a marshmallow root used medicinally to soothe irritated mucous membranes. Chronic antimony poisoning is very similar to arsenic poisoning with symptoms that may include itchy skin, pustules, stomatitis, conjunctivitis, laryngitis, headache, morbid thirst, anorexia (weight loss) and anemia. In acute poisoning, symptoms can include nausea and vomiting, severe diarrhea with mucus and later with blood. Hemorrhagic nephritis (inflammation and degeneration of the kidneys) and hepatitis (inflammation of the liver) may occur concomitantly. Antimony was less frequently used in the case of deliberate poisoning because it has a bitter metallic taste that can be easily detected in food and drink even when highly diluted. However, because it was used medicinally, deliberate overdoses of prescribed antimony certainly occurred. In the 19th century and earlier, its symptoms were often confused with those of tuberculosis.

Mercury is a highly toxic, silver-white liquid metal which is slightly volatile at ordinary temperatures. It is readily absorbed by the skin or through inhalation of its fumes. Mercury salts were widely used in medicine as cathartics, antiseptics, and diuretics, and in topical ointments and salves. As mercurous chloride it was called "calomel" used to induce vomiting. Most people associate the use of mercury with the treatment of syphilis and other venereal diseases, however, it was commonly used to treat a variety of ailments, thus it would be wrong to conclude that if mercury was found in a person's tissues they had been treated for a venereal disease. Every known form of mercuric compound is potentially dangerous, thus intoxication was rather wide-spread. Symptoms of mercurial intoxication can include acute gastrointestinal inflammation, a metallic taste in the mouth, extreme thirst, nausea, vomiting—sometimes of blood—and pain in the pharynx and abdomen. If a person is subjected to subsequent high doses of mercury, he may suffer tenemus (a strong urge to urinate or defecate without result), bloody diarrhea due to hemorrhagic gastritis and colitis, uremia (bloody urine), and circulatory collapse. Low doses of mercury cause stomatitis, gastritis, colitis, and renal tubular failure. If chronically given, mercury may result in excessive salivation, loosening of teeth, fetor oris (bad breath), gingivitis, and ulceration of the mouth. Neurologically, symptoms may include erethism—a mental state of fatigability, easy embarrassment, irritability, or apprehension—tremors of the hands or feet, and uncontrollability of the tongue and lips causing slurred speech. Beethoven suffered some of these symptoms, but apparently did not have those associated with the mouth.

Lead is most readily absorbed through the digestive tract where it is deposited mainly in the liver and kidneys. Like other toxins, it can also be absorbed through the skin via ointments or wet dressings, such as were commonly used in the 19th century. Vitamin D (produced by exposure to sunlight) stimulates the absorption of lead in the system, and Beethoven's healthful addiction to being out-of-doors in the sunshine may have accounted for more than his tanned skin. Symptoms of lead poisoning are more severe in the case of children, where it can cause brain damage. In adults, lead can cause anorexia, weakness, intermittent vomiting, abdominal pain (colic), alternating diarrhea and constipation, and paralysis of wrists and ankles (a symptom not evident in Beethoven). Depending on the dosage, it can also cause one or more of the following: irritability, drowsiness, optic or papilledema atrophym, retinal pigmentation, coma, paralysis of cranial nerves, elevated cerebrospinal fluid protein contents and pressure. An abnormal concentration of lead reportedly was found in Beethoven's hair, causing a Norwegian newspaper to conclude in a recent article that "Fish Became His Fate-Symphony." Because fish was one of Beethoven's favorite foods, the article suggested that the lead content in fish taken from the Danube River had been of such a high level that it caused Beethoven's death. Two things detract from this conclusion: one, lead is not as toxic to adults as it is to children, and adults are able to tolerate moderates amounts of lead in their systems, thus lead absorbed through environmental factors, unless in unusually high concentrations, would not likely be the cause of death in an adult. Two, if the lead content in the Danube fish was high enough to kill Beethoven, why were there no indications whatsoever that Viennese children were dying in unusual numbers or showing symptoms of brain damage? Further, while lead was used in solder and thus could have passed into Beethoven's food or drink via his eating utensils (metal plates, goblets, or silverware), this would not explain why those around him were not similarly affected. Not one of his association, with the possible exception of Stephan von Breuning, showed any symptoms of lead poisoning. If lead had been the poison—or one of them—that did indeed kill Beethoven, then it most likely had been introduced into his system via medical means—through ointments, wet dressings, or in a prescribed medicine—by someone intent upon using it to deliberately eliminate him.

"AQUA TOFFANA"

The higher-than-normal lead concentration found in Beethoven's hair sample may have an interesting historical connection. Rumors about the poisoning of another famous composer, Wolfgang Mozart, were brought into the 20th century by the play—and later by the film of the same name—*Amadeus*, by Peter Schaffer. Although clearly a fictionalized account of Mozart's death, the reader may be interested to know that the play had a historical basis. There was gossip in Vienna that Mozart had been poisoned and the primary suspect had indeed been professional rival, Antonio Salieri. The gossip was even carried to Beethoven via his Conversation Books, written there by his nephew Karl. Beethoven, of course, dismissed the charges as insulting and ludicrous. Nor do scholars attach any credence to the poisoning story. However, the poison which 19th century rumor-mongers guessed had been used to kill Mozart— probably because of his affected kidneys—was called "aqua toffana." Aqua toffana is a combination of antimony, white arsenic, and lead—an interesting consideration because of the high concentrations of lead supposedly found in Beethoven's hair. The poison was named for its creator, a Sicilian woman named Julia Tofana, who used this deadly mixture to commit a few notorious murders.

Because one of the leading experts on poisons in Mozart's time, Dr. Matthias von Sallaba of the University of Vienna, was at Mozart's bedside during his final illness—and he did not give credence to the story—we may be able to put the rumor of Mozart's murder to rest. Two things cause one to wonder, however:

1. As the reader will learn later, it was common practice to ensure the presence of a doctor at the victim's bedside while the latter was being fed poison and

2. Symptoms occurring as a result of ingesting a toxin are usually similar if not identical to natural diseases and the two were very often confused for each other.

My main point here is not to reopen the case of Mozart's alleged poisoning but to illustrate that the toxicity of various substances— including lead, which reportedly was in Beethoven's system in a significant concentration at the time of his death—was rather well known to the population at large. Many "tips" on poisons and techniques of poisoning were described in astonishing detail in newspapers, journals, and popular fiction of the time. Many people were acquainted with a book called *The History of Mme de Brinvilliers*—it was, in fact, read by the wife of Napoleon's poisoner, Montholon—which recounted the story of the sweet and gentle Marquise de Brinvilliers who poisoned her doting father in order to gain his fortune. She was a subtle poisoner, giving her father just enough arsenic to make him unwell and undermine his health without outrightly killing him. His doctors remained confused as to the source of his recurring illness. Over a period of eight months, the Marquise fed her father some 28 to 30 doses of arsenic. When the old man finally died, the doctors conducting the autopsy concluded that he had died a natural death. The Marquise perhaps would have gotten away with murder if she herself had not been so imprudent as to have kept a careful record of her poisonings! We see from this example that a person could be poisoned without suspicions being aroused, particularly if a physician is in regular attendance.

SYMPTOMS: A COMPARISON:

It is useful at this point to compare the symptoms of poisoning with those expressed by Beethoven—in his own letters or by those persons with whom he came in contact—between 1815 and 1818. Since many other common 19th century medicines, if used in excess, could cause severe adverse reactions or even death, the reader may wish to refer to Appendix B for a listing of medications in use during Beethoven's time.

The major symptoms of arsenic poisoning, for example, include frequent headaches, abdominal pain, general fatigue, pain in the limbs, joints and area of the liver, a noticeable change in disposition, and difficulty in walking. All of these were exhibited by Beethoven during this time. Beethoven complained of "colics" (stomach pains) and "rheumatism" (general aches and pains in the joints). He expressed having difficulty in "locomotion" and of extreme fatigue that kept him indoors a great deal and often confined to bed. Further, he reportedly had eye pains (possibly conjunctivitis or similar disease of the eye) which often is another symptom of arsenical poisoning. In his discussion on the poisoning of Napoleon who was known to suffer from arsenical intoxication based on hair sample analysis, Dr. Weider wrote:

> A modern day German pathologist, Dr. A Heffter, a specialist researching in the intricacies of diagnosis in cases of arsenic intoxication, writes that it is unforgivable not to suspect arsenic intoxication when gastric trouble is coupled with conjunctivitis, eczema or weakness in the legs."[7]

Since Beethoven exhibited the same symptoms as Napoleon Bonaparte, a man known to have received dangerous doses of arsenic, it would be remiss not to entertain the likelihood that Beethoven had shared the French leader's fate.

---

[7]Weider, 433

Arsenic and other toxins also cause liver degeneration, mainly because it is this organ which has the task of removing toxins from the bloodstream. As noted, the liver attempts to regenerate when it suffers damage, but repeated exposure to toxic substances causes the condition known as cirrhosis, in which scar tissue interferes with the organ's normal functioning. A toxin ingested by Beethoven during this time, exacerbated by other factors such a moderate consumption of alcohol or contracting an infection, would no doubt have caused the composer's death by liver cirrhosis some ten years later.

Two symptoms of arsenic intoxication not readily apparent in Beethoven are a bronzing of the skin, masked by the fact that Beethoven was normally quite tanned from being outdoors a great deal, and deafness, hidden by Beethoven's already apparent hearing impairment. Interestingly, at this particular time, Beethoven's hearing deteriorated rapidly though previously it had been in a gradual decline. In a short period of time, he lost nearly all his residual hearing, even though his deafness had been on a slow course for the previous 20 years. We have no specific record that he suffered from itching or any other skin problems normally associated with arsenical intoxication, however, he did tell Countess Erdödy that his doctor had told him to rub a volatile ointment all over his body. Neumayr suggested that this was a remedy prescribed for his "rheumatism." But if so, surely his physician would have specified applying it to joints and other affected areas rather than simply "all over his body." Ointments, we recall, were also a viable means of introducing poisons into a body since many are readily absorbed by the skin, while poisonous substances such as lead and mercury were often used in 19th century topical medicines. Other symptoms of arsenical intoxication of which Beethoven complained were a persistent cough and a "feverish cold." We cannot know in the latter case whether this was an actual fever or simply the sensation of fever; thermometers were not common in the 19th century even in doctor's medical bags. It must be noted that both Napoleon—a known victim of poison—and his son, Napoleon II, complained of recurring fevers during their last illnesses. In both cases, when their temperatures were taken with a thermometer—in Napoleon's case, only one of his doctors happened to have such an instrument on hand—it was found to be normal.

Thus we see that Beethoven displayed many of the symptoms of arsenical intoxication associated with low (non-fatal) doses, the amount which can undermine health and cause a general feeling of unwellness without killing the victim outright. It may not have been his poisoner's intent at the time to cause his death, but merely to incapacitate him. When his behavior became even more intolerable in 1826, a time which coincided with upheavals, revolutionary activities, and unrest among student populations, I believe that higher doses of arsenic or a similar toxin were administered to him. As we will see, in 1827, Beethoven exhibited a possible fifteen out of seventeen known symptoms for acute arsenical intoxication. We will explore this time period more in depth later on, but for now we must focus our concentration on an earlier time, a time when Beethoven's health was seriously undermined with bouts of illness that likely had been induced by unnatural means.

BEETHOVEN IN 1815 THROUGH 1819

What indications do we have that the main root of Beethoven's health problems in later years could have been ingestion of a poison? First, the onset of Beethoven's illness in 1816-1817 was acute. Only briefly does he mention being ill during the previous year and nothing either specific or serious, at least not to the extent that it kept him from working. In March 1815, he noted to Joseph von Varena in Graz that he had been unwell but also "very busy."[8] To the Archduke Rudolph he noted only that he was "not yet in the best of health,"[9] a chronic condition for Beethoven. To his friend, Johann Brauchle in the summer he wrote "I am not well... but as soon as I feel better I will visit you." Beethoven did not withhold news of his illnesses, so we can be relatively certain that he was not simply being stoic. He felt "under the weather" because he had genuine medical conditions which caused him to feel somewhat unwell. However, in 1816, his health took an alarmingly rapid decline:

> (February 1816 to Archduke Rudolph) My condition once again deteriorated so that I was able to take a few walks only in the daytime.[10]

> (May 13, 1816 to Maria Erdödy) ...for the last six weeks I have been in very poor health, so much that frequently I have thought of my death.[11]

> (May 15, 1816 to Maria Erdödy) I ... have not been feeling well at all for a considerable time.[12]

---

[8] Anderson 505
[9] Anderson 506
[10] Anderson, 567
[11] Anderson, 577-578
[12] Anderson, 579

> (July 11, 1816, to Archduke Rudolph) Until now the condition of my chest has not allowed me to do so (visit) notwithstanding all the efforts of my doctor, who on that account did not want me to leave Vienna.[13]

Interestingly, once away from Vienna, he made a remarkable recovery, noting to Dr. Johann Bihler in the Summer of 1816 that "This is just to inform you that at present I am at Baden and in excellent health." But then, in November and back in Vienna once again, he wrote:

> (November 3, 1816 to Nikolaus Zmeskall) Since the 14th of last month I have been continually ill and have had to stay in bed and in my room.[14]

> (November 12, 1816 to Archduke Rudolph) At the beginning of last month, i.e. October, I began to feel ill at Baden; and from October 15th until about eight day ago I was confined to my room and to bed. I had a rather dangerous feverish cold and I am still not allowed to be out of doors for very long.[15]

> (December 31, 1816 to Archduke Rudolph) Ever since the concert for the citizens [i.e. December 26th] I have again had to remain in my room; and it will probably be some time before I shall be able to cease worrying about the state of my health[16]

In other letters from the same year (without specific months and days given) he complains:

> ...my state of health, instead of improving, has become worse; and I am very much afraid lest even at Y.I.H's residence (that of the Archduke Rudolph) something might happen to me. The effects of such a heavy feverish cold are extremely slow to disappear.... The doctor assures me that thanks to this favourable weather my condition ought soon to show a marked improvement... [17]

> Since Saturday my condition has again become worse; and it will certainly be some days before I can wait upon Y.I.H. once more...[18]

---

[13] Anderson, #640, II, 584
[14] Anderson, #669, II, 610
[15] Anderson #671, II, 612
[16] Anderson, #688, II, 625
[17] Anderson, #712, II, 637
[18] Anderson, #714, II, 638

> I had not been well for a few days before Your Highness sent me your message... on that very day when Y.I.H. sent the message I became worse and a heavy feverish cold set in.[19]

This "feverish cold" continued throughout 1816.

> To Archduke Rudolph: An attack of colic to which I suddenly succumbed yesterday evening prevents me from waiting upon you today..[20]

His symptoms included problems with his chest, though he did not say specifically what his situation was. He complained of a "feverish cold" more than once, attacks of colic, weakness and difficulty in walking. In addition, his mental state became erratic. He thought of death. He told the Archduke that he had suffered from a "nervous breakdown" (Anderson 636) We see also that he had periods of wellness followed by abrupt relapses, pains in the abdomen, severe cough, and a feeling of fever. By 1817, Beethoven's illnesses became even more severe and more frequent

> (February 15, 1817 to Franz Brentano) As for me, my health has been undermined for a considerable time. ...so far no improvement is to be expected, nay rather, every day there is a further deterioration.[21]

Although better for a while at the end of February, when he noted in a letter on the 23rd to Baroness Dorothea Ertmann that he had suffered "an indisposition which at last seems to be yielding to my healthy constitution,"[22] and yet by the end of March he wrote to his attorney, Johann Kanka that "On October 15th I succumbed to an inflammatory fever, the after effects of which I am still suffering."[23] By April, he told Charles Neate that he was "not yet restored to health"[24] and that his illness had been severe enough even to keep him from composing, which he often did even during bouts of sickness. This same month his illness took an alarming downward turn. His mental health deteriorated even more; he confessed to his friend Nanette Streicher, that he was "in confusion." In a letter to Maria Erdödy written on June 19, 1817, from Heiligenstadt, he described his problems in detail:

> I developed on October 15th a violent feverish cold, so that I had to stay in bed for a very long time; and only after several months was I allowed to go out even for a short while. Until now, the after effects of this illness could not be dispelled. ...

---

[19]Anderson, #728, II, 646 [21]Anderson, #771, II, 676 [23]Anderson, #771, II, 676
[20]Anderson, #   , II, 646 [22]Anderson, #778, II, 679 [24]Anderson, #778, II, 679

> from April 15th until May 4th, I had to take six powders a daily and six bowls of tea. That treatment lasted until May 4th. After that I had to take another kind of powder, also six times daily; and I had to rub myself three times a day with a volatile ointment. ... Since yesterday I have been taking another medicine, namely a tincture, of which I have to swallow 12 spoonfuls daily. ... My hearing has become worse... Everywhere I am abominably treated and am the prey of detestable people. ... my own misery has made me feel depressed. [25]

We note in this letter Beethoven's reference to his hearing, which took a sharp decline. To Nanette Streicher—who, with her husband, took pity on the composer's condition and selflessly ministered to his needs—and at times to others, he began writing a series of letters that show him plunging further and further down into the depths of illness and despair:

> (July 7) There is the distressing prospect that perhaps I may never be cured. I myself am inclined to distrust my present doctor(Staudenheim, who replaced Malfatti) who has finally pronounced my condition to be caused by a disease of the lungs.[26]
>
> (August 21, to Zmeskall) As for me I often despair and would like to die. For I can foresee no end to all my infirmities. God have mercy upon me, I consider myself as good as lost—[27]
>
> (August 25) ...on Friday, became overheated and then felt ill yesterday, which was Sunday, and today I am still far from well—How one feels when one is uncared for, without friends, without everything; left entirely to oneself, and even suffering...[28]
>
> (September 1 to Archduke Rudolph) My ailing condition still persists, and although in some respects there is an improvement yet my complaint is still not absolutely cured. What I have taken and am still taking to cure it are medicines of all kinds and in all forms. Well, at last I must abandon the hope I so often cherished of making a complete recovery—[29]

---

[25] Anderson# 783, II, 683-684
[26] Anderson,#785, II, 686
[27] Anderson, #805, II, 701
[28] Anderson, #806, II, 702
[29] Anderson, #816, II, 708

Drugs and Diseases

> (September 9, to Zmeskall) Owing to a chill I am now feeling very much worse. ... though usually I am very fond of walking, on account of my condition I couldn't go in on foot. ... I now know what it feels like to move daily nearer to my grave.. I shall see you during the next few days, as I must go into town to see the doctor. [30]

> (Autumn) But a few days after you had visited me.... I had a frightful attack of rheumatism, so much so that I am not going out again until tomorrow or the day after.[31]

> (Autumn) I am still feeling unwell... Yesterday and today I had really horrid meals. This person (his servant) can't even think—[32]

Beethoven's mention here of "horrid meals" is of interest because food had to be particularly bad for Beethoven to find it inedible. He will make a similar comment in late 1826 at the home of his brother, when the issue of poisoning arises once again. Some poisons, like antimony, have a bitter taste. The reader might wish to make note of Beethoven's mention of his food here, although I will explore this issue more fully later.

> (December 28) Yesterday I saw your dear kind daughter at my home, but I was so ill that I don't remember very much about her visit. The bitter cold, particularly in this house, gave me a bad chill; and almost the whole day yesterday I could scarcely move a limb. Coughing and the most terrible headaches I have ever had plagued me the whole day. [33]

A few other undated letters[34] from 1817, provide a few more clues:

> I have just received the medicine and fancy that in a few daysI shall be completely cured. I have only one emetic powder. After taking it, should I drink tea frequently? Please let me have a pewter spoon.—

> I have had to take medicine again today.... I feel weaker than than I did yesterday. I tried to go out, but had to turn back after a few minutes.

---

[30] Anderson, #817, II 709
[31] Anderson, #830, II, 716
[32] Anderson, #832, II, 717
[33] Anderson, #839, II, 722-723
[34] All excerpts from Anderson, #850-873, II, 729-740

The housekeeper's departure terrified me so that I was already awake at three o'clock. — My lonely condition demands the assistance of the police.— What a dreadful existence ?!

I am full of vexations today. It is impossible to enumerate them to you. All I can tell you is that I am better, though indeed last night I frequently thought of my death; but in any case such thoughts occur to me occasionally in the daytime as well—

(January 1, 1818) When I got home for the second time, my pain was so severe that all I could do was to lie down on the couch—

(January 1818) I have caught another chill and have a violent cold and cough.

The symptoms Beethoven described are so varied that they do not match any one medical complaint associated with naturally occurring diseases, but they do match remarkably well those associated with arsenical intoxication. When we also look at the health declines in both Napoleon and his son, the reader will no doubt find the similarities as striking and surprising as I did. Both Napoleons had similar patterns of recovery and relapses with symptoms that included cough, severe headache, weakness, stomach pains, pains in the joints, a sensation of fever, anxiety attacks, indications of problems with sleep patterns, and severe depression alternating with optimism.

MENTAL DETERIORATION

Up to this point, I had only mentioned in passing those symptoms relating to mental health. They are, however, significant enough to warrant a more indepth look. Toxins are notorious for the deleterious effects they have upon a person's emotional well-being. It was during this period of time that rumors began circulating in Vienna about Beethoven's impaired mental health. Nettl wrote that "During Beethoven's lifetime, rumors were spread about the condition of his mind and many people intimated that Beethoven might be considered insane. This was especially the case in 1817, (underlining mine) when the Master showed a high degree of excitability and his behavior and appearance deteriorated."[35] After Dr.

---

[35] Nettl, 99

Karl von Bursy visited Beethoven in 1816, the doctor alluded to these rumors in his diary. He described and dismissed Beethoven's attitude... as "*Künstler-Spleen*" (artist's temperament). On December 20 of that same year, the youngest of the Brunswick sisters, Charlotte, made the following statement: "I learned yesterday that Beethoven has become insane. What a terrible loss if this holds true!" Nettl proposed that perhaps these rumors had been started and nourished by Beethoven's sister-in-law, Johanna, who was eager to eliminate Beethoven from the guardianship of her son, Karl. This is not beyond possibility, although this hypothesis ignores Beethoven's own letters which show all too clearly how mentally off-balance he was at this time. Beethoven, however, must have known about these rumors to which Nettl alludes because in a letter he wrote on May 19, 1818 to his friend, Nanette Streicher, he said: "I don't invite you, everything is confused; however they won't lock me up as yet in the madhouse." To the Archduke Rudolph he confessed to having suffered a "nervous breakdown" and he wrote to Wilhelm Christian Müller as late as 1820 that Müller was "not to be misled by the Viennese who regard me as crazy," adding, "if a sincere independent opinion escapes me, as it often does, they think me mad." German composer, Karl Zelter, confided to Goethe in 1819 that "It is said that he is intolerably *maussade*. Some say he is a lunatic." Solomon agreed: "During these years, Beethoven railed openly against the nobility, the courts, and the emperor himself, seemingly oblivious of the possible consequences in Metternich's police state."[36] Nettl pointed out that many psychiatrists confirmed for him that the powers of genius and insanity are closely linked. I cannot dismiss Beethoven's behavior in this way. His extremes in mood coupled with his physical complaints at this time, point not to a peculiarity associated with his genius but to something else quite sinister. It is vital to note that Napoleon Bonaparte suffered similar mental aberrations during times when he most certainly had been poisoned. This brilliant strategist with almost superhuman physical endurance, puzzled his colleagues with his periods of uncertainty, of unwise decisions and confusion.

Although Beethoven certainly was under inordinate amounts of stress at this time (his brother, Caspar Carl had died in 1815; he became embroiled in a bitter custody battle with his sister-in-law Johanna over Carl's son; and his dear friend and confidante, Maria Erdödy had left Vienna to attend to her properties in Padua and Croatia) it is difficult to blame his erratic behavior simply on life circumstances. Paranoia,

---

[36]Solomon, 256

confusion, depression to the point of thinking about death, slovenliness—when personal hygiene had previously been extremely important to him—inordinate flare-ups of temper—even for him—that caused him to hire and fire household staff in rapid succession: this mental state was not exhibited by him even at times when his stress level was as high, such as when faced with the inevitability of deafness. All these manifestations, however, are commonly exhibited by people who have ingested arsenic or other toxins in non-fatal doses. And when did Beethoven most often exhibit these symptoms? At times such as in July of 1816 when he told Frau Streicher that, "Today I have had a fresh plaster put on the nape of my neck." Another time, he talked about having received an "emetic powder" or having been instructed to "rub a volatile ointment all over his body." Is it merely coincidence that his mood swings are connected to these occurrences which just happened to be easy ways to administer poison to a victim?

In July, he wrote an interesting note to Dr. Johann Bihler said that "Doctor Sassafras, whom I told you of, is coming at noon today."[37] Kalischer put forth the idea that Beethoven was referring to Dr. Malfatti in such a way because of his numerous prescriptions. Sassafras is a small tree, the bark of which was used for medicinal purposes, but oil of sassafras is very toxic, causing diarrhea, vomiting and even circulatory collapse in severe cases. Was Beethoven comparing the toxicity of this plant with his doctor? His comment is also curious since he supposedly had dropped Malfatti as his doctor in April; why, then, mention him three months later? Perhaps the initial break had been temporary, but whatever the case, we know that he was in contact with Malfatti's colleague, Andreas Bertolini, throughout 1817.

---

[37] Anderson, #795, II, 694

❖ Interlude ❖
Introducing the Motives

One of the most difficult things to determine in the alleged poisoning of Beethoven has been motive. When I first expressed to a colleague my doubts about his death and suggested that the composer had met a not-quite-so natural end, she was intrigued. No doubt, the symptoms he exhibited at certain points during his life, particularly at the end, closely matched those of Napoleon Bonaparte, known to have been poisoned, and that of Napoleon II, Bonaparte's son whose death is questionable and suspicious. Even so, she was not readily convinced. "What possible motive would someone have for insuring Beethoven's death," she asked, "even if they did not murder him outright? However much he was a genius," she added, "he was still just a composer."

Admittedly, on the surface, she was quite right. It was not readily apparent why anyone should be intent upon ridding Austria of one of its most illustrious composers. The population, and young people in particular, revered and respected him. Nevertheless I was sure that something was amiss in Beethoven's death. Too many things did not add up. Thus despite the fact that my colleague probably thought I was wasting my time pursuing such a crazy notion, I began to search for the elusive motive.

I decided that four things were most important for me to consider in finding this motive. First, I had to look at Beethoven himself, the man he was, the attitudes and philosophies he espoused, the things he believed in. Second, I had to consider the people Beethoven directly associated with, including friends, family, and professional connections, and also with whom they, in turn, associated. Third, it would be important to consider whatever issues or activities—both political and familial—in which Beethoven might have been engaged that might have made his death or incapacitation beneficial to some person or group of persons. Fourth, I felt I needed to understand the times in which Beethoven lived, the political and social climate of Vienna, Austria and the Hapsburg Empire in the early nineteenth century. A study of these four aspects of the Beethoven Homicide Case, as friends jokingly dubbed my inquiry, might provide clues to motive.

There were several possible motives: one, that Beethoven had been eliminated for political reasons, that he had earned enough enemies with his political views and indiscreet speech for someone to think it worthwhile to pursue such a radical course; two, that members of his own family found his behavior so intolerable that they were willing to eliminate him on their own; or three, some combination of the two so that Beethoven's early death was a political-familial collaboration for the benefit of both sides.

But which motive has the most viability? In order to determine this, if not conclusively at least with high probability, we must look at a wide variety of factors which include both the political arena in which Beethoven lived and the family situation in which he found himself during periods of his most suspicious illnesses.

Studying the history of Vienna and Austria during this time period has been a daunting task, requiring the reading and studying of many documents, books and other materials. I will not burden the reader with all the details of this complex time. However, an understanding of the political climate during this crucial time in Beethoven's life is essential. Therefore I beg the reader's indulgence in digressing from Beethoven for a moment to present the following history lesson.

Chapter 3
Austrian Politics 1740-1832

Was the decision to eliminate Beethoven a result of domestic conflicts or could it have been politically motivated? Or both? We cannot begin to answer that until we have a basic understanding of the state of Austria during Beethoven's lifetime. What was the political climate? Could he have been involved in political arenas considered subversive and even dangerous to the Monarchy? Could he have had connections which made those in power nervous? As Erickson pointed out "It may come as a surprise to many readers that the aged Haydn as well as Beethoven and Schubert lived in a Vienna cloaked in an atmosphere of political repression and suspicion."

THE FOUNDATIONS OF THE AUSTRIAN MONARCHY

Empress Maria Theresa came to the throne in 1740 and she was the monarch responsible for creating a vast and complicated state bureaucracy answerable only to the government. At this time Austrians had a very limited concept of constitutional and individual liberty. However, Maria Therese's son and successor, Joseph II, carried out many radical reforms during his ten-year reign (1780-1790). His "Toleration Patent" left Catholicism as the dominant religion of the Monarchy, but allowed other faiths to build their own churches and schools, although he did close some 700 monasteries. Marriage was made a purely civil contract. A new penal code abolished both the death penalty and torture as means to extract confessions. The peasantry was granted some freedoms, including a poor-law relief which could be claimed by anyone with 10-year residency in their parish. On the other hand, Joseph II put down a revolt by Wallachian peasants in 1784 by breaking their leader on the rack and impaling 150 of his followers.

Because Joseph's reforms often served to break the feudal chains that held the peasantry, it was this, and not the fact that many of these reforms had been enacted to make the people more productive sources of labor and income for the crown, that would be remembered and longed for in future years. (Actually, many of Joseph's reforms would be watered down or eliminated by his brother and successor, Leopold II.)

JOSEPH AND THE SECRET POLICE

The Monarchy's secret police force which was to play such a dark role in Austrian life under his successors, was Joseph's creation. In 1782, he converted a crude surveillance network maintained by the courts into a permanent, separate and efficient service. The first head was Count Anton Pergen who hired a great many informers to spy on the army and the bureaucracy. Pergen reported directly to Joseph. Later, Pergen extended secret police coverage to foreigners and political suspects and began to transform it into an instrument of suppression. Within a decade Pergen managed to establish a police ministry and a Hapsburg police system more highly centralized than any other in Europe at the time. It was Pergen who insisted that the secret service could be effective only when combined with the regular police agencies and thus be disguised by them. He felt that if the secret police's activities became evident the public might object to them.

Joseph's primary aim in establishing the secret police force had been to make certain his many edicts and decrees were carried out. The enormous number of such edicts—6000 in a ten-year period—was staggering and difficult to enforce without a strong information network. Thus the police were commissioned to investigate everything. Some of Joseph's decrees were humanistic; others were downright silly. For example, houses were required to have numbers, the local clergy was supposed to be respected, services were to be provided for blind, deaf or crippled children, the sale of contraceptive methods was to be permitted. On the other hand, he decreed that the Schönbrunn Zoo was required to have a zebra. Girls attending mixed schools were prohibited from wearing corsets or any other "body enhancing" clothing. Candles were to be rationed. Coffins were required to be reused. The peasantry was forbidden to bake gingerbread because he believed it had a bad effect on a person's stomach. His object may have been to make his subjects happy, but the end result of his very confining rules was to implant in the people a nervous reverence for state authority. This became a serious situation when Joseph's benevolent and well-meaning reign passed into unscrupulous hands that misused the omnipotence with which Joseph had endowed the Monarchy His "good intentions" eventually gave birth to the "Austrian informer society." Servants were encouraged to spy on and inform on their masters, clerks on their chiefs, priests on their bishops, enlisted men on their colonels, and coachmen on everyone. Even if Joseph's initial intent had been good, the police eventually grew far more powerful than he surely imagined they would. They were instructed to "appear straightforward and sincere so as to dissemble all the more successfully and sound out all the more easily. The police were to conduct themselves with propriety and politeness in searches at the familiar time for surprise, night or early morning. They were to take pains to look through private papers and to show proper consideration when making arrests."[1]

Pergen argued that it was important for the state to tread lightly among the citizenry because only by doing so could it learn reliably the true opinions of subjects and find out the hindrances which secretly lay in the way of its agencies. Only in this way could the police "discover and eradicate (*ausrotten*) the dangerous enemies of internal security which undermine it...."[2]

In ten recommendations about gaining political information, Pergen first mentions scrutiny of government officials (whom Joseph did not trust) to make sure their political opinions did not prevent them from carrying out edicts for which they might lack enthusiasm. Public opinion research was the second task, to discover secretly what the public said about the monarch and the government, and detect any dissatisfaction they had. Third, police spies were to pay special attention to soldiers, the clergy, suspicious foreigners, forgers, and persons spreading "sects and errors" among the credulous rabble. He also recommended the interception of letters with great care so as "not to offend citizens' freedom or the reputation of the mails." He encouraged the recruitment of confidential agents such as servants, although prostitutes also were regularly hired as spies.

Pergen lost some of his power under Joseph's successor, Leopold II who was somewhat more open-minded, and finally resigned on March 3, 1791. However, Leopold intensified censorship in order to combat persons causing "confusions and inflaming minds by nonsensical ideas and by a fantastic swindling spirit (*Schwindelgeist*), in short, causing the destruction of the public peace through the spread of dangerous opinions."

---

[1]Emerson, 12
[2]Emerson, 13-14

When Leopold died and Francis became Emperor, the threat of an overtly aggressive France made it easy for supporters of Pergen's secret police to once again establish power, and Pergen himself was reinstated on December 30, 1792.

The Lower Austrian governor "requested a watch over all actions and people likely to become dangerous to the state, over all public places such as coffee houses and inns, and especially over all secret organizations and societies."[3]

Pergen wrote that the state must "wipe out through effective countermeasures all dangerous impressions which might have been instilled in any class of subjects by sneaking agitators."[4] The police took part in the censorship of the *Wiener Zeitung*, a popular newspaper. They were directed to judge plays to be given in Viennese theaters. They were warned that the theaters tended to spread principles dangerous to the good order and well-being of the state. By 1798 Pergen had a Viennese police directorate of 48, plus a "military police watch" of 354 men. The directorate furnished a daily report on public opinion in the capital to the police.

> Parallel with a war against the French armies was a war against ideas, many but not all of which were associated with France. (Emperor Francis) never tolerated free expression of opinion, at least on political matters. His course had been set early, by the restoration of the notorious Count Pergen to a position of power in the police.[5]

Writing to the provincial governors in 1793, Pergen continued to declare war against dangerous ideas: "In the present conditions when the cult of liberty has gained much ground and all monarchial governments face great unrest, the ordinary arrangements for peace and security are inadequate. Every government must secretly set forces in motion for the good of the state, in order to convert those in error and to wipe out through effective countermeasures all dangerous impressions that might have been instilled in any class of subjects by sneaking agitators."[6]

Baron Franz Hager, first Pergen's deputy and then elevated to Chief of Police upon Pergen's death, assumed the task of continuing the efforts of the secret police. His mission, as he saw it, was to watch all persons of consequence around the clock, to intercept and even filch their correspondence, and to infiltrate all gatherings to seek out subversive activity. Every major household in Vienna had spies attached to it. It was

---

[3]Emerson, 21-22   [6]Emerson, 21-22
[4]Emerson, 23
[5]Emerson, 21-22

their job to rifle trash baskets, snatch crumpled or half-burned letters from stoves and fireplaces, to spy on their assigned family and note the topics discussed around the dinner table or at parties, and then file daily reports on what they observed.

Because Baron Hager became ill in May 1815, he acquired an assistant in Count Joseph Sedlnitzky, a 37-year old Austrian Silesian noblemen. Why Sedlnitzky was chosen is still a mystery. Hager died the following year (August 1, 1816) and 15 days later Sedlnitzky was appointed in his place. He immediately tightened all censorship in an attempt to stop any expression of free thinking. Sedlnitzky worked closely with Metternich from then until they were both removed from office in 1848. Sedlnitzky was eager to maintain the nobility in their proper position, and scorned anyone who attempted to rise within its ranks. He wrote to Metternich in 1817, "I have continually adhered most deeply to the cause of legitimacy and always considered its enemies as enemies of the peace of Europe and of my Monarch."

One thing that cannot be overemphasized is the danger in expressing public opinion that went contrary to the Austrian monarchy.

> Not only foreign diplomats or once powerful French exiles but, at the slightest suspicion, any humble Hapsburg subject or simple traveller in the land was likely to receive the searching attention of the police. For example, a judicial administrator in the Moravian capital of Brünn was called to the police after two or three young people visited his oldest daughter and the group put some candles in the chandelier and danced without notifying the police in advance.... Since the vigilant police were encouraged to discover political opinions, subjects could never know to whom it was safe to talk. Such surveillance encouraged distrust and alienated subjects from one another.[7]

If the simple act of dancing without permission roused the suspicion of the police, how much worse were the uncensored opinions offered in public by Beethoven? After all, as Emerson points out

> the police were not limiting their surveillance to genuine revolutionaries. From this point throughout the reign of Francis—he died in 1835—the police were everywhere in search of the slightest hint of unorthodox ideas among the citizenry. The state's suspicion of intellectuals was such that many citizens who desired careers in government avoided

---

[7]Emerson, 42

higher education in the belief that it would work against their obtaining a position.[8]

Of course, a youthful Beethoven was far more cautious than he was in later years. On August 2, 1794, he wrote to his publisher, Nikolaus Simrock in Bonn, telling him a bit about the Austrian state and his own reaction to it:

> Here very important people have been locked up; it is said that a revolution was about to break out — But I believe that so long as an Austrian can get his brown ale and his little sausages, he is not likely to revolt. People say that the gates leading to the suburbs are to be closed at 10 p.m. The soldiers have loaded their muskets with ball. You dare not raise your voice here or the police will take you into custody.[9]

This, we must remember, was a 23-year-old Beethoven speaking. Once he had established himself and his fame was unquestioned, he was no longer concerned about raising his voice or being taken into custody for doing so.

SCRUTINY OF THE MAIL

The Secret Cipher Chancellery was the bureau in Vienna established for the purpose of reading everyone's private correspondence. It was considered so important for the state that the Emperor maintained it as an independent bureau under his direct control and he eagerly awaited reports from the chancellery on what they had found. Mail was intercepted as far away as the Bohemian spas, such as Karlsbad, which had their own "interception stations." Although most countries had some sort of postal censorship, "it is safe to say that in this sphere no one could hold a candle to the Austrians." [10] All the major post offices had censorship departments called *Logen*. Anything in the Hapsburg mails was likely to be read by the police unless negligence, effective disguise, or sheer chance interfered. The mail of all persons of interest or under any suspicion whatsoever was secretly opened, copied, and resealed in such a way that the recipients supposedly would not know that the letter had been tampered with. Nevertheless, most citizens were aware that this activity was going on, and knew that there was no protection against the police reading private correspondence except to entrust letters to a reliable person for hand delivery. Yet even though Hapsburg subjects tried to keep letters out of the mails, the police worked just as hard to prevent such evasion. More than

---

[8]Emerson, 22
[9]Anderson, #12, I, 18
[10]Musulin, 144

once Beethoven wrote in his letters that he would tell his correspondent "more later by word of mouth." Why he was so careful in writing and so careless in speech is one of those mysteries that have not been solved. Perhaps he perceived the written word—which provides tangible evidence— as more dangerous, while anything said in public less so.

CENSORSHIP: SEARCH AND SEIZURE

Under the guise of protecting the security of the state, the Hapsburg government tried to control not only the physical movements of its subjects, but even their opinions. As Emerson pointed out, police did not limit their surveillance to genuine revolutionaries. Both the Police Ministry and the Foreign Office made many attempts to influence opinion by hiring writers to supply propaganda to the local newspapers. But more than that, they sought to control the outlook of subjects by elaborate and stringent censorship. In 1801, Count Pergen had gained the right of censorship for the Police Ministry which then kept hold of the role for another 47 years. The Foreign Office, as well as the Police Ministry, took part in the censorship of newspapers and periodicals, books, and plays, and many other things that attempted to influence public opinion. Those who dared read these "subversive" materials were under constant suspicion.

Those who violated censorship laws were severely punished. In Vienna under Francis I, it was dangerous to speak and write freely. Although the police did not employ brutality or terror to enforce censorship laws or to suppress ideas, simply the threat of arrest, the loss of one's job, and other deterrents made more drastic measures unnecessary.

The police harassed everyone, even the members of the *Ludlamhöhle*, a harmless if sometimes rowdy social club. The police had heard rumors that secret and dangerous activities were going on within the club and raided its meeting place. All papers—even music!—were confiscated. Members' houses were searched. Poet Franz Grillparzer, who happened to be a member of this innocuous little club, was interrogated, had all his papers taken, and was given one day's house arrest.

The police used customs officials to search the premises of suspects for papers and other incriminating evidence. Such searches and seizures took place simply at the whim of the Police Ministry, the Foreign Office, or other administrative sections such as the police directorates. The police arrested and interrogated suspects at will and without great provocation. When the police cared to, they held suspects a very long time for investigation without submitting charges for judicial examination or even bringing them to trial. Prisoners generally were held in one of

Vienna's fortresses, such as the Spielberg, where conditions were scandalously unhealthy and miserable. Torture, however, was not employed to extract information.

THE PERCEIVED THREAT OF FREEMASONRY

Not without some reason, Joseph came to fear the growth of Masonic societies and other secret organizations. Joseph did not persecute the Masons in the early part of his reign since his own father had been a Grand Master. However, toward the end he grew intolerant of these radicals about whom Pergen's secret police were constantly reporting. After all, the lodges were directly engaged in political operations and supported social reform in Vienna. Outwardly they sponsored seemingly harmless banquets, lectures, and musical performances while at the same time were engaged in secretive political activism. Not all these groups were outwardly revolutionary in nature, but Joseph did not see any distinction between them. He wrote, "The so-called Freemason societies are increasing the spreading of their ideas even to the small towns; left alone, without supervision, they might become dangerous in their excess to religion, order, and morals..." In December 1785, Joseph passed into law the *Freimaurerpatent* which decreed that Vienna was allowed only two lodges, thereby disbanding six others. Provincial capitals could have only one lodge, and lists of members were to be submitted to the police every three months. Lodges were also subject to random inspections.

The most famous Freemason was Wolfgang Mozart, who flaunted Masonic ritual in his opera, *Die Zauberflöte*. As Joseph was already uneasy about Mozart, it was just as well that he died a year before *The Magic Flute* was written. Some biographers have put forth the claim that Beethoven was also a Freemason. This aspect of Beethoven will be discussed more fully in the next chapter dealing with Beethoven's politics.

In a general survey of the secret societies, Sedlnitzky traced the Carbonari to Masonic groups in Naples who spread to Roman territory seeking Italian independence when Napoleon added territory in the peninsula to his French empire. There was talk of revolutionary plots in Italy in 1816, and as a result the governor of Milan began a highly productive enterprise in political espionage. About that time, Count Sedlnitzky inquired about a new "half-Masonic sect" in Piedmont, and Metternich was eager to discover what connections Masons had with dissatisfaction in Lombardy. Deputy Police Minister Saurau sent two agents, Captain Parutta and Chevalier Dumnt—known for their political duplicity—to northwest Italy and southern France in 1816 During the summer of that year, disquieting reports about unrest in Italy continued to trickle in to Vienna. Sedlnitzky complained that independence seekers were stirring up public sentiment. The Carbonari were said to be gaining ground throughout the Papal States. Austria closely watched both the Carbonari and Freemasons, and any other "sects" with suspicious names. It is interesting to note, once again, that that fateful year of 1816 appears so prominently in the history of Austrian suppression.

Metternich's obsessive fear of Freemasons is evident in this notation from Emerson:

> With his burdensome and undiscriminating delight in detail, he frequently gave petty instructions about the security of the state, as when he wished to know in 1824 whether tie-pins worn in Florence, outside his own lands, were in fact a secret mark of Masonic groups who menaced the peace of Italy and the Hapsburg position there.[11]

UPRISING AND SUPPRESSION: 1816-1818

> In the absolutist state that controlled and kept watch on Austrian society after the Congress of Vienna... public life was impossible, and it had become dangerous to discuss public affairs even in a private salon.[12]

It may be of interest to the reader to learn of some seemingly innocuous individuals—who indeed probably were completely harmless—who suffered from the irrational suppression of ideas in Austria. If these men suffered forms of persecution, can we assume that the very outspoken Beethoven had been immune from censure?

The Teacher

An historian whose troubles with rigorous Hapsburg censorship became exceedingly well known in his time was Julius Franz Schneller, professor at the lyceum at Graz, and a man who figures prominently in Beethoven's conversation books. The first volumes of his *Political History of Imperial Austria* appeared from 1817 to 1819 in spite of difficulties with the censors. Hormayr, then imperial historiographer, attacked the work in the official *Wiener Jahrbücher* for its "bad tendency and its glorification of Josephinism." Schneller's fifth volume was rejected outright. "Yesterday I wished I had a thunderbolt to smash the yokels at the

---

[11]Emerson, 32

[12]Heindl, 41

censorship," Schneller wrote. He appealed and resubmitted his manuscript, appealing to friends such as the wife of High Chancellor Count Saurau, former Governor of Lombardy. Metternich consulted Gentz on the issue, who condemned the work. In Gentz's opinion, every work which contained liberal opinions should be forbidden even when the objectionable parts were deleted. The work went unapproved. Realizing that the subject of history was too dangerous for a writer, Schneller sought appointment as professor of aesthetics in Vienna. After a long wait, he finally learned that the Emperor had rejected his appointment on the advice of the police. As this professor continued his "subversive" activities, the Foreign Office assured Sedlnitzky that they would take every opportunity to point out to potential employers how detrimental to public welfare were his principles.

The Writer

"I was terrified" wrote journalist Heinrich Börnstein in his memoirs regarding his friends' suggestion that he become a Vienna correspondent for foreign journals outside the empire, "for such a thing was then like an invitation to robbery or burglary." Writing for foreign papers or attempting to publish works abroad without first receiving the approval of the Austrian censorship office was forbidden with heavy punishments imposed on violators. Under Sedlnitzky's rule correspondents of foreign papers were pursued unsparingly and punished like criminals. Börnstein's friends assured him that there were means to cleverly send messages that avoided any danger. Correspondence was often carried on by freight wagons and used such merchants (in places such as Berlin or Leipzig) as book dealers, stocking manufacturers or shoemakers as go-betweens who then forwarded what they received to the appropriate recipient. Addresses were changed very two months. The only "news" routinely smuggled out of Austria was gossip concerning Viennese society, anecdotes about the court, little scandals, and other delights forbidden in Viennese papers. "One may regret," wrote Emerson, "that censorship gave false worth to these trivialities which the 'popular press' was to inflate."

One day, however the communication system broke down. The authorities learned the means by which articles were being smuggled out of Austria and were furious. They organized a search of all houses where such activities were suspected. Just in time, Börnstein managed to burn all his papers, even his laundry tickets. The police arrived soon after he had managed to rid himself of anything incriminating. They looked everywhere in his house for evidence, even in his straw mattress, but found nothing suspicious. The raid on Börnstein's house terrified his landlord who demanded that he move. Börnstein immediately gave up his job as a foreign correspondent. He wrote in his *Memoirs*:

> Today no one can any longer comprehend my anxiety, but then it was justified. At that time many journalist or correspondent out of favor disappeared into the cells of the Spielberg or the casements of Munkacs for ever, for the good Emperor Francis was very jealous of his authority as Emperor, and let people who committed a crime in word or deed against the divinely established sanctity of the crown rot without pity, burdened by the heaviest chains, in the deepest cells of the Spielberg.[13]

Börnstein, operating under the rumor that such "heretics and criminals" were severely punished, exaggerated the consequences which Hapsburg journalists suffered because of infractions against the rigorous censorship. Yet his anxiety strongly reflected the fears of the population at large of the government's watchfulness and the impact of its brutal measures. While journalists did not experience the severe penalties which Börnstein recounted in his Memoirs, the police controls on publication were oppressive enough. In 1816, for example, when the Vienna Police Directorate recommended a retraction and reprimand for an editor whose criticism of Hapsburg troops had been published abroad, Sedlnitzky ordered three days of police arrest for the editor on the charge of conducting forbidden foreign correspondence.

THE PROBLEM WITH NAPOLEON

Napoleon's rise to power threatened the existence of the Hapsburg Monarchy. He was, after all, a commoner, a mere general and commander-in-chief of the French army. In 1797, he battled his way across Europe to within sixty miles of Vienna. At that point, the emperor, now Francis I who would later become Napoleon's father-in-law, negotiated for an armistice. A humiliated Austria ceded to France its provinces in southern Netherlands (Belgium) and acknowledged the new Republic of Lombardy. Three years later, when Napoleon again struck at Austria, it was as First Consul of the Republic of France. In June of 1800, he again crushed the Austrian army, once more obliging Francis to sue for peace. Austria was forced to recognize the Rhine, the Alps and the Pyrenees as France's natural

---

[13]Börnstein, 142

frontiers. At this point, Beethoven was a great admirer of Napoleon, and he was not alone. To many, Napoleon represented freedom from the monarchy's control: enlightenment, republicanism, equality.

Although Beethoven's admiration temporarily turned to bitter disappointment when Napoleon declared himself emperor of the French in December 1804 (and thus became, to Beethoven "just another tyrant"), it was actually Joseph Fouché, Napoleon's police chiefs who had caused Napoleon to assume his imperial title. Fouché argued that if Napoleon sired a son, under a hereditary empire succession would be ensured, even if Napoleon himself were to be assassinated. Fouché had uncovered an English-financed plot to do exactly that, prompting his suggestion. Beethoven either did not see the "logic" in this move or perhaps did not know the reason for it, prompting his anger; in later years, however, his disappointment would give way once again to admiration. The French empire was proclaimed in May 1804 and on December 2 of that year, Napoleon crowned himself Emperor, supplanting Pope Pius VII at the last minute. This act was a direct challenge to the Hapsburgs and their hereditary title of "Emperor of the Holy Roman Empire" Franz did not quite meet the challenge: he changed his title to "Hereditary Emperor of Austria" yet petuantly maintained that he was "Roman Emperor Elect."

Taking to the battlefield once again, Napoleon crushed the combined Austrian and Russian armies at Austerlitz, killing 15,000 and taking 20,000 prisoner. In the Peace of Pressburg which followed on December 26th, Austria lost the Venetian Republic, Tyrol and Vorarlberg were ceded to Bavaria, and the rest of the Hapsburg's other Germanic possessions were taken by Baden and Wüttemberg, Napoleon's allies, which removed Austria from Western Germany entirely. These German states declared themselves to be the "Confederation of the Rhine," with Napoleon a self-declared "Protector of the Confederacy."

By 1806, Napoleon had declared the old Roman empire to be defunct. With the loss of the "Rhine Confederacy," Franz declared that it was "impossible for us to discharge any longer our imperial office," and thus on August 6, 1806, he dissolved the Holy Roman Empire which had existed intact for 1000 years, since the time of Charlemagne. All that Franz retained was the old symbol of the Holy Roman Empire: the double-headed eagle and the traditional colors of the German empire: gold and black.

In 1809, Napoleon again marched on Vienna, while Franz fled to Hungary. By May 13, Napoleon was living in Vienna's Schönbrunn Palace and it was there, on October 14, that Austria had to sign yet another peace pact with France. Austria gave up Poland, parts of Carinthia, Carniola and Croatia, what was left of its Adriatic possessions, and some German possessions along the Bavarian border. In one blow, Franz lost three and quarter million of his subjects. Six months later, on March 11, 1810, believing an alliance was better than wars he kept losing, Franz gave his daughter, the Archduchess Marie-Louise to Napoleon as his bride. (The two were actually married by proxy, with the Archduke Charles, one of Napoleon's most formidable opponents on the battlefield, standing in for the bridegroom). Interestingly, there was no anti-French sentiment among the Austrian people. The English, by contrast, would have rioted had one of their princesses been given in marriage to "Boney," as Napoleon was nicknamed. Perhaps the great legal reforms that Napoleon had brought about in the wake of his conquering army had sown the seeds of liberalism among the Austrian population. The only real resistance came not from swords but pens, the most prolific being wielded by Metternich's advisor, Friedrich von Gentz, a Prussian who had entered the service of the Hapsburgs in 1802. He and colleagues like Friedrich Schlegel, produced a number of manifestos and newspaper articles to try to mobilize resistance against Napoleon. Yet their efforts were directed toward "the German people" rather than Austrians or the Viennese and had little effect.

Napoleon's power was not broken completely until 1815, when he was exiled and the famous Congress of Vienna came together to trace the new frontiers of Europe. In the midst of this, a new power was on the rise: Metternich. Clement Wenceslas Lothar von Metternich-Winneburg-Beilstein, was from an old Rhenish family (based primarily in Coblenz, several miles south of Bonn) and for 33 years would dominate Viennese and Austrian government.

The translation of Sir Walter Scott's *Life of Napoleon* appeared in 1824, three years after the general's death, even though it contained many objectionable details. The censors permitted it to be published after these parts had been deleted. The censors hesitated to ban it entirely because they feared that foreign critics and so-called liberal writers would have used its prohibition to denounce Austrian censorship. Beethoven saw and commented on this book to his friend, Carl Czerny, noting his feelings of admiration for the late emperor.

THE RISE OF METTERNICH

In 1790 when Metternich was 17, he was presented by his father, Count Francis (serving in the diplomatic corps) to the Hapsburg monarchy. The occasion had been the coronation of Leopold II, brother of Joseph the reformer, as Holy Roman Emperor. The family arrived in style: 98 coaches were needed to convey the entire family into town. In 1792, Leopold died, and 24-year-old Francis came to the throne, and with him came Clements Metternich, first as an ambassador, then as Foreign Minister, and finally as Chancellor. Metternich was raised to the status of prince following the Battle of Leipzig (at which he was merely a spectator!) It was Metternich who orchestrated the marriage of Francis's daughter to Napoleon, said to be "an intrigue after his own heart, for it was partly conducted by overtures at masked balls where the amorous Metternich was just as much at home as at his office desk." [14]

After Napoleon's defeat, it was Metternich who acquired four million new subjects for his emperor: Austria regained Lombardy and Tyrol, kept Salzburg, extended its domain to Venetia, Istria and Dalmatia, as well as keeping Hungary and Bohemia. Metternich knew, however, that this over-extended empire could continue to exist only as long as nothing came along to disturb it... and that meant preventing anything that could revive the liberal spirit of Bonaparte. The Republic of France could not be allowed to return as a conqueror. The empire required continuity and continuity required that the dynasties be allowed to continue undisturbed. In France, the Bourbons under Louis XVIII, had been returned to power, and Metternich knew that that was exactly the way it needed to remain, otherwise the delicate balance of power would topple. France, now a royalist country once again, was a full participant in the Congress of Vienna. At this Congress, the four allies—Austria, Russia, Prussia and Britain—pledged to join together to fight any revolutionary attempts which might be reborn in France. This pledge birthed the "Congress System," which was designed to convene if anything threatened the status quo. (It was, in fact, convened repeatedly during Metternich's era.) "The Austrians... continued to be smothered under the dynastic purple. Indeed for the burgeoning liberals inside the Monarchy, the Congress emerged as an instrument of domestic repression."[15]

Metternich was always suspicious of the universities as hotbeds of revolution, and in October 1817, his suspicions were confirmed. A few hundred students from Jena, Kiel, Vienna, and Berlin gathered at the Castle of Wartburg in the Grand Duchy of Weimar for a joint demonstration. Although they claimed to be celebrating the 300th anniversary of the Lutheran Reformation and the more recent victory over Napoleon at

---

[14]Brook-Shepherd, 42
[15]Brook-Shepherd, 43

Leipzig in 1813, slogans abounded denouncing tyranny and one student provided a copy of the Final Treaty of Vienna and tossed it into a bonfire. "For Metternich, this was as heinous as burning the Bible itself."[16] Although Metternich had been fully informed by his police spies about the growth of student societies within German universities, this Wartburg gathering—which had been organized without his knowledge—alarmed him. As a result, in August 1819, he convened the Austrian-Prussian Congress of Karlsbad for the specific purpose of tightening state control over the universities and the freedom of the printed word. The Karlsbad Decrees, which Metternich essentially drafted, gave every German state the right to suppress any publication of more than 20 pages. A central commission was established in Mainz to monitor the political tenor of lectures at every university and monitor any "revolutionary activities." Within Austria, the secret police monitored the books that professors borrowed from libraries. Foreigners were forbidden to be employed anywhere as teachers, even as private tutors. Staffs of state schools had to undergo a three-year probationary period during which their activities were closely monitored before their appointments were confirmed. Gentz warned on July 25, 1818 that "We are completely convinced that all of the evils afflicting Germany today, even including the licentiousness of the press, this student nuisance is the greatest, the most urgent, and the most threatening."[17] As historian Brook-Shepherd noted,"All this fell short of a reign of terror."

And how did the Viennese fare in this atmosphere of oppression? Some found they could avoid trouble with the law by walking a careful line between what was allowed and what was not. Others preferred to take refuge in a cozy world of non-politics.

Into this society came one of Austria's greatest poets, Franz Grillparzer, who was a close friend of Beethoven's and, in fact, would write his funeral oration many years later. During Grillparzer's lengthy and illustrious career, he had quite a few clashes with the Metternich regime. For example, he narrowly escaped dismissal in 1819 when a poem he wrote about ancient Rome seemed to Sedlnitzky's "thought police" to be too close a parallel to the fragile Austrian monarchy. Fortunately, most of Grillparzer's works—which often were based on works of Schiller, such as *Don Carlos*, *William Tell*, or *Wallenstein* and had anti-Hapsburg themes—were performed in theaters under the direction of the very liberal Joseph Shreyvogel, who also happened to be a friend of Beethoven's.

---

[16]Brook-Shepherd, 45
[17]Emerson, 110

And what about music? It was not like the written word which could be inflammatory, was it? And yet composers wishing to give concerts were required to inform the police of the date and time of the concert and submit to the censorship office for approval all printed materials. That included the program, the libretto, and concert posters. Passing the censors was not always easy. Music was seen as the means to give the people a glimpse of an ideal, a vehicle for attaining a higher state of existence, as something akin to and perhaps substituting for religion. Both the Police and Foreign Ministries scrutinized not only newspapers, books and periodicals, but also virtually everything believed to influence feelings and outlook, and that included music.

LATER YEARS OF SUPPRESSION: 1822 TO 1830

Sedlnitzky believed that most of the troubles facing the monarchy stemmed from the ideals of the Enlightenment and the French Revolution which were still espoused even though the revolution had been over for a quarter century. Prussian minister Gampz wrote in March of 1824, "All branches of the public administration are more or less affected by this evil. It is not sufficient to limit surveillance to high traitors."

Metternich had denounced a young professor of statistics at the University of Prague, George Norbert Schnabel, and tried to have him fired from his position. The efforts of Metternich and the Police Ministry went unrewarded: Schnabel remained in his chair at Prague. In January 1822, the Foreign Office hoped to silence him by their characteristic means if direct action was impossible. And why had this teacher suffered such abuse? Because Metternich believed that the professor's encyclopedia contained positions which led into "those errors dangerous for the state to which Rousseau's social contract had broken the fatal path."

In autumn 1823, Franz Grillparzer submitted his play *König Ottokars Glück und Ende* for censorship. For the Emperor, this showed too clearly that this poet of genius was little more than a trouble-making minor official to be fired if he erred again. On December 21, 1823 the Police Ministry asked the Foreign Office whether *King Ottokar* should be forbidden or returned to the author for revision. They were afraid that this latest play by Court Clerk (*Hofkonzipist*) Grillparzer in the Finance Ministry would remind the public of Napoleon and also cause bad feelings among different groups of Austrian subjects, particularly in Bohemia. On New Year's Eve, the regular Foreign Office censor reinforced these fears and declared that the bad effect of the play on any audience made it impossible for an Austrian state to produce it. Furthermore, the play should not even be printed. (This statement was kept secret by Austria until 1905.) News of the rejection shocked Grillparzer and astonished his friends. The play eventually was produced because the censors had not offered to the Emperor any reasons why it could not; they had simply rejected it.

This effort to suppress Grillparzer's *King Ottokar* epitomized the suffocating approach of the high censors to intellectual life in the Hapsburg empire. Grillparzer continued to be a civil servant, although he failed to receive an appointment as librarian which he had hoped for. He was not physically punished or technically mistreated. He continued to write. Yet the stifling censorship hung over all his efforts and achievements. By their petty political judgments of the moment the censors were able to stifle creative imagination, even if they could not extinguish it completely.

"The regular contribution of Metternich and his Ministry was pettiness, chicanery, and suppression. Through (chief censor) Bretfield he helped make that system most obnoxious as his Foreign Office regularly sought to control public opinion. ... However much of the detail of censorship Metternich left to his subordinates, he actively controlled opinions when he believed the issue sufficiently important."[18]

---

[18]Emerson, 167

Chapter 4
Beethoven and His Politics

Anton Schindler knew Beethoven for slightly more than the last ten years of his life. They had a falling out which led to an estrangement of several years during that time period, but Schindler does offer interesting insights into the composer's life and attitudes. It is unfortunate that Schindler has come to represent an unreliable source. Without a doubt he burned many of Beethoven's conversation books and doctored the contents of those he saved. His opinions of various persons in Beethoven's life, such as his brother Johann and nephew Karl are so one-sided — supposedly because of personal malice—that he cannot be taken as an objective observer. He has not been treated kindly by modern scholars who believe that self-serving motives drove him to alter or destroy what could have been valuable primary source material. They claim that he did away with anything that placed him in a bad light or showed him as anything but Beethoven's closest and most trusted friend and confidante. Of course there may be some truth to this. However, when one looks at Schindler within the context of the times in which he lived, one cannot help but wonder whether his motives more correctly could be said to have involved self-preservation. We have already seen how ruthless the Austrian government was in suppressing what they considered subversive talk, writing, and actions. Perhaps Schindler had legitimate political reasons for destroying the material he did.

One person who helps corroborate the idea that Schindler's motives may have been political in nature is Dr. Johann Baptist Bach. Dr. Bach was a court lawyer, considered one of the foremost juridical authorities in the imperial capital. He was also Beethoven's friend and served as his attorney in several legal affairs. Schindler had been employed in Bach's office as a clerk during his student years. It was Bach who helped edit Schindler's original manuscript on Beethoven in 1840—some eight years before the downfall of Metternich's rigid regime. Schindler noted that anything questionable was deleted by Dr. Bach "in his own interests no less than in mine." Schindler tells us that

> With considerable misgivings I sent the manuscript to be censored in Vienna, but nothing was found unacceptable there. On the other hand, I was very surprised at the liberal use my patron (i.e. Bach) made of his red pencil. Factual material having to do with the history of the times was in his opinion liable to put both of us in a dangerous position, even when it served to illustrate certain facets of Beethoven's character. Accordingly much of what I had written was struck out for no apparent reason. Much of the material he deleted has been included in this edition.[1]

Much material previously deleted had been restored, but apparently not all. It would be interesting know what had remained forever stricken from Schindler's biography. Schindler echoed the sentiments of others describing the restrictions placed on speech and writing during these times, and had the same fears other speakers and authors experienced:

> In short, the first edition appeared—but under the restrictions and limitations that had been agreed upon. The author was safe from the gallows or the wheel, but he was subject to suspicion and intrigue that was sufficient to do considerable harm to his work without his being able to vindicate himself openly.[2]

What were Beethoven's political inclinations that Schindler was so reluctant to reveal? As we will see, Beethoven was an outspoken proponent of personal liberty and governmental reform. He hardly could have been well tolerated by the monarchy he continually—and often loudly—condemned. By 1860, when Schindler revised and reissued his biography, he was able to include some of the statements he had deleted in the earlier edition.

> Fortunately, however, Austria today (i.e. 1860) is entirely different from the Austria of Beethoven's time, and it is no longer inadvisable to set forth openly the things that are a part of history in general and that bore a special relationship to Beethoven's life. If Dr. Bach had realized that the hour of Austria's political reform was not far away ... he would not have

---

[1]Schindler, 27-28
[2]IBID

felt that his social position made caution imperative, and would have withheld his red pencil. But like thousands of middle-class subjects of the Emperor, he had long since despaired of any improvement in the political structure. The inexorable Fates cut his life's thread in 1847, almost on the eve of the Austrian people's long-awaited new day.

With the collapse of Metternich's restrictions, Schindler also was able declare:

> Continuing our history of events and their ramifications in as orderly a sequence as possible, we encounter now for the first time a new and unexpected interest, one that has to do not with music but with political science. We must, however, come to expect to find our composer concerned with this area of human activity, for though it seems far removed from his essential domain, yet one side of his nature inclined irresistibly in a political direction. We shall, therefore, often find him concerned with matters of politics.[3]

We see already, just from Schindler's opening remarks in his discussion of Beethoven's political attitudes, that he was hardly "just a composer" as some people believe. He was not a political leader and held no post of importance; he was not a rebel leader in the truest sense of the word. But we have already learned that free speech was not acceptable in the Hapsburg empire. We also know that Beethoven was well admired by the populace, in particular young people and students. And who did Metternich and his police force fear and persecute the most?

"I AM OFTEN VERY FREE IN SPEECH"

Beethoven once remarked to a friend he had unwittingly offended that he must be excused for such unintentional woundings because "sometimes I am very naughty—... I hate any kind of restraint. I am often very free in speech." [4] Nowhere was this more true than in the realm of expressing his political views.

> Beethoven held strong republican sympathies, personally inclined as he was towards unimpeded freedom and independence. Beethoven wished to bring about a general political change in the world, including the world of art, such that the whole structure of social standards and relationships would be raised to a higher plane. [5]

---

[3]Schindler, 111   [4]Anderson, 173   [5]Schindler, 112

Most of the published criticisms of Beethoven as a political figure start from the premise that he was one of the many so-called harmless 'tavern politicians,' whose ire could be aroused by a single catch-word. Most of these critics were foreigners very little acquainted with the situation prevailing in Austria and totally ignorant of the attainments and culture of the people, especially in the large cities. They were equally ignorant of this aspect of Beethoven's character, and they drew their conclusions from what they had heard him say during one or two casual encounters.[6]

Although Schindler believed Beethoven had been wise enough not to "expose his most secret thoughts before strangers" the comments of others show us that the composer did not usually exercise caution in expressing his opinions openly. Ignaz Seyfried, who knew Beethoven many years, wrote in his *Beethovens Studien*: "Within the circle of his intimate friends his favourite topic of conversation was politics, on which he would speak with an enlightened power of observation, correct interpretation, and clear vision such as one would never expect even from a votary of the diplomatic corps living solely for the exercise of his art." But not only his friends made such observations. Friedrich Rochlitz saw Beethoven only three times during the summer of 1822, and was no more than a casual acquaintance. Nevertheless, he was privy to many of Beethoven's "secret thoughts" concerning the politics of the time. In his book *Für Freunde der Tonkunst,* Rochlitz wrote:"Within the circle of his intimate friends his favorite topic of conversation was politics." Nephew Karl urged caution, writing: "Silence! The walls have ears," and then later, "The Baron is a chamberlain of the Emperor. I think that you should not speak against the regime with him." Apparently his advice was ignored.[7]

Admirer Dr. W. C. Müller, founder of the society concerts in Bremen, who like Rochlitz was no more than an acquaintance of Beethoven's, visited the composer in 1820 on his way to Italy, and wrote an article called "Something About Ludwig van Beethoven" Beethoven apparently had not been all that discreet with him either. Müller noted:

> This sense of freedom as a citizen of the world...may well have been the reason that in restaurants he would talk continuously, expressing himself openly and without reserve, critically or satirically, on everything; the government, the police, the morals of the nobility. The police knew it but they left him

---

[6]Schindler, 243-244
[7]Schünemann, III, 284

alone, either because they considered him a crackpot or out of deference for his genius as an artist.[8]

Beethoven's name appears in the secret police files from the Congress of Vienna in 1815, so Müller's observation that the police knew all too well how outspoken Beethoven was against the monarchy was correct. But did the police really "leave him alone" as Müller thought? Certainly they would not have censored him openly. He was well-admired and well-known. The last thing the police wanted was to cause public outcry against their treatment of a much-beloved composer. But would they have simply done nothing, trusting that the public would simply dismiss Beethoven's "ravings" as those of an eccentric?

Schindler wrote that

> In Beethoven's time no democrat dared question the divine right of the Emperor, and no prince ever took his divine right more personally than Emperor Franz. For this reason alone democratic tendencies, if known to the police, were interpreted as political disobedience.[9]

Schindler's observations have been echoed by many others, so why would the Emperor, a man "notorious for his low opinion of artistic genius and his esteem only for 'the useful man.'" have allowed Beethoven to speak out without consequence? Emperor Franz detested Beethoven, and he refused to attend any concert where Beethoven's music was to be played. The emperor's court composer, Teyber, elevated himself in his monarch's eyes by never failing "to take advantage of his opportunities to discredit the great master at court. An emperor's composer enjoyed far more prestige than a Beethoven, and could with high good humour ridicule and revile him."[10]

Schindler tells us further that "He was fond on such occasions (when around friends) of giving full play to his wit and sarcasm, though he was sometimes indiscreet, especially in expressing his outspoken political and social views." From this comment we might presume that Beethoven spoke his revolutionary thoughts only around those he trusted, and perhaps that was his intention. But is that a valid assumption? I believe we must consider that being hard of hearing often made him speak more loudly than he realized. At times, he wrote down his thoughts, knowing that he could not trust himself to modulate his voice and speak in a low enough tone not to be overheard. And even if his friends could be trusted,

---

[8]AmZ XXIX, 1827, 345   [10]Schindler, 247
[9]Schindler, 246-247

were they always completely alone? Were their conversations never overheard? As we know, spies were everywhere, from shopkeepers to coachmen. We can be relatively certain that Beethoven's views were common knowledge and that friends sometimes warned him about his outspokenness. A conversation book entry for 1819 reads "Do not speak so loud. Your situation is too well known; — that is the inconvenience of public places, one is completely limited; everybody listens and hears."[11] Madame Cherubini also corroborates this in her memoirs. She wrote that "(Beethoven) simply ridiculed their (the aristocracy's) high and mighty prejudices, and showed no more deference to a princess than to a bourgeois."

Other close acquaintances of Beethoven's tell us similar stories. Friend Karl Amenda noted that in 1816 Beethoven "told me a great deal about Vienna and his life here. Venom and rancor raged within him. He defies everything and is dissatisfied with everything and blasphemes against Austria and especially against Vienna." He said further that Beethoven had told him that "There is nobody you can trust... one has nothing in Austria since everything is worthless, that is, paper."

In that same year, 1816, one of Beethoven's long-time friends and publisher, Nikolaus Simrock, said that everywhere in public, Beethoven railed at Emperor Franz because of the reduction of the paper money. "Such a rascal ought to be hanged to the first tree," Simrock said Beethoven told him.

AN ANGLOPHILE

After Englishman Edward Schutz met with Beethoven in 1823, he published a story about his visit in the *Harmonicom*: "He is a great enemy to all gêne, and I believe that there is not another individual in Vienna who speaks with so little restraint on all kinds of subjects, even political ones." Schutz also commented that Beethoven and his music was "well admired by the young artists in Vienna," and also that "He appears, uniformly, to entertain the most favourable opinion of the British nation." Johann Stumpff, a harp manufacturer of German descent who lived in London, corroborated Beethoven's love for the English, noting after a visit with Beethoven in 1824 that "Beethoven had an exaggerated opinion of London and its highly cultured inhabitants." Stumpff said that their conversation had centered mainly around Beethoven's condemnation of the frivolity and bad musical taste of the Viennese and showed "excessive laudation of everything English."

---

[11]Thayer 746-747

Beethoven much admired the English ideals of personal liberty and constitutional government. The English with their "radical" ideas were not well liked by the Austrian monarchy and anyone who was as enthusiastic an Anglophile as Beethoven naturally would be suspect. The composer was particularly fond of reading about parliamentary debates and was very enthusiastic about the speeches made by Henry Peter, Lord Brougham, first Baron of Brougham and Vauz, (1778-1868), who entered Parliament in 1810. He was a vigorous opponent of slavery and became a liberal leader in the House of Commons. He introduced educational and legal reforms and was one of the founders of both The Society for the Diffusion of Useful Knowledge, and of the University of London. As a role model, the Austrians did not consider him suitable. Once again we find Beethoven applauding personages and opinions the monarchy condemned.

A READER OF THE FORBIDDEN

In part, Beethoven's political inclinations were a result of his being an avid follower of world affairs. He made it a point to read the *Allgemeine Zeitung* every day in order to broaden his knowledge of politics. The Austrian government did not approve of this "subversive" publication. In keeping with their strict rules of censorship, the Foreign Office and the Police Ministry naturally made all decisions about what foreign newspapers and magazines would be permitted in the Hapsburg Monarchy. (The *AZ* was a German publication.) They were reluctant to simply ban or confiscate foreign newspapers which the public readily read on arrival because they feared generating even more interest in such "forbidden fruit" than they already enjoyed. However, they did remove from the "accepted" list of what Austrian subjects could legally subscribe to and receive through the mails any publication "which in the course of the year had expressed an evil spirit."[12]

Although the *Allgemeine Zeitung* was soundly and repeatedly criticized by the Police Minister in 1817, initially it was decided that its misdeeds were not bad enough to warrant prohibition. However in 1819 Sedlnitzky at last was able to change that opinion. He claimed that among all the papers most frequently read in Vienna, the *Allgemeine Zeitung* "distinguished itself for its evil tendencies." He complained that the correspondents and editors of the paper had been seized with the new evil spirit of the times and wrote in a revolutionary sense and tried to make the people receptive to revolutionary ideas. At the very least, he urged, Metternich should severely warn the editors and owners of the paper.

---

[12]Emerson, 145

By the spring of 1820 Sedlnitzky continued to develop his campaign against the *Allgemeine Zeitung* claiming that despite warnings it continued to reprint "all those violent Jacobin utterances and principles which were recently expressed in ultra-liberal French papers." By 1822 Sedlnitzky finally managed to prohibit the distribution of the *Allgemeine Zeitung* so that it could only be acquired (legally) by selected readers. Exactly how Beethoven acquired the copies he read "every day" is not known although Schindler reported that he had the paper delivered to his home. Metternich noted, "No one knows better than I how very much the German papers in general and the *Allgemeine Zeitung* in particular corrupt public opinion. But just because the evil is so wide-spread this special measure seems to me insufficient; it is necessary to use more vigorous measures." They proposed increasing the tax on the paper as a way of making it less attractive to the public, but no definitive way of dealing with the *Allgemeine Zeitung* was achieved in Beethoven's lifetime and, much to the chagrin of the government, many citizens still managed to acquire and read the *AZ*. Beethoven's admiration for the articles contained in the *AZ* is yet another mark against him in the minds of the Hapsburg government.

It is appropriate here to mention another publication frowned upon by the Police Ministry. *Der Wanderer* was soundly reprimanded for publishing the final declaration of the Allied Ministers in Aachen because an official and carefully edited report was to appear first in the *Wiener Zeitung*, a government-sanctioned and controlled publication. The editor of *Der Wanderer* was none other than Baron Ignaz von Seyfried, a close friend of Beethoven for more than twenty years. Seyfried himself was threatened with banishment and the papers' owners with severe penalties if such a misdeed occurred again. Beethoven's choice of friends surely did not earn him any favor with the court, either.

BEETHOVEN AND THE ARISTOCRACY

After Joseph II had given his people a taste of freedom, it was inevitable that the concepts of democracy and nationalism—both threats to the Monarchy—should begin to grow in favor with the populace. Yet both in Joseph's time and for a long time after him, the population formed a rigid pyramid. At the top was the Hapsburg emperor and his family consisting of a great many archdukes who were almost deities in terms of their political power. Underneath them was a "thick wedge of nobility." Then was a class of non-noble bureaucrats, university graduates, and professional men, defined in the 1780 census as "Honoratior." Beneath them was a relatively small class of "burghers" in towns, and finally, the largest group, the peasantry that provided most of the Monarchy's wealth. The Monarchy

> drew a firm and very thick line between itself and all but a handful of even the high nobility. Only 21 families (15 princely and six headed by counts) enjoyed the privilege of automatic access to the court and the right to marry into the imperial family. A whole chapter would be needed to describe the intrigues surrounding the selection process.... This Hochadel kept itself leagues apart from the great mass of society below. Nobles occupied the top posts in the army, in diplomacy, in domestic administration, and largely even in the Church. Their wealth came from their estates, some of them the size of English counties. The lesser nobility, especially in Hungary, stood closer to the ordinary people, and therefore were a potential force for change.[13]

Beethoven was one of the very few who dared to insinuate himself—a commoner—into the society of the nobility. By his bearing, by his lack of deference to their higher social status and authority, he presumed himself to be their equal. Such a stance seems laudable to our American society which bases itself in principle—if not always in fact—on the premise that "all men are created equal." In Beethoven's day, however, it was heresy to suggest such a premise. Yet many members of the aristocracy—including the Archduke Rudolph who was not only one of Beethoven's staunchest friends and patrons but also a younger brother of the Emperor Franz—accepted the ill-bred Beethoven into their society. Prince Lichnowsky had even approved of Beethoven's association with Countess Josephine Brunswick and encouraged a marriage between them. The aristocrats with whom Beethoven interacted socially deferred when he refused to follow their protocols. They did not object when he moved as an equal among them, nor did they complain too loudly when he rebuked them. Why did they allow Beethoven to "get away with" such a thing? Perhaps in their eyes it was his great genius that lifted him above the common ranks and allowed them to overlook his humble roots. Yet it is difficult to imagine that every member of the nobility was so willing to accept a commoner in their midst or even entertain the notion that such a thing should be allowed even in the case of a Beethoven. After all, Mozart also was a great musical genius, and yet he knew and maintained his "proper place" in society which Beethoven refused to do. I suspect that a

---

[13]Brook-Shepherd,31

number of them strongly objected to—albeit, perhaps secretly—and felt threatened by his presumptions of equality. After all, the very idea was revolutionary in itself. Theirs was a society where the upper classes ruled. It had always been that way. If the lower classes were allowed to infiltrate that exalted arena of power, then the entire ruling structure could topple, leading to the unthinkable: a democracy, a republic, an overthrow of the monarchy itself. Who can believe that someone like Metternich—who was so desperate and determined to maintain the status quo, that carefully constructed pyramid—wanting or allowing anyone as visible, as admired, as influential as a Beethoven to give the impression that equality was achievable? It was all too evident that the young in particular, the very same students whom Metternich feared the most, would find a role-model in Beethoven. Thus Beethoven's insistence upon being treated as a peer among the nobles must have disturbed many in the upper ranks of the Empire and perhaps even placed him in a dangerous situation to which he was oblivious.

BEETHOVEN AND SECRET SOCIETIES

The Josephinists

Schindler reported that "He [Beethoven] invited me to come often at 4 o'clock in the afternoon to the same place where he was in the habit of coming almost every day to read the newspapers. We had met in a remote room of the tavern *Zum Blumenstock* in the Ballgässchen. I became a regular visitor to the place, and before long I realized that it was a sort of cell of a small number of Josephinists of the truest dye."

Josephinists was the name given those people who voiced strong opposition to the police-state rule imposed by Metternich. The name referred to Emperor Joseph II (1741-1790) who was viewed as a revolutionary reformer. They held him up as a model ruler who had attempted to do away with the class system and institute a society based on equality and security for the masses, with rewards meted out based on merit rather than birth. Although the passage of time shined Joseph's reign somewhat, he had made some positive reforms that had benefited his subjects, and in many minds he had been a monarch far superior to his successors. These views were long espoused by Beethoven, as Schindler corroborates:

"Our composer was not in the least out of place in this company, for his republican views had suffered a serious blow as a result of his becoming acquainted at this time with the British constitution." Schindler added that "A captain in the Emperor's bodyguards and Herr Pinterics, a man generally known in Viennese musical circles and one who played an important part in Franz Schubert's artistic life, were the master's closest associates in this society and in the exchange of political opinions, his seconds who would both stimulate him and agree with him."

Although technically not a Josephinist, perhaps Beethoven's close association with members of the group was intimate enough to give the government cause to suspect his involvement in their activities.

The Carbonari

The Carbonari were a secret society which flourished in Italy, Spain and France in the early 19th century. They were thought to have derived from Freemasonry because it was organized similarly with rituals, symbolic languages, and a hierarchy. Beyond advocating political freedom, its aims were very vague. The group had primary responsibility for uprisings in Spain, Naples and Piedmont in 1820 and 1821.

In that same year of 1820, Napoleon escaped from Elba, and suddenly the police were hearing loudly expressed sympathies expressed for the French leader by the Austrian people. That, coupled with uprisings instigated by the Carbonari, meant that anyone who moved from one place to another automatically aroused the suspicions of the police force. Young people—students in particular—were especially vocal in their support of Napoleon, and Schindler admitted that he was no exception. When a group of students rioted at the university in Brünn (now Brno) in southern Czechoslovakia, the police stepped in. Schindler's papers had not been in proper order and he had been arrested. Later he was cleared, but the experience had left him shaken. After making Beethoven's acquaintance, Schindler related the story to him and Schindler remarked that Beethoven had been "very interested in and sympathetic to his plight."[14] And Karl Peters wrote in Beethoven's Conversation Book, "You are a revolutionary, a Carbonaro." Although Beethoven was not truly a member of the Carbonari, it was not difficult for anyone to see that he supported their desire for political freedom.

The Freemasons

Having noted that the Austrian government was extremely uneasy about Freemasonry and its tenets, the question must be asked: was Beethoven a Freemason? Although modern scholar Paul Nettl (and others) felt that the issue of whether Beethoven was a Mason was uncertain, Victorian scholars such as Alexander Thayer and the editor of Thayer's original edition in German, Hugo Riemann, took it for granted

---

[14]Schindler, 203

that he was a member of the brotherhood and assumed he had dropped his membership when he lost his hearing and could no longer attend meetings in which he could not participate. Nettl felt their observation was untrue because he was under the mistaken notion that Masonry had been abolished in Austria when actually its activities had simply been curtailed. We do know that Beethoven wrote Masonic music. In 1810 we find a letter in which he offered to replace one of his songs sung at the lodge to whom his friend, Franz Wegeler, belonged in Coblenz, with something better. It also was noted that when Beethoven met Schindler for the first time, they supposedly greeted each other with "a certain handshake" taken to have been Masonic in origin, although this seems unlikely. Schindler's first encounter with Beethoven had been as a messenger only. And though Thayer noted as evidence the fact that Beethoven referred to Schindler in a few notes as "Samothracier" this could simply have been following Beethoven's habit of giving his friends amusing nicknames. "Samothracier" actually refers to a resident of one of the Greek islands known for its music (Beethoven was known to be fond of ancient Greek poetry) and not necessarily to a mystic brotherhood. Also, while this might point in some vague way to Schindler's membership in Masonry—though Schindler himself says not—it does not necessarily follow that this reference proves Beethoven also held a membership. On the other hand, Beethoven's personal philosophy of equality, universal brotherhood and personal freedom fits very well within the confines of Masonic belief. While he was not a man for observing rituals—religious or otherwise—nevertheless it is not difficult to believe that he was an adherent to some form of Freemasonry or at least the ideals espoused by them. Certainly his Ninth Symphony, with its climactic "Ode to Joy" which sings of the brotherhood of mankind, was as Masonic in theme as Mozart's *Magic Flute*. Beethoven's connection to this group, or even simply his perceived connection, could have been one of those "fatal links" which made the Monarchy uneasy about him. It would have mattered very little whether he was an official member of a group.

HAVING THE WRONG FRIENDS

Beethoven's conversation books show that he and his friends had much in common when it came to the Monarchy; they were all bitterly disenchanted with the Austrian government and routinely expressed their complaints. Currency was devalued and the economy was poor. Beethoven grumbled over "worthless Austrian paper" that passed for money. Beethoven and his friends also held the common opinion that the aristocracy received too much preferential treatment. F. X. Gebauer wrote, "The aristocrats are again receiving charity in Austria and the republican spirit smolders only faintly in the ashes." Many members of Beethoven's intimate circle of friends—including Oliva, Blöchlinger, Schindler, Bernard, and Grillparzer—railed against Austrian censorship. Grillparzer wrote, "The censor has broken me down—One must emigrate to North America in order to give his ideas free expression." Holz wrote, "The poets are worse off then the composers with the censor, which works for obscurantism and the introduction of stupidity."

> To Beethoven, whose intellectual development took place within the context of the German striving for Gedankenfreiheit (freedom of thought) there could be no greater evil than the suppression of ideas and of rational inquiry. Accordingly he despised the Austrian government, with its network of police agents and its rigid censorship.[15]

And so, it seems, did most of his associates.

Beethoven made dedications of pieces of his music to several prominent people who espoused enlightened ideas. In 1801 he dedicated his Sonata in D, op. 28 to Joseph von Sonnenfels who was an intimate of and adviser to Joseph II. And in 1803, to Tsar Alexander—who was a reformer of sorts in his own country—Beethoven dedicated his sonata for violin and piano, Op. 30. These were unpaid and totally honorary dedications, unlike many which were made to patrons or students.

Many of the those with whom Beethoven had close personal relationships were people often in trouble with the police. They were not criminals in the true sense of the word, but as writers and thinkers, their philosophies clashed with political sentiments of the times. We see the same names in Beethoven's letters as appear in the police files.

Josef Bernard (1775-1850) was a close friend of Beethoven's. Born in Bohemia, Bernard came to Vienna in 1800 as a member of the "Hofkriegsrat." He became editor of the *Wiener Zeitschriff* in 1818 and editor-in-chief by 1819. Bernard also was the founder of the *Wiener Kunst und Industrie Comptoir,* a publishing house. Bernard met Beethoven around 1815—a familiar year to us by now—and is mentioned regularly in the conversation books in later years. Nettl notes that "For many years, Bernard was Beethoven's friend and knew more about the Master's daily life than anyone else, except for Schindler."[16] Bernard apparently was one

---

[15]Solomon, 260

[16]Nettl, 12

of those involved in Josephinism, for he wrote in the Conversation Book, "Before the French Revolution there was great freedom of thought and political liberty here. N [apoleon] should have been let out for ten years"— that is, to set things straight.

Johann Baptiste Julius Bernadotte (1764-1844) spent his military career and gained fame under Napoleon. In 1797 he became the French ambassador in Vienna but left as a consequence of having raised the French tricolor on top of the embassy. Bernadotte was adopted by Charles XIII of Sweden and Norway in 1818. In 1823, Beethoven wrote to him, recalling to him "old times" and thanking him for having conferred on him membership in the Swedish Academy of Music. Bernadotte may have been officially a Swede/Norwegian but his origins and his political allegiances were decidedly French and Napoleonic. Schindler's asserted that it was Bernadotte who inspired Beethoven to write the "Eroica" symphony for Napoleon, but there is no corroboration for that. In fact, Bernadotte seems to have fallen out of favor with Napoleon before Beethoven met him.

August Kotzebue (1761-assassinated 1819) was one of the few pro-Austrians mentioned in Beethoven's correspondence. Originally he was a writer and lawyer in Weimar (Goethe's hometown) but had earned a title while in Russia. Kotzebue went to Vienna in 1798 and was director of the *Burgtheater*. After establishing himself as a playwright, he left Vienna in 1799 to go back to Russia and promptly was arrested on grounds of being "politically unreliable." Kotzebue was taken to Siberia. The Tsar released him the following year and made him director of the German theater in Petersburg. In his *Literarisches Wochenblatt* founded in 1818, he ridiculed the liberal ideas and national enthusiasm of German youth. Consequently he was looked upon as a Russian spy and killed by K.L. Sand, a university student. His magazine *Der Freimütige* contains a number of excellent remarks and observations about Beethoven. He reviewed both the *Christus am Ölberg,* the Fourth Symphony, and the *Coriolan Overture.* Kotzebue wrote three texts for the opening of the new Hungarian theater in February 9, 1812, which were given to Beethoven to set to music. Beethoven considered him a "dramatic genius."

Eulogius Schneider (1756-guillotined 1794) had been a Franciscan monk turned French revolutionary turned poet. His revolutionary poems impressed Beethoven. Nettl noted that "It might be assumed that Schneider had a considerable influence on Beethoven's development. Beethoven's liberal and revolutionary philosophy, expressed in many of his works and in his daily life, seemed to be foreshadowed by the enthusiastic poems of

Schneider."[17] It was Schneider who was responsible for Beethoven's composition of the funeral cantata on the death of Joseph II who as we have seen, was the beloved posthumous patron saint of the outlaw Josephinist group. Schneider's name appeared in a conversation book from 1819 as part of a political discussion between Beethoven and Oliva.

Julius Franz Borgias Schneller (1777-1832) wrote under the pseudonym Velox. Gleichenstein was a mutual friend of Beethoven's and Schneller's, and in fact it was Gleichenstein who introduced Schneller to Beethoven. In 1811, Schneller worked as an enthusiastic promoter of Beethoven's music in Graz, where Louis Bonaparte, Napoleon's third brother, became another one of his close friends. Schneller was an ardent admirer of both Great Britain and America, as was Beethoven, and considered them model countries. These progressive ideas made him many enemies. In Vienna he applied for a professorship at the University of Vienna, but the Emperor Franz himself had rejected his appointment on the advice of the police. Back in Graz his liberal ideas likewise made him enemies, and was told that if he continued his subversive activities the Foreign Office would take every opportunity to point out to potential employers who detrimental his ideas were to public welfare. He eventually moved to Freiburg in 1823 where he apparently learned the value of discretion.

Franz Grillparzer (1791-1872) was a famous dramatic poet who met Beethoven in 1805 at the home of his uncle, Joseph Sonnleithner. His official occupation was Court Clerk (Hofkonzipist) in the Finance Ministry. Grillparzer and Beethoven hoped to collaborate on an opera, but it never came to fruition. Grillparzer suffered numerous reproofs from the Emperor and the police for his poetry and plays, particularly *König Ottokars Glück und Ende* which the censors felt would remind the public too much of Napoleon and cause dissention among different groups of people. He was told he would be fired from his position if he persisted in trying to publish such works. Grillparzer was never fired or outwardly punished, but he never received the higher appointments to which he aspired. "He continued to write. Yet the stifling censorship hung over all his efforts and achievements... By their petty political judgments of the moment (the censors) clouded the light of creative imagination, if they could not extinguish it."[18] It was Grillparzer who asked Beethoven via his Conversation Book, "Does the censor know what you think while you are composing?"

Joseph Schreyvogel (1768-1832, allegedly of cholera) another writer with an unsavory reputation, was known under the pseudonym

---
[17]Nettl, 219   [18]Emerson, 165

Thomas West. His official job was Secretary to the Court Theaters. He founded, with Köhler, the *Kunst und Industrie-Comptoir* noted earlier. There are numerous connections between Schreyvogel and Beethoven and his name appears many times in letters and conversation books.

And just for one more interesting little connection between Beethoven and Napoleon I should present Anna Milder-Hauptman who was the lead singer in Beethoven's opera, *Fidelio*, in 1814. Beethoven was very fond of her and admired her singing greatly. When Napoleon occupied Schönbrunn Palace in Vienna, she had sung for him. Napoleon had been so thrilled by her singing that he wanted to steal her away from Vienna for the Paris opera house.

We see that another "problem" with Beethoven from the police's point of view must have been in the company he kept.

CONNECTIONS TO A SPY

There is a curious bit of information in Solomon's Beethoven biography relating to a man named Moritz Trenck von Tonder. Trenck, a Viennese banker whom Solomon notesd was "previously unknown" in the Beethoven literature," wrote several letters to a friend of Beethoven's, Antonie Brentano, in Frankfurt. The letters, three of them, were written on March 28, 1827—two days after Beethoven's death—and on April 27 and May 10 of the same year. Trenck wrote:

"I hesitate to bring you sorrow through the sad news concerning our friend Beethoven, but I know what great interest you, honored lady, take in his fate." Trenck supplied Frau Brentano with details of Beethoven's last sufferings—seemingly sparing her none of the grisly details despite his assertion of wanting to spare her sorrow!—along with a full description of his funeral and related ceremonies. Trenck enclosed newspaper clippings, a handwritten copy of Grillparzer's funeral address, poems eulogizing Beethoven, obituary notices, and news of concerts held in Beethoven's honor. He also enclosed the report on Beethoven's last days that was written by Beethoven's brother, Johann.

One curious thing about Trenck's correspondence with Frau Brentano is in his reference to "*our* friend, Beethoven," rather than *your* friend. There is no existent letter written by Beethoven to him, nor from Trenck to Beethoven. There is no mention of him in anyone else's correspondence. He neither wrote in nor was written about in Beethoven's Conversation Books. How then did he count himself among Beethoven's friends? The second, and even more curious thing about Trenck and his interest in Beethoven is that Trenck was far more than a simple banker. He was, in fact, a close associate of Metternich. In private correspondence between Metternich and Gentz, the former referred to Trenck as "the best of all possible spies." Unfortunately there is too little existent information on Trenck to speculate on why a top Metternich spy wrote a detailed series of reports on Beethoven's death to Antonie Brentano (supposedly a dear friend and the woman Solomon put forth as the "Immortal Beloved" despite counter evidence), or why he represented himself as Beethoven's friend when it seems he was not. Whether there is any significance which can be attached to this curiosity cannot be determined at this time, yet it was too interesting to avoid including here in this study of Beethoven's likely unnatural death. Was he—or perhaps Frau Brentano—yet another fatal link?

BEETHOVEN AND NAPOLEON

Beethoven had so many entanglements with people who knew, admired, or served under Napoleon that I would be remiss if I did not address Beethoven's feelings about the French leader himself. His connections to Napoleon are another "fatal link." After all, the last thing that the Austrian government wanted was for Napoleon to regain power and remove the royalist house of Bourbon from the French throne. Anyone supporting anything Napoleonic was certainly considered an enemy of the state.

It should not surprising that Beethoven admired Napoleon; many of his contemporaries did. Goethe owned a bust of Napoleon and had remarked about him in 1829, eight years after Bonaparte's death, that "Napoleon managed the world as Hummel his piano, both achievements appear wonderful, we do not understand one more than the other, yet so it is, and the whole is done before our eyes." Hegel called Napoleon "a soul of worldwide significance" in 1806. And Grillparzer wrote in his *Autobiography* that "I myself was no less an enemy of the French than my father, and yet Napoleon fascinated me with a magic power."

Carl Czerny, who visited Beethoven in Baden in 1824, reported a remark made the by composer regarding Napoleon: "In 1824 I went with Beethoven once to a coffeehouse in Baden where we found many newspapers on the table. In one I read an announcement of Walter Scott's *Life of Napoleon* and showed it to Beethoven. 'Napoleon,' he said, "earlier I couldn't have tolerated him. Now I think completely otherwise."[19] Some people may find Beethoven's change of heart about Napoleon surprising. No doubt most call to mind the story of his third symphony, the *Eroica*,

---

[19]Thayer, 920

composed with Napoleon—a man Beethoven much admired at the time—in mind. His fight for freedom and equality had greatly appealed to the composer. But then, when he heard that Napoleon had declared himself emperor of the French, Beethoven's disappointment manifested itself in outrage. He angrily scribbled out the dedication to Napoleon and substituted "In memory of a great man," instead. The myth goes that Beethoven maintained this feeling for quite a few years, however we see from his remark to Czerny that he had changed his mind about Napoleon and once again admired him. In fact, Beethoven's opinion of Napoleon may have reversed itself fairly quickly. In a letter to his publishers, Breitkopf and Härtel, written August 24, 1804, Beethoven noted that: "—the title of the symphony is really 'Bonaparte.'"[20] On the score of the symphony itself is written in the copyist's handwriting:

Sinfonia Grande
Intitulata Bonaparte (later lightly crossed out)
(1804) *im August* (added later by an unknown)
de Sigr.
Louis van Beethoven
Gescrieben auf Bonaparte (pencilled in by Beethoven)
Sinfonie 3 Op. 55 (added later by an unknown)

Solomon noted that for Beethoven to

> have kept Bonaparte—either as title or as dedication—at a moment when renewed war between France and Austria was imminent [e.g. 1805] would have marked Beethoven as a philo-Jacobin, a supporter of a radical cause and of a hostile power. It would have led not merely to the loss of a patron [Lobkowitz] but to the possibility of reprisals in anti-Revolutionary Austria as well....Viennese authorities kept constant watch upon all expression of social or political dissent. And of all forms of dissent, support for France was considered the most dangerous.[21]

Max Unger found a note written by Beethoven on October 8, 1810 that read, "The Mass [in C major, op. 86] could perhaps be dedicated to Napoleon."[22] Beethoven's reconnections with Napoleon also were intimated by Joseph Heer, in his *"Der Graf von Waldstein und sein Verhältnis au Beethoven,"* which attributed Beethoven's rift with his old friend Count

---

[20]Anderson #96 [21]Solomon, 137
[22]Unger, "Beethoven's vaterländische Musik," *Musik im Kriege*, 1, 1943, 170 ff, citation from D.W. MacArdle, *Beethoven Abstracts*, Detroit, Information Coordinators, 1973, p. 156

Waldstein—to whom the famous sonata by the same name was dedicated—to their different political views. Waldstein was a zealous Austrian patriot who took every opportunity to agitate against the French "usurper" [Napoleon] even after the war ended. Beethoven apparently did not share Waldstein's view of the French leader and felt strongly enough to break off relations with Waldstein.

Louis-Philippe-Joseph-Girod de Vienney (1799-1852), the Baron de Trémont, visited Beethoven in 1809, six years after the *Eroica* incident and during Napoleon's assault on Austria. Trémont tried to entice Beethoven to come with him and visit Paris, an idea that at length came to appeal to the composer (although the proposed visit never happened). Trémont tells us that

> [Beethoven's] mind was much occupied with the greatness of Napoleon and he often spoke to me about it. Through all of his resentment I could see that he admired his rise from such obscure beginnings; his democratic ideas were flattered by it. One day he remarked, "If I go to Paris, shall I be obliged to salute your emperor?" I assured him he would not, unless commanded for an audience. "And do you think he would command me?" "I do not doubt that he would, if he appreciated your importance ..." This question made me think that, despite his opinions, he would have felt flattered by any mark of distinction from Napoleon. ... When Napoleon took possession of Vienna for the second time, his brother Jerome, then King of Westphalia, proposed to Beethoven that he should become his maître de chapelle, at a salary of 7000 francs... I think I did well in advising him not to accept the offer.[23]

I will return to Beethoven's connection to Napoleon later in a discussion of Napoleon's son, the Duke of Reichstadt.

BEETHOVEN'S COMPLAINTS

What did Beethoven denounce in speaking about the government? Nearly everything, it seems, if Schindler can be given the least bit of credence. He disliked Austria as a whole, calling it the "Austrian Barbary" and believing it to be a land of crude, uncultured people who did not appreciate art. He hated the entire governmental system, and the imperial court in particular; as such he could hardly have been a favorite with the monarchy! Schindler enumerates Beethoven's favorite topics of conversation.

---

[23]Sonneck, 74-75)

One, the legal system, particularly that practiced by the lower courts. There is little doubt that his bitter experiences during his custody battle over his nephew's guardianship soured him against this group of government agents. Even the upper court, the *Obervormundschaft* he referred to with a derogatory epithet, calling them the "Ober-Arsch Hinterschaft," which I trust needs no translation. Whim and bribery abounded, sanctioned by centuries of common practice. Judges had a free hand to abuse their authority, and lawyers on both sides practiced every kind of harassment to humiliate all the parties involved in a case.

Two, Beethoven detested the police and the way they overstepped their already extensive powers. Even petty officials were given broad areas in which they could exercise every kind of caprice and satisfy their personal desires. No one judged them, and not too many dared challenge them. As we have seen, those who did generally found themselves punished in some way.

Three, the bureaucracy found in all branches of the state. Beethoven felt that government officials lacked any notion of the humanity or citizenship of the people, but regarded them merely as subjects who should obey them. His strong sense of personal liberty could not condone such actions. He complained incessantly about the devaluation of currency and heavy taxation imposed on the people.

Four, although he socialized among them, Beethoven found the aristocracy in general to be decadent and felt they indulged too often in crude excesses. Schindler noted that during and after the Congress of Vienna, virtue and morality had disappeared from the highest strata of the capital's society. A man with Beethoven's strict moral values could not find such behavior acceptable.

Five, Beethoven voiced loud complaints regarding the stinginess of the imperial court in the support of the arts and sciences and its lack of interest in anything outside the palace. Any activities connected to music vanished with the death of the Emperor's second wife in 1807.

Six, Beethoven felt the monarchy took no interest in the religious education of the people Schindler notes that

> It may seem surprising, indeed almost incredible, to learn about a musician who was deeply concerned about matters far removed from his own field, since musicians are especially notorious for their lack of interest in anything not connected in some way with notes. Yet...the composer exhibited a profound interest in the hearts and minds of the people. An eager spirit like Beethoven's with its broad powers of knowledge and understanding, could not encounter a single significant field of

inquiry without interest and critical comment. The amazing part of it is that such a busy musician should take the time and trouble to agitate for the religious education of the people in order to elevate them to a better knowledge of God and His creation.[24]

Schindler noted that Beethoven was particularly fond of the two-volume work by Christoph Christian Sturm called *Betrachtungen über die Werke Gottes im Reiche der Natur und der Vorsehung auf alle Tage des Jahres*. ("Considerations Over the Works of God in the Richness of Nature and the Providence of all the Days of the Year.") As it seemed to Beethoven to be a clear summary of everything people needed to know, he recommended it to several priests but they paid no attention to him. Thus in his later years, he never uttered another word about the religious culture of the people unless it was to voice a piece of bitter sarcasm.

THE NINTH SYMPHONY

On May 7, 1824, Beethoven premiered his Ninth Symphony in D minor, the "Choral," Op. 125 which set to music Friedrich Schiller's poem "To Joy," now more commonly known as the "Ode to Joy." It had been Beethoven's intention to set Schiller's poem to music for some twenty years, first entertaining the notion before he even left Bonn. Schiller was one of those writers whose works were regularly banned by the censors, and it was not until 1808 that his works once again began reappearing in public. Schiller wrote "To arrive at a solution even in the political problem, the road of aesthetics must be pursued, because it is through beauty that we arrive at freedom." Schiller was clearly one of those—whose membership included Kant and Goethe—who felt that only art would lead mankind toward a new social order that would include the freedom to attain one's full potential. With the paranoia rampant in the upper echelons of the aristocracy at this time, it is easy to see why Schiller's beliefs, and anything associated with him or which espoused his views, would cause political unease within in the monarchy.

Neumayr believed that in this symphony Beethoven wanted "to underscore the programmic nature of the work as a kind of counter statement to the politics of the so-called French (i.e. Bourbon) Restoration of 1814." Whether this is true or not, the Choral Symphony unequivocally presented the ideal of universal brotherhood in which all men would be brothers. Although in Beethoven's version of the poem he stressed that this

---

[24]Schindler, 247

universal brotherhood would take place under God rather than within society, it was still a bold statement of the principles of the Enlightenment which Beethoven had championed most of his life. Further, while Beethoven removed from Schiller's poem some of the more inflammatory stanzas such as

> Safety from the tyrant's power!
> Mercy e'en to traitors base!

and rewrote "Beggars shall be brothers of princes" to a gentler "Thy magic power reunites/All that custom has divided," the symphony still embodied Nietzche's interpretation which said "Now the slave emerges as a freeman; all the rigid, hostile walls which... despotism has erected between men are shattered." Basil Deane wrote, that the *Ode* was "the nearest German equivalent to the hymns and odes to brotherhood, liberty and humanity set to music by the revolutionary composers in France."[25] Indeed, the story was often bantered about that Schiller had originally written this poem as an "Ode to Freedom," *Freiheit* rather than *Freude*, though this is not supported by historical evidence. Nevertheless, perception is often as powerful as fact.

It is a testament to the reception the monarchy gave this work that, despite a personal invitation issued by Beethoven to the Emperor and Empress to attend the premier the imperial box at the theater remained conspicuously empty. Although they had promised to attend, the two shunned the performance and left Vienna a few days before the concert. Even Beethoven's friend, the Archduke Rudolph, was absent, having been in Olmütz at the time. The general public, however, received the work with great enthusiasm. Schindler reported to Beethoven (who could not hear the acclaim) that when for the fifth time the audience broke out in riotous applause, the Police Commissioner gave an order for silence so that the performance could continue.

To this review, Schindler added "Yesterday I still feared secretly that the Mass (*Missa Solemnis*) would be prohibited because I heard that the Archbishop had protested against it."[26] Beethoven's music, it seems, did not meet with approval from the Court and its associates. And, interestingly, despite what seems to have been wild acclaim by the public for this symphony at its premier, when the concert was repeated less than three weeks later (May 23rd), the theater was not even half filled and the concert lost money. Did the public see the absence of the Imperial Family as condemnation of this work and fear giving approval to it with their

---

[25]Scherman & Biancolli, 312-313
[26]Thayer III, 166

attendance? Perhaps this revolutionary symphony also made the Court wonder how much further Beethoven might go in expressing his republican views.

A PROVERBIAL THORN

We have seen already that Beethoven, far from being "just a composer," was a man who read the "wrong" books and newspapers, associated with the "wrong" people, and espoused the "wrong" views loudly and in public. He vehemently supported the ideas of liberty and equality and just as rigorously condemned the government under which he lived. He was associated with, if not an official member of, groups whose activities were considered dangerous and subversive and little more than political outlaws such as the Josephinists and the Freemasons. He was much admired by a population that included the very people the government feared and tried to control the most: the young, the university students. He showed the common folk that a man of humble birth could rise through the hallowed strata of the noblity if he had enough confidence in himself. His insistence upon being treated as an equal by the aristocracy was a threat to the social order and the status quo.

Beethoven also was one of the writers' favorites. "Among other writers in the first decades of the nineteenth century, transcendental views about arts and artists attached increasingly to the singular figure of Beethoven. A kind of mythology grew up around this composer in which his manner and habits were seen as a representative illustration of the life of the artist. He appeared to live mainly outside the mainstream of society and its conventions."[25]

It is apparent from Beethoven's strong political leanings and his unwillingness to be discreet about his feelings, that Austria's government officials often must have pondered how they could rid themselves of this nuisance with "mythological proportions" who was in a position to influence the thinking of others. Unfortunately for them, their options were limited. As a freelance and independent artist, his livelihood did not depend upon the patronage of the aristocracy. They could keep professors from teaching and authors from writing articles and plays, and businesses from publishing and selling controversial materials. But they could not separate Beethoven from his music, nor from the love the public had for this music and the man who wrote it. They could make life hard for him (and probably did) through the state-owned theaters by making it difficult

---

[25]Plantinga, 88-89

for Beethoven to hold concerts for his financial benefit. But generally he was above any sanctions such as they were able to levy against others, as they did against Grillparzer and others like him. Most of the publishers of his music were foreign, based in Leipzig and London. The police officials could not even threaten him for their threats were empty ones; they could not afford to make a martyr of him even by imprisoning him, for both the students they feared and the public-at-large would certainly have rallied around someone they so admired. Many a revolution has been founded when the people were given a martyr around whom to rally. For a long time it surely seemed to the Monarchy that Beethoven would remain a thorn that could not be extracted without seriously harming the patient.

Then, in the midst of this dilemma, a fortuitous situation made itself apparent. Frau Johanna van Beethoven, who was already known to the police for her unscrupulous behavior, who was the widow of Carl Caspar and sister-in-law to Ludwig, became involved in a bitter custody battle over her son, Karl, with none other than that very same Ludwig who had become such a thorn in the monarchy's side. One can only imagine the delight of the court officials when a possible pawn in the Court's campaign to eliminate Beethoven came to their attention. The woman and the court, it seemed, shared a common problem in this man Beethoven. Might they not have attempted to use this mutuality to their advantage?

Second, another possible pawn may have been realized as well, for Metternich's personal physician was one Dr. Johann Malfatti, doctor and friend of the composer. Beethoven had rejected and disappointed the doctor's niece and had railed against the doctor's medical ability several times, no doubt causing some hard feelings on the doctor's part. A more indepth look at these two people may give us some clues as to whether they might have been pawns in the Monarchy's attempt to deal with the problem of Beethoven.

Chapter 5
The Sister-in-Law
Johanna Reiss van Beethoven

Few details remain about the wife of Carl Caspar and the mother of Karl who caused Ludwig—either deliberately or inadvertently—so much vexation for much of the last dozen years of the composer's life. Theresia Johanna Reiss was born between 1784 or 1786, the daughter of Anton Reiss, a well-to-do upholsterer and his wife, Theresia, daughter of Paul Lamarche, a wine merchant and burgomeister from Retz in Lower Austria. She married the middle Beethoven brother on May 25, 1806 when she was little more than a girl and her husband was some 10 to 12 years her senior, bringing to the marriage a considerable dowry of 2000 florins. This monetary gift allowed the couple to purchase a large house in the Alservorstadt, part of which they used as rental property to earn a substantial income. A few months later, on September 4th, she gave birth to the couple's only child, a son Karl, and his "premature" birth was the first indication to Beethoven that, as far as he was concerned, Johanna's morality left something to be desired. (Exactly what he thought about his brother's involvement in her fall from grace is unknown, although he did remark in a 1823 conversation book that "My brother's marriage was as much an indication of his immorality as of his folly.") There are indications that the marriage of Johanna and Carl was not a happy one. Carl had his elder brother's temper, and disagreements between the couple sometimes erupted into violence. There is some possibility that at least once Carl considered divorcing his wife, and Johanna claimed that a scar she retained on her hand into old age was the result of her husband stabbing her with a table knife. Yet Johanna's own behavior—which included theft and adultery—was far from exemplary and it is likely she often goaded her husband into violence. Brother Ludwig once noted that "Although I could never defend, still less approve her actions, yet I warded off my brother's anger from her."[1] Johanna's daughter-in-law, Caroline, would later claim

---
[1] Anderson, #1009, II, 876

that she was forceful and emotional, noting that through her letters she could "present her poverty and despair in burning colors with dramatic effect." She had at least one affair—with a medical student—during the course of their marriage, and it was suggested that she was carrying on with another man while her husband lay dying. Several years after Carl's death, she bore an illegitimate daughter, Ludovica, whose father was Finance Councillor Joseph Hofbauer.

In 1811, her husband had her arrested for having stolen some money from him. (She would later also be charged by her husband with immorality, which in the 19th century was an offense that could be punishable by banishment from the Hapsburg Empire. In 1823, Beethoven would seek—though unsuccessfully—to have his other sister-in-law, Therese, sent away for this very reason.) Although one could argue that "his" money was also "her" money, most married couples do not take money from each other without asking for permission first. Johanna, however had been raised in a rather larcenous household. Her father told her he would never give her any money, but if she could take it from him without him catching her, she could have what she was able to steal. Little wonder that she continued this habit after she was married. She was placed under house arrest for a year although her husband forgave her. A draft of a letter from Ludwig to her says, "I must again reluctantly regret that my brother has rescued you from your deserved punishment." Although Solomon sees no consistent hostility between Beethoven and his sister-in-law prior to their fight over the boy, it is all too evident in the former's *Tagebuch* (journal), that he disliked and distrusted Johanna intensely. Before his brother died, Beethoven wrote a draft of a letter to her in his journal that indicated he felt she "lived under a great delusion" about herself and he accused her of having "vented your spite on me, you then tried to make it up with some friendliness."

A BROTHER'S DEATH

Johanna and Carl Caspar were married just nine years when he finally succumbed to tuberculosis, a disease from which he had suffered over a ten-year period and with which he was severely ill since 1813. Carl's illness provided another source of friction between Ludwig and the government. Virtually during Carl's death throes—indeed, barely three weeks before he died—his employer, Herberstein at the Royal Treasury Office, sent him the following heartless letter, excerpted here:

> Neither from the most mediocre request for a leave of absence... nor the hitherto submitted certificate from Joseph Pelar, Chief Surgeon in the (General Hospital) ... is the cashier Carl von [sic] Beethoven to be seen as suffering from an incurable disease, and consequently totally unfit for further service. Rather, one has much more sufficient reason to come to the last-named conclusion on the basis of his inappropriate employment, constantly interrupted for three; on his specific and punishable disinclination for his duties; and on his customary negligence. ...Cashier Carl von Beethoven will, without fail, be ordered on November 2 of this year to begin his cashier's position at the Chief Treasury Office; to work regularly and without interruption... If he fails to do so, one would be compelled to view this as an unseemly example to all the other treasury officials and to treat it severely.... [2]

Brother Ludwig was understandably enraged by this letter from an employer who blatantly ignored statements by Carl's doctor attesting to the severity of his illness, and later wrote on it this note:

> This miserable bureaucratic product caused the death of my brother, since he really was so sick that he could not perform his duties without hastening his death— A fine monument to these uncouth high officials. L. van Beeth.

Beethoven seemed to think that Carl Caspar's health had made too sharp a decline in his last days, making him suspect that Johanna had poisoned him. He would not believe otherwise until Dr. Bertolini had performed a post-mortem examination and declared Beethoven's suspicions groundless. Because the symptoms of some toxins resemble tuberculosis and fooled other doctors before Bertolini, it is possible that Bertolini had made a mistake. However, there is no proof that he did, and he was specifically looking for toxins in Carl's body, therefore we must give Johanna the benefit of the doubt. Even if Johanna was blameless, it is clear from Beethoven's suspicions that long before any custody battle over Karl had managed to embitter Beethoven toward Johanna, he already considered her to be a "bad wife," and blamed her for his brother's untimely death. At the end of 1815, just after his brother's death, Beethoven wrote in his journal:

> O look down, brother, yes I have wept for you and still weep for you. O why were you not more open with me? you would still

---

[2]Albrecht, II, #211, 80

be alive and certainly would not have perished so miserably, had you earlier distanced yourself— and come wholly to me.

This note showing that Beethoven blamed his sister-in-law for his brother's death—despite Bertolini's findings—is hardly surprising when one understands Beethoven's staunch adherence to standards of morality. Johanna's infidelity—a character flaw Beethoven found intolerable—her dishonesty, as well as her lack of concern for his brother, did more than anything else to turn Beethoven against her.

A BROTHER'S LAST WILL

When Carl Caspar died on November 15, 1815, he left behind an ambiguous will that eventually pitted his brother Ludwig against his wife Johanna with his young son Karl as the prize. His original will, signed the day before his death, gave his brother full guardianship of his son. According to a statement Ludwig made to the Landrecht in 1815, Carl Caspar had already indicated he wanted him to assume the guardianship of his son on April 12, 1813, and presented a "Document B" to that effect. This document which the 1961 translator of Beethoven's letters, Emily Anderson, mistakenly thought to be lost, and which subsequent biographers have likewise taken to be missing, was identified by Albrecht as the following, written when Carl was seriously ill and thought his death was imminent:

Declaration, April 12, 1813

Since I am convinced of the openhearted disposition of my brother Ludwig van Beethoven, I desire, that, after my death, he undertake the guardianship of my surviving minor son, Karl Beethoven. I therefore request the honorable court to appoint my said brother to this guardianship upon my death, and beg my dear brother to undertake this office and, like a father, to assist my child with word and deed in all circumstances.[3]

It was signed by both Carl and Ludwig and, as witnesses, Baron Johann von Pasqualati, Peter von Leber, and Franz Oliva. In the will iteself, a line that read, "Along with my wife, I appoint my elder brother, Ludwig, as co-guardian of my son, Karl," was amended and the "along with my wife" and "co-" were stricken out. (Although Maynard Solomon used this to accuse Beethoven of underhandedness, the composer readily explained why he had wanted this phrase amended. He had not wished to

---

[3] Albrecht, #171, II, 6

be "bound up with such a bad woman in the matter of such importance as the education of the child" and had asked his brother to strike out this phrase.) Shortly thereafter, Johanna prevailed upon Carl to write a codicil that stated his wish that young Karl not be taken away from her, but that she and Ludwig should share custody of the boy. Why the gravely ill Carl Caspar—who died the very next day—had signed this is unclear. Had he been fully cognizant of the consequences of signing such a document? Had he signed it of his own free will and by his own initiative? Or had he not been quite so sound of mind and been easily coerced to add this statement to his will? The circumstances under which this codicil had been written are difficult to discern. In a letter to the Court, Ludwig offered Anna Wildmann, who had nursed Carl Caspar during his final illness, as a witness to his contention that the codicil had been written under duress and that Carl had wanted to retrieve it. For some reason the woman was never called to testify. However, the court—the Landrecht, which heard the cases of the nobility—apparently agreed with Beethoven's assessment of his sister-in-law's character—which claimed she lacked the "moral and intellectual qualities" needed to raise her son. They issued a statement on January 9, 1816, that having reviewed Beethoven's petition and Johanna's criminal history, they were abolishing the decree of co-guardianship that had been granted on November 22, 1815.[4]

GUARDIANSHIP AND ILLNESS

It was interesting to me to note that Beethoven's serious decline in health handily coincided with his custody battle with Johanna over the boy, Karl. Immediately after the death of his brother, Beethoven took steps to exclude Johanna from the life of her son, a move he considered necessary in order to safeguard the moral health of the boy. At first the court agreed with him, and on January 9, 1816, granted him full custody, but awarded Johanna visitation rights to be established by the boy's guardian—that is, by Beethoven. At the time, Beethoven was in no position to have the boy live with him—given his haphazard way of living, his habit of moving from place to place, and the general chaos of his quarters—so he arranged for Karl to attend a boarding school, owned by Giannatasio del Rio, where he hoped the family-like atmosphere would prove beneficial. Johanna was never far away from either Karl or Beethoven. Beethoven wrote to Giannatasio:

---

[4]Albrecht, #216, II, 89

> The Queen of the Night paid us a surprise visit yesterday (February 20, 1816) and, what is more, uttered a dreadful imprecation upon you. Her usual sauciness and impertinence to me was displayed on this occasion also; it startled me for a moment and almost made me believe that what she stated was perhaps the truth. ... The enclosed "suitable" little book was given to Karl yesterday in secret by his mother who forbade him to tell me anything about it — ... you will realize also that we must be on our guard.[5]

Johanna got into the habit of visiting with her son at the boarding school, which she considered "neutral territory." Though not an ideal arrangement, she found it tolerable, and certainly preferable to Karl living with his uncle. The schoolmaster, however, found her visits to be disruptive to the school in general and to Karl's emotional well-being. Giannatasio wrote a letter to Beethoven hoping to stop Johanna's visits to Karl at his school.

> (February 11) ...I have to insist that you, as guardian, show me formal authority in a few lines by which power I can, without further ado, refuse to allow her to take the son with her.[6]

Although Giannatasio noted that this could be a "severe privation" for a mother, he felt it was a necessary step to insure the good education of the child and the undisturbed order of his school. And thus he insisted that Beethoven provide him with the legal authority by which he would "forcefully offer resistance to the presumptions of the mother." To this, Beethoven replied:

> (February 22, 1816 to Giannatasio) In regard to Karl's mother I have now decided to comply fully with your desire that she should not see him at all at your school. This arrangement is much more suitable and safer for our dear Karl. — I will now arrange for her to be able to see him at my home... [6]

This "arrangement," that Johanna see Karl only at the home of the brother-in-law whom she detested as much as he did her, certainly was not suitable to Karl's mother. However, Beethoven prevailed. The Landrecht handed down a decision on February 20th to the effect that if Johanna wished to see Karl, she had to apply to the guardian who would then make the arrangements. Karl was to remain under the headmaster's supervision, and under no circumstances was Johanna to visit Karl at school.

---

[5]Anderson, #611, II, 561   [6]Albrecht, #220, II, 93
[7]Anderson, #613, II, 563

Johanna made no attempt to present herself as a model citizen and thereby convince the court as to her suitability to be Karl's guardian. Beethoven noted that "Last night that Queen of the Night [Johanna] was at the Artists' Ball until three a.m. exposing not only her mental but her bodily nakedness—it was whispered that she — was willing to hire herself — for 20 gulden!" [8] She also did not hesitate to spread rumors about her brother-in-law which disturbed him greatly. These rumors, which were spread for many years, were perhaps her way of waging war against him.

> (February, 1816) ...the Queen of the Night (who) never ceases to let out all the sails of her vindictiveness against me.... The idle talk of that wicked woman has upset me so much that I cannot reply to everything today. You will receive full information about everything tomorrow. But in no circumstances whatever must you allow her to see Karl...[9]

> (1820, to the Court of Appeal).... she declared that I had done her son a physical injury on account of which he had to remain in bed for three months. [Dr. Smetana supplied supporting evidence in the form of a certificate attesting to the boy's health.][10]

> (1820, to the Court of Appeal) ...P[iuk] again retailed the the well-worn complaints of Fr[au] B[eethoven] about me, even adding 'that I am supposed to be in love with her,' etc and more rubbish of that kind.[11]

At the end of July 1816, Beethoven wrote to Giannatasio that "Several circumstances induce me to have Karl to live with me" and told him that he planned to begin this arrangement at the end of the school quarter. The "circumstances" to which he alluded had to do with Johanna, though he did not say specifically what. He did enclose a note from her to Giannatasio, which unfortunately has not been preserved, commenting,

> How much we can count on her improvement, you will see from the disgusting scrawl which I am enclosing; the only reason why I am sending it to you is that you may see how right I am to hold fast to the attitude I have adopted towards her once and for all.[12]

---

[8]Anderson, #611, II, 562 [10]Anderson, p. 1393, Appendix C, Document 14
[9]Anderson, #616, II, 566 [11]Anderson, p. 1400, Appendix C, Document 14
[12]Anderson #644, II, 589

Beethoven did not get a chance to realize his plan for establishing a home for himself and his nephew, because before the end of the school term, Beethoven became seriously ill. Was this merely a coincidence? On November 3rd, he noted to his friend, Zmeskall, that he had been seriously ill since the middle of October, was still very ill, and lamented that "All my plans for my nephew have collapsed on account of those wretched people."[13] We can see here that Beethoven blamed his ill health on his servants, which may well be something to consider, although others might well have been at work undermining his health. He was compelled to ask Giannatasio to keep Karl on as a student and boarder for at least another quarter.

APPEAL TO AN EMPEROR

In November 1817, Beethoven once again told Giannatasio that he was considering taking his nephew out of his school and having him come live with him and be taught by a private tutor. At the time, however, he was not feeling well and could give him neither a definite decision nor a timeframe for withdrawing Karl from the school, but told Giannatasio he would do so soon. Thus once again, Karl's placement in the neutral territory of Giannatasio's school where Johanna could feel comfortable about her son's situation and her ability to visit with him, was threatened. Although Beethoven began to suffer "the most terrible headaches" and could "scarcely move a limb," (December 28, 1817) and complained on January 11th that he had "caught another chill" and had a sudden "violent cold and cough," this time he stuck with his plan to bring Karl into his home. On January 24, 1818, Beethoven withdrew Karl from Giannatasio's Institute and brought the boy to live with him, supplying him with a private tutor. His intent in making this move is shown in his journal, written at the end of 1817: "A thousand beautiful moments vanish when children are in wooden institutions," he wrote, "whereas at home with good parents, they could be receiving impressions full of deep feeling..." They vacationed a short time in Mödling, then when they returned to Vienna, Beethoven placed Karl in the *Akademisches Gymnasium.*

Johanna tolerated the situation for the better part of the year, but then in September 1818 she petitioned the Landrecht to reconsider their decision on Karl's guardianship. Her petition was denied, but, undeterred, she made a second appeal, this time to place Karl in a state school. This plea also was rejected. On December 3rd, Karl ran away from the Gymnasium

---

[13]Anderson #669,II, 619

and went to his mother's. Letters between the Giannatasios and Beethoven's housekeeper—whom they had secured for him—indicated that the boy had been abusive toward Beethoven's servants and taken money from them and spent it on sweets. To our 20th century eyes these do not seem to be very grave offenses, but in Beethoven's day an unruly child was viewed as a source of genuine concern. Karl was taken back to Beethoven by the police and Beethoven re-enrolled the boy in Giannatasio's institution until he could make other arrangements. While at his mother's Karl told her that his uncle had "threatened to throttle him" when he caught him, but to Beethoven, Karl said that his mother had instructed him to make false accusations against him if asked in court. We cannot know where the truth lies. Had Johanna made up the "throttling" story to discredit Beethoven? Had Karl simply told his uncle what he thought he wanted to hear? Had he been playing one against the other?

At this point Johanna enlisted the aid of Court Secretary Jakob Hotschevar, a distant relation of hers, to argue the case. Hotschevar was the husband of Johanna's mother's step-sister, a convoluted relationship which made him a vague sort of uncle to her. It is perhaps of note that it was during this hearing with Hotschevar involved that the Landrecht—the legal body that had been involved with the custody case for three years—first questioned Beethoven in regard to his "nobility." From the transcript of the testimony given, we see that the Landrecht had asked Johanna—the first to be questioned—completely out of the blue, whether her husband had been of noble birth. Johanna hedged on the issue, saying that the brothers (Caspar Carl and Ludwig) had led her to believe they were of noble birth, and that the documentary proof was said to be in the hands of the eldest brother. It is difficult to believe that Johanna could have been so ignorant or näive that for nearly a decade she had remained under the impression that her working class husband, a mere treasury clerk, had actually been a member of the nobility. When his turn came to be interviewed, Ludwig said he had no such documents. He freely admitted that he had no claim to the aristocracy and that "van" was simply a Dutch predicate, as opposed to the German "von" which implied a noble heritage. There had been no deliberate deception on Beethoven's part, since both his family's origins and the social status of he and his brothers were well known in the community. By law, the Landrecht only could hear cases involving the aristocracy, therefore the issue was transferred to the Magistrat, the civil court for common citizens. According to Schindler, Beethoven considered their decision the "grossest insult." Not only did he consider the Civil Magistrat to have an unfavorable reputation, but since his primary associations since arriving in Vienna had been with members of the aristocracy, it is likely he never considered bringing his case to a "court for commoners."

This move, which I believe may have been orchestrated by Hotschevar in order to place the case before Judges who would be more sympathetic toward his client, caused a radical—albeit temporary—change in the custody battle. Unlike the Landrecht which had repeatedly upheld Beethoven's guardianship, the Magistrat immediately returned Karl to his mother, displaying, as Thayer noted, "unusual, not to say unjudicial zeal in her behalf." Thayer also expressed his curiosity about the fact that the Magistrat, unlike the Landrecht, had nothing whatsoever to say about Johanna's criminal history—minor though it may have been—nor about her morality, which should have been called into question especially since she gave birth to an illegitimate daughter while the case was still pending! Deiters remarked about this that

> No doubt Beethoven had hoped to attain his ends by general statements and thus spare himself the shame and humiliation which would have followed had he presented the truth, even in disguise, touching the lewdness and shameless life of his own sister-in-law; and her legal advisers, and the members of the Magisterial Court knew how to turn this fact to their own advantage.[14]

The Magistrat was unmoved by Beethoven's arguments both against Johanna and on his own behalf, and took Karl's guardianship from him, appointing Councillor Matthias von Tuscher in his place on March 26th. Naturally Beethoven appealed the decision, accusing Johanna of wanting sole custody of her son so that she could keep all of her pension and not be required to relinquish part of it to his upkeep. The complicated issue of Karl's guardianship remained in flux until the Court of Appeals reversed the Magistrat's decision and granted Beethoven co-guardianship (with *Hofrat* Karl Peters) of Karl in 1820. It was at this point that Johanna made her appeal to the Emperor. Every Wednesday, Emperor Franz would hear complaints from common citizens and then refer them to appropriate members of his court for resolution. Beethoven referred to these audiences as Franz's "public deceptions." As a result of Johanna's petition before him, Emperor Franz asked for a report on the boy, and Deputy Sedlnitzky supplied the following:

---

[14]Thayer, III, 28)

It is evident that this boy, now 13 years old, even before the death of his father (a treasury official) seven [sic, 5] years ago, ran wild to some extent under the influence of his uneconomical mother, who did not have the best reputation. For a year now, at his uncle's expense, he has been in the private school of a certain Blöchinger [sic, Blöchlinger] in the Josephstadt, and is now in the third grammatical class. His talent and application are praised, and if he commits many thoughtless and youthful pranks immediately afterward, they are ascribed much more to his imprudence, combined with a passionate temperament and the habit of doing violence to obedience and decorum in outbreaks of irresponsibility and mischievousness, than to ill will; and therefore, in this respect, there is cause to expect his improvement.[15]

The Court of Appeal did not grant Johanna's petition and Beethoven remained Karl's guardian, along with Karl Peters. Up to this point it seems that Beethoven had been able to thwart Johanna's every recourse in regaining custody of her son. But had she played the last card in the hand she had been dealt? We will revisit Johanna later, in 1826, when she again comes under suspicion. For now, let us review her involvement in Beethoven's illnesses in 1815-1818.

JOHANNA AS SUSPECT

As far as motive is concerned, there was hardly anyone in Vienna with a better reason to do Beethoven harm. His incapacitation through illness—and certainly his death—could only have been to her advantage. While she might not have had murderous intentions, it is not hard to imagine her wanting to make her brother-in-law sick enough so that he could not fulfill his duties as guardian, thus perhaps allowing the custody of her son to default to her or one of her relations. Or, to Johanna's way of thinking, perhaps anyone would have been preferable to Ludwig van Beethoven!

An interesting if somewhat indefinite pattern seems to appear when one looks at the correlation between Beethoven's intentions to take Karl out of Giannatasio's school, in order to have the boy live with him, and his health. Twice these plans coincide with the onset of serious illnesses. The first time Beethoven wanted to withdraw Karl he became violently ill and could not follow through with his plans. The second time, he also became suddenly and acutely ill, but withdrew Karl despite his indisposition. Certainly illness had successfully prevented Beethoven's

---

[15]Albrecht, #270, II, 183

first attempt, so it would not be surprising if his second bout with illness had been caused by someone wanting to once again thwart his plans. Because this cause-and-effect did only happen twice, it is difficult to say with certainty that there was a definite correlation between Beethoven's intentions and his illnesses. Nevertheless, I feel it is curious enough to warrant our consideration.

Although means is not of great importance given the easy availability of poisons to the public at large, it is interesting to note that during her marriage to Caspar Carl, Johanna had had an affair with a medical student who could have given her a "crash course" in the art of successful poisoning. Certainly Ludwig thought her capable of such an act in the case of his own brother's death.

As for opportunity, Beethoven himself noted that Johanna would pay him surprise visits, when she easily could have placed in his apartments a doctored bottle of wine he would naturally have assumed to have been purchased by his housekeeper. It is also a possibility that Johanna did not work alone.

ACCOMPLICES?

If Johanna did have a hand in poisoning her brother-in-law, could she have had assistance from the servants who worked for Beethoven during this time? In his letters we note repeated references to Nanni, Baberl (Barbara), Peppi, and others, and none are complimentary. Although some scholars have chalked up Beethoven's negative feelings about them to his tendency to exhibit paranoia, it is as the saying goes: you are not paranoid if someone really is out to get you. From Beethoven's letters, even if we allow for some exaggeration, it seems as if they were not savory characters, and if we could have had testimony from his friend, Frau Streicher, she may well have corroborated his uneasy feelings about them.

> To Giannatasio del Rio, February 1, 1816: I beg you once more in no circumstances to allow his mother to influence him. How or when she is to see him, all this I will arrange with you tomorrow in greater detail. But you yourself must have some sort of watch kept on your servant, for she has already bribed my servant, though for another purpose![16]

---

[16]Anderson, #603, II, 554-555

September 3, 1816, to Zmeskall: I have a servant who makes his way into other people's rooms with counterfeit keys. So it is an urgent matter. [17]

November 3, 1816, to Zmeskall: Please let me have at once through Herr Schlemmer the papers, testimonials, and so forth which you have about them (his servants)— I have reason to entertain strong suspicions that they have committed a theft— Since the 14th of last month I have been continually ill and have had to stay in bed and in my room---[18]

To Frau Streicher he complained in December 1817:

...the younger one behaved yesterday so impudently and pertly that I threatened, if she was naughty again either to me or to other people, to turn her out of the house immediately; you will notice that we are receiving practically the same treatment from both of them. This propensity is ingrained in their characters, and particularly in the really evil character of the younger one —[19]

In a lengthy letter to Frau Streicher written from Mödling, June 18, 1818, he enumerated the concerns he had had with his servants for a long time: (The italics indicate my emphasis, showing the servants' connections to and sympathies with Johanna. Underlines indicate Beethoven's emphases.)

I noticed that Frau D. in particular was preventing Karl from confessing everything; 'He really ought to spare his mother,' she told him; and Peppi (the new cook) backed her up. Of course they didn't want to be discovered; *both of them have joined forces* quite shamefully and allowed Frau van Beethoven to make use of them; both have *accepted presents* of coffee and sugar from her, and Peppi has been given <u>money,</u> and the <u>old woman</u> presumably too. For there is no doubt whatever that she herself went to Karl's mother. *Moreover she told Karl that if I dismissed her from my service, she would go at once to his mother.* She said this on one occasion when I reprimanded her for her behavior, with which I frequently had cause to be dissatisfied. Peppi, who often listened to what Karl and I were talking about, seemed to be tempted to confess the truth. But the old woman taxed her with being stupid and roundly abused her— Hence Peppi's attitude hardened again and she tried to

---

[17]Anderson, #640, II, 592-593   [19]Anderson,# 841, II, 724-725
[18]Anderson, #669, II, 610

> put me off the scent— The story of this horrible treachery may have been going on for almost six weeks.
>
> In the case of the old woman... hatred may have been a contributory cause, for she always believed that she was being kept down. But just from her <u>sneering expression</u> one day when Karl was embracing me, I suspected <u>treachery</u> and thought how shameful and mischievous such an old woman could be.
>
> ...on the eve of my departure *I received an anonymous letter, the contents of which filled me with terror*; but they were little more than suppositions. Karl, whom I pounced on that very evening, immediately disclosed a little, but not all. ...The old traitress, in particular, tried to prevent him from confessing the truth. ... I know only too well his intriguing and passionate mother.[20]

Beethoven talked about bribery, counterfeit keys, treachery, betrayal, anonymous threats. True, this could have been merely an delusion on his part, brought about by illness and deafness. He had always had a suspicious nature, and it worsened—as it often does in the hard-of-hearing—as he grew older and more isolated from others. Still, Frau Streicher apparently did not attempt to allay his fears, nor did Zmeskall to whom he also complained, nor does it seem that either of them ever contradicted him in any way, though Beethoven continually confided his thoughts to them. While it is possible that they simply were humoring a sick man, it is also possible that they agreed with his assessment. It is not difficult to imagine Beethoven's servants—whom he did not treat very well—siding with Karl's mother. She was their peer; they were all women and thus more likely to understand her position as a mother. If she had asked them to help her make him sick enough so that he would be prevented from taking her son away from her, might they not have helped her? After all, she was not asking them to commit murder. Nor do I feel that Johanna herself had murderous intentions. But the fact is, she was desperate to keep her son. The legal system had failed her, and nothing she had done, not spreading rumors about Beethoven, nor accusing him of mistreating Karl, nor even complaining to the Emperor himself, had helped her case. Under such circumstances it often happens that desperate people will resort to desperate measures.

---

[20] Anderson, #904, II, 767-771

Chapter 6
Doctor Under Suspicion: Johann Malfatti

While Johanna van Beethoven is a viable suspect in the 1816-1819 poisoning of Beethoven, we have another suspect to consider: Beethoven's own doctor, Johann Malfatti. The suggestion that a practitioner of medicine, a man supposedly sworn to preserve life and alleviate suffering could be involved in such a criminal undertaking may seem offensive to some. Perhaps that is one reason modern physicians who have studied Beethoven's illnesses have not even considered the possibility that his ailments had an unnatural cause. Yet doctors in history have not always had sterling characters. They were not only healers of the sick, but also political creatures, sometimes victims of their times and circumstances, sometimes people who acted out of self-preservation or misguided loyalty. Even those seemingly above temptation can be tempted. History has known its share of unlikely murderers in the guise of family members and persons holding esteemed positions in society. One of Metternich's most successful spies was, in fact, Abbé Altieri, a man of the cloth, and if a man who is sworn to uphold righteousness can be drawn into political intrigue, then why could not a physician be enticed to use his skills for ill? There is the possibility that Malfatti was convinced that such an act—eliminating a person potentially harmful to the Monarchy and future of Austria—was one of patriotism. On the other hand, more than one doctor in history has been known to grossly violate the Hippocratic Oath. The reader may be interested to know that one of the most notorious serial killers of the Victorian Age was, in fact, a physician, Dr. William Palmer, who murdered—with poison, seemingly a physician's weapon of choice—his wife, his wife's mother, his brother, and his infant children. Palmer, who was a respected practitioner admired by his patients and his community, remained above suspicion for many years. His associates later were shocked to learn that he had managed to poison so many without detection. Thus a person's credentials—even if they involve the saving of lives—should not allow us to eliminate them from the list of suspects. Malfatti's life had enough contradictions and little mysteries associated with it that it must lead us to at least wonder.

A BRIEF BIOGRAPHY

Dr. Giovanni (aka Johann) Malfatti von Montereggio was born in Lucca, Italy in 1775. He studied medicine with two renowned men of medicine: Dr. Luigi Galvani (1737-1798) in Bologna and Dr. Johann Peter Frank in Pavia. His early work with Galvani[1] had interested him in galvanic treatments which once involved him in an unpleasant court case, although he emerged from it unscathed. It was as an assistant to Dr. Frank that Malfatti arrived in Vienna in 1795, at the beginnings of Austria's reign of suppression. He became a resident physician at the Vienna General Hospital and founded the society of general practitioners—the "Vienna Society of Physicians"—in 1802. When Dr. Frank left Vienna in 1805, Malfatti went into private practive. By 1809 he had published a book entitled *A Plan for Pathogenesis,* (the science of tracing the origin and development of disease) and had already acquired a high reputation as an eminent physician throughout Europe. Interestingly, he had looked after the health of the brother and sister of Napoleon Bonaparte, King Louis Bonaparte of Italy and Elisa Bacciochi. The latter passed away in 1820 while under Malfatti's care, a year before her famous brother. Malfatti also served as the personal physician to the Austrian Archduke Charles (1771-1847) and the Archduchess Beatrix von Este, though neither seemed the worse for it. Because of his outstanding reputation, many foreign heads of state who were in the city in 1815 for the Congress of Vienna placed themselves in Malfatti's care. Although the citizenry at large may have believed he had an outstanding reputation as a physician, his colleagues had a slightly different view. Malfatti was a man of fashionable exterior and pleasant approach, gifted in the art of conversation. Basically, his colleagues saw him as "society's pet, a role for which he had undoubted

---

[1]Galvani was a professor of anatomy, noted as a surgeon and for research in comparative anatomy. He devised an arc of two metals with which contractions in limbs, such as the legs of frogs, could be induced. His controversy with Volta—who was correct in his assumption that the electricity originated in the metal rather than in the animal subject as Galvani believed—led to future research on electrotherapy. Beethoven tried galvanism, unsuccessfully, of course, in a hope to restore his hearing. Dr. Johann Schmidt—who was Beethoven's doctor until he died of a stroke in 1808, at which time Malfatti assumed the role—and Malfatti both were proponents of galvanism.

talent since he was much less a scientist than a man of the world. His lively chatter and the pleasant taste of his medicines had endeared him to everybody."[2] The gift of gab along with a bag full of good-tasting medicine were no doubt the main reasons that so many were willing to place themselves in his care. In 1831 he even was asked by Metternich to treat his son Viktor, when the boy fell seriously ill. In 1837 the Austrian government rewarded him for his excellent service by giving Malfatti a title and making him a member of the nobility. Malfatti became a rather wealthy man and owned both a villa in the Hietzing district near Schönebrunn Palace and a country estate in the Währing suburb.

BEETHOVEN AND THE MALFATTI FAMILY

In 1809, Beethoven quarreled bitterly with Marie Erdödy, the woman he called his "Father Confessor" (*Beichtvater*) because of his intimate relationship with her. He had been living happily in her house as a member of her family[3] from early November 1808, but some six months later, he listened to the unfounded gossip of some servants and came to the erroneous conclusion that she had been unfaithful to him and given her sexual favors to his servant. Although he later apologized when he realized he had made a grave mistake, his jealous anger initially clouded his better judgment and he stormed out of her house. He moved into the only apartment immediately available to him: a miserable room on the top floor of a brothel. There he lived in emotional and physical squalor for a short time until better accomodations could be found. Badly hurt by his accusation against her, Countess Erdödy could not find it in her heart to forgive him readily, and there was a period of estrangement between them. Fortunately, Beethoven was rescued from his resulting loneliness by the good intentions of his long-time friend, Ignaz Gleichtenstein, who introduced him back into society and who attached him to the Malfatti family who embraced the emotionally vulnerable Beethoven warmly and gave him some semblance of the sense of belonging he had enjoyed with his beloved Erdödys whom he had temporarily lost.

The Malfatti family with whom Beethoven became acquainted consisted of Jakob, his wife, their two daughters, Anna and Therese, Jakob's grandfather Mathias, and Jakob's three brothers one of whom, Giovanni (Johann), was a doctor. As Beethoven's doctor, Johann Schmidt

---

[2]Aubry, 190

[3]The Erdödy family consisted of Countess Marie (neé Niczky) estranged from her husband Peter, her eldest daughter also named Marie (called Mimi), her second daughter, Frederike (Fritzi) and her youngest child, a son, August (Gusti).

had only just died a short while before in late 1808 and the composer did not yet have another physician to attend him, Beethoven put himself under Malfatti's care. Beethoven even wrote a little cantata for him (WoO 103) in 1814 in celebration of Malfatti's name day on June 24 called *"Un lieto brindisi."*

Baron Gleichtenstein married Anna Malfatti in May 1811. The myth of Beethoven's romantic involvement with Anna's elder sister, Therese, has long persisted despite the fact that all evidence for it is circumstantial and exceedingly flimsy and Beethoven's own letters can be offered as counter evidence. Beethoven's sole letter written to Therese alone (his others were written to the family as a whole) is tepid and betrays little emotion on his part beyond his disappointment in her shallow view on life. Therese was fickle and flighty, shared none of his interests—even music she took without serious concern—and he could not have considered such an unworthy creature as a potential wife even in his most desperate moments. It may have been that the family had hoped to make the famous composer one of its own, but Beethoven had the presence of mind not to allow it to happen. His refusal to become a member of the Malfatti family and thus making the immature Therese unhappy may not have been well received. Therese eventually married Baron von Drosdick in 1816; it is questionable whether the union was a happy one.

A DOCTOR'S ASSISTANT

Another person to factor into this equation is Dr. Andreas Bertolini. Bertolini was an assistant to Dr. Malfatti, but had become friends with Beethoven three years earlier in 1806. He became one of Beethoven's doctors around 1808 along with Malfatti. Apparently no other doctor enjoyed the personal friendship with Beethoven as did Bertolini. The latter was very fond of music and advised Beethoven in 1814 as to which theme would be best for a polonaise the composer was writing for the Empress of Russia. Interestingly, there was a rupture in their relationship around 1815—and by now the reader may be attuned to that particular year— when supposedly Bertolini secured a commission from Major-General Alexander Kyd for Beethoven to write a symphony. As the story goes, Kyd had intimated to Bertolini that he wanted "something simple, like his earliest works." When Bertolini passed on the request to Beethoven, the composer became incensed by this stipulation. He was not one who allowed others to dictate to him the direction of his creativity. The story ends with Beethoven taking his rage out on Bertolini and breaking off his relationship with him.

How much credence can we give this story? Where did it come from? Why would Beethoven decide to "kill the messenger?" It had not been Bertolini who had demanded, nor even urged, that Beethoven write "simple music," but Kyd, the man who had requested the piece. Why would Beethoven blame his friend for another's rudeness, especially when he had accepted suggestions from Bertolini before? Even if he had been angry initially, Beethoven was well known for thinking things over later when his temper abated, realizing his error, and then making great efforts to apologize and mend the rift. No such overture of conciliation was ever made to Bertolini.

It was at this time, 1816, that Beethoven, under Malfatti's care, developed his peculiar illness which included a variety of symptoms not readily associated with any particular disease. Modern physicians studying the case have offered many opinions, but no definite conclusions have been drawn. The symptoms, as we have noted, do match those of arsenical intoxication. What if, instead of a rift coming as the result of a musical issue, Bertolini had told Beethoven something which the latter did not want to believe: namely, that his doctor and friend, Malfatti, was deliberately doing him harm? What if Bertolini had discovered by accident, or even simply became suspicious of the fact that Malfatti was involved in a scheme to administer doses of poison to Beethoven so that his health would gradually break down and maybe even eventually kill him? As Weider pointed out in his book about Napoleon, a person who uncovers something of this nature usually knows that they must keep their mouths shut or end up becoming victims of "sudden and mysterious illness" themselves. Likely Bertolini only intimated to Beethoven that something was amiss, but it was enough to cause an angry reaction in the composer. The Malfatti family, after all, had become friends of his. He spent many evenings in their company. He helped them in a selection of a piano and wrote music for them. In fact, it was for Malfatti's niece, Therese, that Beethoven had written the piano student's standby, *Für Elise*. Many biographers have supposed that it was to Therese Malfatti that Beethoven had proposed marriage in 1810. Personally, I have found the story to be highly suspect, though it does suggest a closeness to the family. It is far more likely that it was Therese who wanted to marry Beethoven—not the other way around—or that the Malfattis wanted to pull the famous composer into the family. The latter might even have been on the suggestion of certain government officials who thought that such an alliance might cause Beethoven to be more discreet in his talk so as not to hurt his wife and her relations. Whatever the reason Therese ended up in Beethoven's path, his letters indicate that he had gently rejected the spoiled, flighty girl knowing that she could never be his intellectual or emotional equal. Beethoven's rejection of Malfatti's niece might even have helped smoothe away the doctor's reluctance to take part in a scheme to remove him from the picture.

As his physical condition declined over the next eighteen months or so, it is likely that Beethoven began thinking about Bertolini's cautious and subtle warning. In April 1817, Beethoven made an abrupt break with Malfatti. In June he wrote to Maria Erdödy his foremost confidante (with whom he had by now made amends) that

> I changed my doctors, because my own doctor, a wily Italian, had powerful secondary motives where I was concerned and lacked both honesty and intelligence.[4]

All of a sudden, his "friend" was dishonest; Beethoven believed he had motives which did not simply include treating his illnesses. It is unfortunate that he was not more specific about what he had learned or had been told about Malfatti. Perhaps Bertolini had intimated that Malfatti had been cheating him—rather than putting forth the more honest revelation that he was undermining his health. Whatever happened, Beethoven apparently leveled some accusation at Malfatti (which, as we will see, the latter would dredge up again some ten years later) and ended their relationship. It is also interesting to note that after this break, Beethoven's health gradually improved. Arsenic is very slow to leave the body and its effects can be felt for a long time after it is no longer being ingested, but by 1819, Beethoven's health was relatively good once again, albeit only for a short time.

There is one other interesting piece to this puzzling little scenario: Bertolini's burned notes. In his book *Music and Medicine*, Neumayr noted that "They (Beethoven and Bertolini) unquestionably discussed many highly personal matters that Bertolini did not want to become public."[5] What caused Neumayr and others to come to that conclusion? Many years later, in 1831—the year that the Napoleon's son was growing closer to death with Dr. Malfatti at his side —Bertolini fell seriously ill with what he thought was cholera. While it is possible that he actually had contracted cholera which was epidemic in Europe that year, the mortality rate for the disease at that period in history was approximately 95%. That Bertolini had contracted cholera at an advanced age and yet survived was nothing short of miraculous.

---

[4]Anderson #783, II, 683
[5]Neumayr, 341

HOW IT COULD HAVE PLAYED OUT....

Let me present a possible scenario to explain Bertolini and his mysterious, burned notes: Seeing the approaching death of Napoleon's 20-year-old son, again with Malfatti in attendance, Bertolini is spurred into taking action. He had not spoken out when Beethoven lay dying, but now his conscience cannot take on the burden of another unnatural death. He tells Malfatti of his suspicions and threatens to expose him. He says that he had notes on Malfatti's treatment of Beethoven in 1817—perhaps even suggests he has information on Malfatti's second involvement with Beethoven in 1827. Although Malfatti's efforts to rid Austria of the "embarassment" that the Duke of Reichstadt has become is supported by the government itself, it certainly would have been a scandal for news of deliberate harm being done to the popular young man—not to mention the much-beloved Beethoven—to come out. Obviously Bertolini could not be allowed to make his suspicions public. Coincidentally, at that very moment, Bertolini falls ill with "cholera"—a disease that conveniently has symptoms matching those of arsenical intoxication. To protect his family and perhaps even to save his own life, Bertolini burns all his letters and notes concerning Beethoven. This act which presumably guards a delicate secret caused many biographers to assume that Bertolini had burned notes relating to his treatment of Beethoven for syphilis, and that in doing so, he had wished to save his friend's reputation from damage by spurious gossip. Two things fail to support that contention: today's physicians have found no evidence whatsoever that Beethoven had ever had syphilis. Nothing in his medical history or autopsy even remotely suggests that he had contracted the disease, and reputable historians today reject the notion that the composer had had this venereal disease. Second, if Bertolini's purpose in burning his notes was to protect Beethoven's reputation, why wait until four years after his death to destroy these records? Why not burn them after he had ceased being Beethoven's physician, at a time when a living Beethoven would have cared about his reputation? Or directly after Beethoven's death in 1827 when stories about the "dead hero" circulated? Why wait until 1831, when his own health and well-being were in jeopardy, to suddenly have concern for the reputation of a man dead four years? It seems to me far more likely that Bertolini's frantic note-burning had been motivated by fear of reprisal, and that the notes themselves were dangerous because they were political in nature rather than medical.

MALFATTI AS SUSPECT, 1817

A cursory look at Malfatti's life does not raise any suspicions. It is only when one gives attention to his patients and his treatment of them, and to the comments of his colleagues, that doubt about his reputation begins to creep into the picture. I have not yet revealed very much about Franz Joseph, Duke of Reichstadt, Napoleon Bonaparte's son, and his life and death under Malfatti's care. It will be appropriate to do so later, so that parallels can be drawn between Beethoven's death in 1827 (when he experienced symptoms similar to those in 1817), and the Duke's death at age 21 in 1832. For the time being, I will note that despite the fact that nearly all the other physicians who visited the Duke of Reichstadt questioned both Malfatti's diagnosis and treatment, his reputation as an outstanding doctor was never tarnished.

Although we will look at his treatment of Beethoven more thoroughly when we discuss the composer's final illness—for there the inconsistencies are most apparent—we must already wonder about some curiosities in Malfatti's life. He was involved in a lawsuit, and yet seems not to have suffered from it. Financially Malfatti was always well off despite fluctuations in the value of Austrian currency and an often disappointing economy. At a time when money was devalued because of war, his fortune never faltered. His colleagues repeatedly were puzzled by his "misdiagnoses" and treatments of patients, and yet he was given a title and retained as physician to the court of Emperor Franz I and to Metternich and his family. How can a man make so many "wrong" decisions—which ultimately result in the deaths of his patients—and yet rise so high in his profession?

I believe that the reader will soon see yet another "fatal link" between Beethoven and the Napoleons become apparent, that link being Dr. Johann Malfatti.

Interlude
Beethoven from 1822-1826

Beethoven had a brief respite in his health problems between the beginning of 1819 and mid-1821 when he was bedridden for approximately six weeks with "rheumatism." His health, however, soon worsended again. Liver damage first made itself apparent in jaundice which he reported in a letter to the Archduke Rudolph written on July 18, 1821. A November 12th letter to Franz Brentano shows that diarrhea had been added to his problems. On April 6, 1822, Beethoven's letter to Ferdinand Ries reports that he had been ill for "the past half year." By 1823, letters show that he was plagued with intestinal difficulties, including repeated attacks of diarrhea, an inflammation of the eyes which included pain and sensitivity to light, and symptoms he believed were associated with "catarrh and a cold." These symptoms persisted into 1824. In August 1823, he wrote to the Archduke that

> Yesteday my doctor assured me my illness was getting better, but I still must pour down a whole portion of medicine within 24 hours which, because it purges the bowels, leaves me feeling extremely weak.

Neumayr attributed Beethoven's problem to viral hepatitis, but it is extremely rare for the symptoms of hepatitis to continue for more than six months, let alone two years. His symptoms were also intermittent, not persistent, with periods of wellness followed by severe relapses.

Beethoven continued to add varied symptoms to his list of health complaints. If he had indeed suffered from viral hepatitis and worsening cirrhosis of the liver as well as whatever diseases were causing his eye problems, bleeding, coughing and respiratory difficulties, should we not be amazed that he survived as long as he did?

In 1825 Beethoven lost confidence in Dr. Staudenheim who had been treating him for several years without improvement, and enlisted the services of Dr. Anton Branhofer in mid-April. Branhofer, a no-nonsense physician, put his unruly patient on a strict dietetic regiment, which included abstaining from wine and coffee, and to which Beethoven apparently adhered. Yet there were no positive results. On May 15, 1825, Beethoven reported that he was coughing or spitting up blood and having frequent nosebleeds. His stomach and "general physical condition" were "terribly weak." His Conversation Books indicate that he was also suffering from fever or fever-like symptoms. Braunhofer wrote, "Every fever lasts a little while, yours is already going away."

No better by June 9, Beethoven wrote that "my weakness often comes really to the edge of fainting." His disposition worsened and he was prone to irritability and moodiness to the point which was odd even for a Beethoven whose emotions were normally volatile.

In autumn of 1825, Beethoven took his usual summer residence in Baden and his health showed almost immediate improvement. He attended parties and his disposition became almost cheerful; he exhibited an almost boisterousness which had not been evident in Beethoven for some time. Despite a periodically bad stomach, his health stablized. Is it not interesting that he should show such a dramatic improvement once removed from Vienna? Could the source of his troubles have been in the city?

Back in Vienna by January 1826, he began to once again suffer "gout pains," particularly evident in his lower back around the area of the kidneys. Yet other than one complaint in February about "gout on the chest," the rest of the year showed an improvement in his health, until the end of that fateful year.

CORRELATIONS

If we recall Beethoven's political situation at this time, we see that he had become more and more outspoken against the Monarchy, caring not at all how inflammatory his remarks were nor who heard them. His works, most notably the Ninth Symphony, had taken on a revolutionary air. In family matters, bitter altercations with a teenaged nephew often escalated into violence. Beethoven complained that Karl "began seeing his mother on the sly again," and thought he might have been assisted in this endeavor by Johann. In 1825, Beethoven wrote a note to Karl saying,

> As God is my witness my only dream is of being totally separated from you and from my wretched brother and this detestable family that's been wished on me. May God hear my prayers, for I can't trust you anymore.

Yet his strong sense of responsibility toward his "detestable family" and a love for his nephew that, despite everything could not be extinguished, counteracted whatever desires he had for separating from these persons who caused him such deep personal anguish. If this prayer could indeed have been answered—if Beethoven himself had allowed it to have come true—who knows whether he might have had a few more years of life.

Ludwig van Beethoven
engraving ca. 1818
Source: Louis Nohl, 1890

The Brothers Beethoven

Johann van Beethoven
oil painting by Leopold Grosz
1841

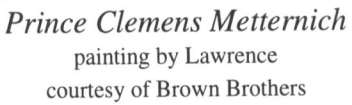

Prince Clemens Metternich
painting by Lawrence
courtesy of Brown Brothers

*Count Joseph
Sedlnitzky*

Dr. Johann Malfatti
Source: Photo Archives,
Institute for Medical History,
University of Vienna

Dr. Andreas Wawruch
Source: Photo Archives,
Institute for Medical History,
University of Vienna

Franz Karl, Duke of Reichstadt, King of Rome
Lithograph c. 1830, Source: Hofbibliotek Vienna

Karl van Beethoven
Unsigned photograph c. mid-1850s
Source: Bekker

*Karl van Beethoven
as a Cadet*
miniature on ivory

Anton Schindler
undated photograph

Karl Holz
miniature on ivory
by Barbara Fröhlich-Bogner
February, 1824
Source: Historisches Museum,
Vienna

Chapter 7
Beethoven's Last Four Months

A detective in search of an unknown killer will first inform himself of any peculiarly significant circumstances surrounding the crime, then search for the most obvious enemies of the victim.[1]

How did Beethoven die? The answer has been given without much hesitation: cirrhosis of the liver, with the additional complication of pneumonia. And what had brought him to this early grave, and given him the liver disease that had claimed his life? Again, there has been an answer: alcohol, many say, had been the cause of the damage to his liver. This causality was even put forth by Neumayr, who had softened previous biographers' accusations that Beethoven had been a heavy drinker and therefore that his own weaknesses in this regard had been at the root of his health problems. Neumayr suggested that he may have had a genetic sensitivity to alcohol, so that even a small amount would have been dangerous to his health . Any amount of drinking, even in the moderate amounts Beethoven consumed was enough to become the ultimate cause of the composer's death at the age of 56.

On the surface, and despite assertions by Beethoven's contemporaries that he drank very little and that his favorite beverages were spring water and coffee, there has not been much reason to doubt the diagnoses of the experts. Yet, there are enough inconsistencies in various reports about Beethoven's life and death, that have led me to believe that perhaps these experts had been wrong all along.

One of the most thorough accountings of Beethoven's last months of life came from Dr. Andreas Wawruch, one of the physicians who attended the composer during his final illness and who, officially at least, had been in charge of his case. Many experts drew their conclusions about

---
[1]Weider, 529

the cause of Beethoven's death from Wawruch's report, but seemingly have ignored the questions that arise—or at least arose in my mind—in reading it. Before going further, allow me to digress a moment to present a brief biographical sketch of Beethoven's last official doctor. At times unfairly maligned by Schindler, he presents qualifications that often surpassed those of the much-lauded Malfatti.

ANDREAS JOHANN WAWRUCH (1772-1842)

Despite Malfatti's reputation with the nobility, Dr. Andreas Wawruch was the far more experienced and capable doctor. Modern physicians have called his treatment of Beethoven "completely appropriate and correct and expertly applied." In fact his treatments, the "tappings" he administered to Beethoven where an incision was made in the abdomen in order to draw off excess fluid, are still used to treat similar cases of edema today, albeit done under far more sanitary and less painful conditions. Wawruch was a professor of pathology and pharmacology at the University of Prague, and was one of its most popular teachers. He became director of the medical clinic in Vienna in 1819 and served as professor of clinical pathology and internal therapy for advanced surgeons at the Vienna University until his death in 1842. He was a member of the Imperial Doctors' Society in Vienna and a contributor to the imperial medical journal in which many of his essays were published. Wawruch's expertise as a pharmacologist could have caused Malfatti to make up the story of Beethoven's excessive love of alcohol so that Wawruch would not become unduly suspicious about Malfatti's "prescription:" an alcoholic punch.

WAWRUCH'S REPORT

I present to the reader Wawruch's report, written approximately two months after Beethoven's death (May 20, 1827). We find our first clues, the first inconsistencies, here:

> Ludwig van Beethoven declared that from earliest youth he had possessed a rugged, permanently good constitution, hardened by many privations, which even the most strenuous toil at his favorite occupation and continual profound study had been unable in the slightest degree to impair. When he entered his thirtieth year, however, he began to suffer from hemorrhoidal complaints and an annoying roaring and buzzing in both ears.

Although the first problem with Wawruch's report does not relate to Beethoven's final illness, it does show that the doctor was not infallible when it came to reporting on the composer's medical history. Far from having a "permanently good constitution," Beethoven still as a young man commented to his friend Franz Wegeler, "Was I not always a sickly fellow?" Second, Beethoven entered his thirtieth year two weeks before the end of 1800, but it was quite a few years prior to that that Beethoven had first noticed a change in his hearing. In his *Heiligenstadt Testament,* a will he wrote on October 6 and 10, 1802, he noted that he had started having difficulties with his hearing some six years previously, when he was still in his mid-twenties.

> Soon his hearing began to fail, and for all he often would enjoy untroubled intervals lasting for months at a time, his disability finally ended in complete deafness.

Wawruch does not say when this totality of deafness occurred, but Beethoven became profoundly deaf around 1817. As I have already noted, this was significant.

> At about this same time Beethoven noticed that his digestion began to suffer; loss of appetite was followed by indigestion, and annoying belching, an alternate obstinate constipation and frequent diarrhoea.

Again, in addition to the complete loss of what had previously been erratic hearing ability, Beethoven was beset with a variety of other medical complaints. These same symptoms appeared in the cases of both Napoleon—a known vicitm of arsenical intoxication—and his son, the Duke of Reichstadt. Their health gradually declined, and loss of appetite and weight headed their list of initial symptoms. Weider wrote "To (Napoleon's) chronic ill-health has now been added *une maladie de langueur*, a wasting illness." Like Beethoven, he suffered from alternating constipation and diarrhea and his appetite was severely affected. If we understand Wawruch's report correctly, these symptoms noted in connection with Beethoven occurred simultaneously, around 1817.

> At no time accustomed to taking medical advice seriously, he began to develop a liking for spiritous beverages in order to stimulate his decreasing appetite, and to aid his stomachic weakness by excessive use of strong punch and iced drinks, and long, tiring excursions on foot.

No other person of Beethoven's acquaintance, with the exception of Holz, a youthful "drinking buddy" Beethoven acquired late in life, has ever mentioned the composer's excessive use of alcohol. (I will cover Holz and his interesting relationship to Beethoven later on.) Schindler, who knew him from 1814 until his death, noted that Beethoven's favorite beverages were coffee and spring water which he often drank by the quart. And however bad Wawruch thought walking and "excessive exercise" was for a person, it is clear to us now that this was a healthy addiction on Beethoven's part. His health problems most definitely did not relate to his habit of taking long walks, and, perhaps, the stamina he gained from his regular walks helped him stave off death for as long as he did.

> It was this very alteration of his mode of life which, some seven years earlier, had led him to the brink of the grave. He contracted a severe inflammation of the intestines, which, though it yielded to treatment, later on often gave rise to intestinal pains and aching colics and which, in part, must have favored his eventual development of his mortal illness.

Wawruch's "seven years earlier" does not make it clear exactly to what time period he was referring. Seven years earlier than when he had lost his hearing entirely? Not so, because Beethoven did not suffer a catastrophic illness in 1810. Possibly Wawruch was referring to seven years earlier than the present time, which would have put his severe illness around the year 1819, again, as we know, a significant date in our pursuit of who and what killed Beethoven.

> In the late fall of the year just passed (1826) Beethoven felt an irresistable urge... to go to the country to recuperate.

Recuperation was not Beethoven's reason for wanting to go to his brother's country home in Gneixendorf. First, Beethoven's letters for 1826 do not reflect any illness for six months prior to this time. The last time he mentions illness—and Beethoven was not one for keeping his sicknesses a secret—was in February of that year, when he noted that he had a "gout on the chest." Thus there was nothing from which he felt he needed to recuperate. Beethoven's decision to go to the country stemmed from his desire to take his nephew Karl away from the city, the police, and his mother. Karl had attempted suicide, a criminal offense at the time, although he was not incarcerated or kept under police surveillance for very long (another one of those odd coincidences which I will return to later). Once released from the hospital, Karl wanted to stay with his mother whom Beethoven still felt would be a bad influence on the boy (who was hardly a "boy" except under Austrian law which did not recognize a person as an adult until they were 24). In order to avoid her, Beethoven decided to leave Vienna with Karl, accepting his brother Johann's offer to come and stay with him in Gneixendorf. Wawruch's next statements confirm that Beethoven could not possibly have been very ill when he arrived at his brother's.

> Often, with rare endurance, he worked at his compositions on a wooded hillside and his work done, still aglow with reflection, he would not infrequently run about for hours in the most inhospitable surroundings, defying every change of temperature, and often daring the heaviest snowfalls.

It is difficult to imagine a man who is seriously ill running through the woods in the cold and snow. In addition to this, Beethoven accompanied his brother on several excursions to nearby towns, and they took long walks around Johann's property which covered some 400 acres. Eventually, however, illness did creep up on Beethoven.

> His feet, always from time to time edematous, would begin to swell and since (as he insisted) he had to do without every comfort of life, every solacing refreshment, his illness soon got the upper hand of him.

What was Beethoven's "solacing refreshment" with which he did without? Could it have been alcohol? If so, then it was not that which worsened his health. Swollen legs and feet are symptomatic of arsenical intoxication.

> Itimidated by the sad prospect, in the gloomy future, of finding himself helpless in the country should he fall sick

Here we see Wawruch contradict himself. According to an earlier statement in his report, Beethoven had already been ill. How then could he "fall sick" in the future if he was already ill?

> he longed to be back in Vienna, and as he himself jovially said, used the devil's own most wretched conveyance, a milk-wagon, to carry him home.

It is unclear exactly how Beethoven and his nephew made the trip from Gneixendorf to Vienna. We do know that they made one overnight stop on his way to his brother's house, and likewise stopped for the night on the return trip. Coaches ran from St. Pölten or from Krems—each about an hour's distance from Johann's estate—to Vienna, but not from

Gneixendorf directly. Thus Beethoven and Karl had to take some other conveyance to one of these in order to catch a regular coach back home. Johann's wife had taken his carriage into Vienna, so it was unavailable. Some sort of wagon apparently transported them.

At midnight of the day they left Gneixendorf, Beethoven became suddenly and violently ill. We note that Beethoven was not, according to Wawruch and the account that Beethoven gave him, very ill at the point of his departure. Wawruch writes only that he traveled in inclimate weather "driven on by an inner anxiety, a gloomy foreboding of disaster." From Karl, the only eyewitness to this tragic trip, we have no account. There is no gradual onset, no progressive development of symptoms. All at once Beethoven is plunged toward death's door:

> Toward midnight he had his first attack of feverish chills and a dry hacking cough accompanied by terrible thirst and pains in his side. When the fever began, he drank two quarts of ice-cold water and, in his helplessness, longed for the first light of day. He was laid, sick and feeble, in the wagon and finally arrived, exhausted and spent, in Vienna. I was not called until the third day.

Beethoven's symptoms could have come directly from a textbook on toxicology: sensation of fever, chills, a dry cough, pain in his side, and the tell-tale burning thirst, followed by extreme weakness. It was the oddity of his "terrible thirst" that first made me suspicious, for this is not symptomatic of either cirrhosis or pneumonia, and further, it is a symptom both of the Napoleons shared with Beethoven.

BACK IN VIENNA

We finish out this chapter with the rest of Wawruch's report, which discusses what happened to Beethoven immediately following his return to Vienna and the arrival of Wawruch on the scene on December 5th.

> I found Beethoven afflicted with the most serious symptoms of pneumonia, his face was burning, he was spitting blood, suffocation threatened his breathing, and the pains in his side made it agonizing for him to lie on his back.

From Wawruch's report one might assume that Beethoven had been violently ill the entire time, from midnight on December 1st to the time when Wawruch first encountered him. on the 5th. But Beethoven had a brief "remission" starting around December 2nd or 3rd. At that pont, his letter to Holz says only that he was *umpässlich*, that is "indisposed." If

Beethoven was sick, he never hid that fact, so despite his violent episode on the road, he must have had a somewhat remarkable recovery after arriving back in Vienna. But then, a few days later, as Wawruch arrives on the scene, he once again was violently ill. Allow me to digress a moment and compare Wawruch's initial observations of his patient with those made by Napoleon's doctors. According to them Napoleon had a "persistent cough and his breathing was labored (certainly pneumonia-like symptoms). The lower part of his legs and feet were swollen. He had pain in the region of the liver. He spit blood. He had sensations of fever without a rise in temperature. We note that Wawruch did not take Beethoven's temperature, only noted he had a "burning face" and assumed a fever from that observation. Redness of the face is another one of those tell-tale signs of arsenic poisoning because the toxin dialates blood vessels in the skin.

Amazingly, Beethoven again recovered from this catastrophic onslaught—although it now took about five days to do so, rather than the three it had taken after his first "attack"—so that Wawruch reported

> he was able to sit up on the fifth day and tell me with much animation about the difficulties he had endured up to then. On the seventh day, he felt so much better he was able to get up and walk around, and read and write. On the eighth day, I was no little alarmed. At the morning visit, I found him stricken and suffering from jaundice all over his entire body, the most dreadful vomiting and diarrhea had threatened to kill him the night before. Shivering and shaking, he was doubled up with pains raging in his liver and intestines, and his legs, which up to then were only moderately bloated, were terribly swollen. From now on, dropsy began to develop; the amount of urine voided was sparcer... nightly attacks of suffocation (pulmonary edema) appeared...

Again we turn to Weider and his account of Napoleon's state of health: "Napoleon's health was sometimes better, sometimes worse. Each time he fell ill the familiar symptoms would recur, though new ones might be added... Bertrand noted that Napoleon's skin had become yellow, suggesting his liver was affected. Later he was also diagnosed as having developed pleurisy.... Napoleon's doctor noted that he had a dry and persistent cough and his breathing was labored. He could urinate only slowly and in strictured pain. The lower part of his legs and feet were swollen."

Not only are the symptoms of the two men remarkably similar, but in each case the observation of the men's urine output is interesting: a lessening in the secretion of urine is typical of intoxication by arsenic.

What also is notable about Wawruch's account is the rapid onset of Beethoven's symptoms. He went from feeling fairly well, being able to get out of bed, read, write, and walk around to that very same day being doubled over with pain, suffering from vomiting and diarrhea, his legs swollen, his ability to urinate impaired, his breathing labored, his skin jaundiced.

Weider again: Napoleon had a sensation of fever along with chills, without any rise in actual body temperature. This was accompanied by difficulty in breathing, nausea, abdominal pain, vomiting, dizziness, and severe sweating. And in the case of Napoleon's son, we see the same symptoms again: his skin became yellow, his liver swollen and tender, he had periods of recuperation followed by severe "relapses," his appetite worsened and he lost a lot of weight, he had difficulty in breathing and his feet and legs were swollen. "Fever" came on periodically, followed by copious sweating (caused by the body's attempt to rid itself of the toxin), leaving the duke very weak. He was jaundiced. Occasionally he would spit blood. By now, these symptoms must seem all too familiar to the reader.

I will continue with Wawruch's report in the course of looking at Beethoven's last days and last medical treatments. An old acquaintance—Dr. Johann Malfatti—is soon to make his appearance under odd circumstances, and at virtually the same time, Karl will depart to join his regiment and to make his new life in the army.

Chapter 8
Beethoven's Last Treatments

We saw that after arriving in Vienna, Beethoven's condition improved. He had one brief respite a day or so after returning home, followed by another serious episode after which Wawruch found him violently ill, and then he again was considerably better from days five through seven, so much so that he could sit up and walk about. On the eighth day he had an unexpected and violent relapse that alarmed Wawruch. The doctor found him jaundiced, suffering from vomiting and diarrhea, feeling an intense pain in his side, and having serious swelling of his lower legs and feet.

Beethoven generally did not trust doctors—and considering the barbarism of 19th century medical "treatment" it is not hard to imagine why—and Wawruch was completely unknown to him. Despite the fact that Wawruch was a skilled physician for his time and came highly recommended, Beethoven did not like having a stranger attend him. In cases of extreme illness or stress, it is not unusual for a patient to find the familiar more comforting. But who had suggested Johann Malfatti to him, a man he had not seen in ten years? We do not know. We know only that Beethoven had prevailed upon Schindler to try to persuade Malfatti to come and help him. Schindler obliged him but at first was unsuccessful. He recalled that

> ... when I went on the master's behalf and asked Malfatti to come, he would not listen, and turned me coldly away. Never shall I forget the harsh words of that man which he commissioned me to bear to the friend and teacher who lay mortally ill... I repeatedly carried to him the urgent requests of Beethoven that he should come to his help or he should die. ... To all these representations Malfatti answered me coldly and drily, "Say to Beethoven that he, as a master of harmony, must know that I must also live in harmony with my colleagues." Beethoven

> wept bitter tears when I brought him this reply. ... I dared a second and even third attempt at arousing his compassion for the suffering composer. ... Malfatti finally took pity on poor Beethoven... [1]

Repeatedly, Malfatti refused to visit his old patient and one-time friend. His attitude was one of cold-blooded anger. Beethoven would die without him, Schindler had said, and Malfatti had been unmoved. How was it that Malfatti still bore Beethoven a grudge even though a decade had elapsed since their falling-out? Malfatti gave the excuse that an act of kindness toward Beethoven on his part would incur the disapproval of his "colleagues." Yet it is difficult for me to believe that Malfatti's fellow doctors would have seen his ministering to a desperately sick man as an act of betrayal against them. Would they not rather have lauded his ability to forgive an old friend a transgression from ten years before? Exactly who then were these mysterious colleagues of Malfatti's who, like Malfatti himself, bore Beethoven such ill-will?

Then in a surprisingly abrupt move, these disapproving colleague were forgotten and Malfatti changed his mind. Were the opinions of the fellow physicians no longer relevant? And if not, why not? Might we not wonder if this sudden turn-about which occurred so close on the heels of Karl's departure was more than mere coincidence? Had Malfatti been prevailed upon to "take up where Karl had left off" in the matter of his uncle? Exactly who or what had changed Malfatti's mind can only be speculated, but to have such a sudden change of heart after he had treated Schindler with such coldness is very odd. Schindler continues:

> At last I prevailed upon him to give the patient at least the pleasure of a professional visit as if he were going to the bedside of a complete stranger. He expressed the wish that this visit (to Beethoven) should take place in the presence of the physician who was in charge of the case.[2]

This is an interesting request. Why would Malfatti insist upon having another physician present? In other instances of poisonings in history, there is an interesting pattern: in almost all cases a physician was present when the poisoning took place. In his discussion of poisoning in general, Weider gave an example of the infamous Marquise de Brinvillier and her systematic administration of arsenic to her father which eventually lead to his death. Over a period of eight months, she gave her father approximately 30 doses of the poison. He noted that,

---

[1]Schindler, 320. [2]IBID

It was part of the Marquise de Brinvillier's famous practice of killing off her dear and wealthy relatives that a physician should be at the victim's bedside and prescribe the final deadly poison. The physician's dosage would naturally be corrected appropriately as opportunity permitted. A doctor must be in attendance. Who would suspect a physician of deliberately administering a deadly poison?[3]

Who would suspect a man of poisoning a patient with another doctor in attendance? How much easier to avoid suspicion if one has medical attention standing by as the poison is being administered. Seen in that light, Malfatti's request that Wawruch be present when he attended Beethoven perhaps is not so strange at all.

From that day on, Malfatti would visit Beethoven every day, but always with Wawruch along. For some reason, Wawruch acquiesced to Malfatti's supposed expertise—perhaps because Malfatti was quite well thought of both in Vienna at large and at the court of the emperor in particular, and was known to have once enjoyed a personal acquaintance with Beethoven. Malfatti immediately stopped all of Wawruch's prescribed treatments and in their place substituted only a "frozen punch"— a combination of sugar, rum, and tea or fruit juice. Schindler noted later that this punch was prescribed in "rather large quantities" and that "Under this regiment the patient felt refreshed, and was sometimes so strengthened that he thought he would be able to compose again, and even that he would recover entirely." This is not a surprising reaction since the alcohol would have eased Beethoven's discomfort and allowed him to get much-needed rest.

Johann Baptist Jenger commented about Malfatti's reversal of Wawruch's treatment in a letter he wrote to Marie Koschak-Pachler, a gifted pianist who had once delighted Beethoven with the way she executed his works. Jenger reported that Dr. Malfatti had said Professor Wawruch's treatment of Beethoven up to that point had been "entirely wrong." Neumayr, perhaps wanting to give Malfatti the benefit of the doubt, assumed that what Malfatti had meant was that Wawruch's prescriptions had been wrong from a *psychological* point of view. But I am more inclined to believe that Malfatti wanted to discredit Wawruch so that he could essentially take over the case—while still leaving Wawruch officially in charge—and prescribe his own remedies. As we will see, everything that Malfatti prescribed for Beethoven worsened his condition. not alleviating his suffering, but increasing it.

---

[3]Weider, 293-294

About this prescription for iced punch, Wawruch wrote the following statement as recorded by Thayer. Several things about this statement raised more suspicions in my mind about Malfatti and his intentions. Wawruch begins:

> Then Dr. Malfatti, who thenceforth supported me with his advice, and who, as a friend of Beethoven's long years' standing understood his predominant inclination for spirituous liquors hit upon the notion of administering frozen punch. I must confess that the treatment produced excellent results for a few days at least. Beethoven felt himself so refreshed by the ice with its alcoholic contents that already in the first night he slept quietly throughout the night and began to perspire profusely. He grew cheerful and was full of witty conceits and even dreamed of being able to compose the oratorio 'Saul and David' which he had begun.[4]

It was true that Malfatti had known Beethoven for several years, and served as his physician between the years 1809 and 1817, but he had not seen him for ten years. And yet the glib Malfatti somehow convinced Wawruch that he was still Beethoven's close and long-time friend who knew him better than anyone. Was Wawruch oblivious to the fact that until a short time before Malfatti had still borne Beethoven animosity?

The next interesting statement Wawruch makes is that "Dr. Malfatti ... understood [Beethoven's] predominant inclination for spiritous liquors." When Schindler later read Wawruch's account, it is obvious from his reaction that he did not catch the implications of Wawruch's remarks. Schindler took offense and complained in his book that Wawruch had called Beethoven a drunkard. Wawruch's statement does not specifically say that, but it did imply that Beethoven was predisposed to drink large amounts of alcohol and that supposedly Beethoven's predilection for "spirituous beverages" had first manifested itself at the age of 30—*and that it had been Malfatti who had led him to believe this.* Wawruch formed this opinion because *Malfatti* had told him that Beethoven drank to excess; after all, Wawruch did not even know Beethoven until a few months before his death and Wawruch was in no position to know one way or the other, He simply accepted what Malfatti had led him to believe was the truth. Since Malfatti was a renown physician and a colleague who professed to have had an intimate friendship with Beethoven, Wawruch had no reason to doubt him. I once again call upon Weider's account of Napoleon's fatal illness for an interesting parallel:

---

[4]Thayer, III, 1030

We might do well to observe that Montholon (Napoleon's poisoner) wanted it established that Napoleon customarily drank orgeat (the orange drink in which the poison was to be administered) on St. Helena, and not just during his last weeks.[5]

Is this not surprisingly similar to the actions of Malfatti, who likewise wanted it established with Wawruch that Beethoven was very fond of alcohol?

Wawruch then writes, "But this joy...did not last long. [Beethoven] began to abuse the prescription." Again we have a contradiction of which none of the participants seemingly were aware. At first Malfatti warned Beethoven against drinking the punch in excess and would not allow him to take it in liquid form, that is, he could only dissolve the ice in his mouth. Thayer wrote that "But this was only in the beginning; when he saw the inevitable end approaching, he waived all injunctions as to quantity." However, this waiver was not given at the very end of Beethoven's life, but at a time when he was actually feeling better, so there was no "inevitable end" to be seen at that time. Modern physicians with sophisticated tests who are able to examine the results of blood work, x-rays and biopsies might make such a realistic prediction, but we cannot ascribe such an ability to the practitioners of 19th century medicine. Beethoven had survived catastrophic illnesses before, and his doctors had no evidence at hand that could have told them that his prognosis was so bleak. They surely would have viewed his rallying as a sign that his health was improving and that he might even achieve a full recovery.

From a teaspoon's dosage, Malfatti soon allowed Beethoven to drink one glass a day, then gave Beethoven free rein and said to him, "Drink all you want." Since it had been Malfatti who had prescribed the large quantities of alcohol, how could Beethoven have "abused" this prescription as Wawruch complained he had? Wawruch's umbrage should have been directed at his colleague, not his patient.

Beethoven soon came to look forward to the refreshment and relief that Malfatti's remedy afforded him. Then one day, after drinking some of Malfatti's iced punch which had previously given him relief from suffering, Beethoven had a sudden and violent reaction. An alarmed Wawruch wrote

> The spirits soon caused a violent pressure of the blood upon the brain [severe headache]; he grew soporous (sleepy), breathed stertoriously like an intoxicated person, began to wander in his

---

[5]Weider, 404

speech, and a few times inflammatory pains in the throat were paired with hoarseness and even aphony [inability to speak] He became more unruly and when, because of the cooling of the bowels, colic and diarrhea resulted, it was high time to deprive him of this precious refreshment. [Wawruch also noted that the swelling in Beethoven's feet had worsened.]

Shall we compare this to what Napoleon's doctor noted about him after having one of his "refreshments?" He had a dry and persistent cough and his breathing was labored. The lower part of his legs and feet were swollen. His pulse was irregular. He was sleepy and weak. He had a terrible headache and soon became "so hoarse that he could not speak." He exhibited excitability. He suffered from periods of diarrhea followed by constipation. Interestingly, Napoleon was also rendered deaf, a symptom no one would have taken into account in Beethoven's case.

Shall we also compare Beethoven's symptoms to those exhibited by Napoleon's son as he lay dying? Malfatti, who also was the Duke of Reichstadt's doctor at the end of the young man's life, wrote in his report that the Duke was often "so hoarse that he could not utter a sound." He was jaundiced, his liver swollen and tender. He had periods of recuperation followed by severe relapses. He lost weight and was weak. He had periods of temper. He slept badly. He had difficulty breathing, suffered a persistent cough, and his feet and lower legs were swollen. He would spit blood. And at the end, he, too, was hearing impaired and almost completely deaf in his left ear.

It would be difficult to list the symptoms exhibited by each of these men as they lay on their deathbeds and determine to which one of them they applied. And yet each one of them had their deaths ascribed by their attending physicians and those who performed their autopsies to different reasons: Napoleon to cancer, his son to tuberculosis, Beethoven to cirrhosis and pneumonia.

The iced punch was not the only suspicious "medication" that Malfatti gave to Beethoven. On February 22, the composer wrote to Schott Söhne publishers that "My doctor has ordered me to drink very good, old Rheine wine." Beethoven was jaundiced and suffered pains in the region of the liver as well as edema in the feet, legs and abdomen. His doctor surely must have suspected a problem with his liver, and yet he *ordered* Beethoven to drink wine. In another letter to Baron Pasqualati written on March 16, just ten days before his death, Beethoven wrote, "Now as regards wine: Malfatti first wanted me to have Moselle wine; but since you can't get the genuine thing here, he says, <u>he himself gave me several bottles</u>

of wine from Gumpoldskirchen (a wine-producing region just outside Vienna) and asserted they were the best for my health because there is no genuine Moselle wine to be had here." The underlinings are mine to emphasize that it was *Malfatti* who provided the wine for Beethoven to drink. Thus because of Malfatti Beethoven was still drinking wine—and whatever else was in it—even after Wawruch had forbidden it. Again we find an interesting parallel with Napoleon. Weider writes:

> Special wines not usually enjoyed by the rest of his suite were put aside for Napoleon. On occasion, Napoleon would give away a bottle of this wine and the recipient usually fell ill.

One recipient of a gift of wine from Napoleon's special stock was his attendant, Gourgand. About him Weider wrote that he "displayed liver symptoms, considerable mental anxiety and distress, watering of the eyes, muscular spasms and diarrhoea. All these symptoms are typical of acute arsenical intoxication, but there is no mention of the doctors suspecting more than a particularly puzzling kind of dysentery." Gourgand had had "several dangerous crises in the course of it. After the worst of them, however... he recovered amazingly quickly." Then yet another of Napoleon's entourage, Noverraz, fell ill, very suddenly and violently, and in his case the doctor diagnosed "an extremely violent liver crisis." His illness and recovery was followed by that of Las Cases the Younger —his father was also on St. Helena with Napoleon— who "suffered from periods of severe difficulty in breathing and palpitations of the heart. He fainted several times." The doctors decided the boy had a "congenital heart defect." Interestingly, just as members of Napoleon's entourage sometimes took sick and even died, so did a particular member of Beethoven's circle: Stephan von Breuning, who just coincidentally became Karl's guardian upon Beethoven's death. Breuning who felt ill all the while he attended Beethoven on his sickbed, died just six weeks after Beethoven, and Karl's guardianship—again, so coincidentally—transferred to Jakob Hotschevar, Johanna's champion during the Beethoven vs. Beethoven custody battle many years before. Breuning's son, who later became a physician, attributed his father's untimely death to the stress of dealing with his friend's loss. Physicians today attribute his death to pneumonia, a disease with symptoms similar to and often confused with those associated with arsenical intoxication. But what had been the official cause of death at the time? A familiar old diagnosis: liver disease.

At the end of February, Malfatti claimed he was ill and no longer could visit Beethoven. Was he then assured that Beethoven's death could no longer be avoided, that he had been weakened to the point where even his stamina and amazing will to survive could no longer save him? Was he anxious to remove himself from the case and put himself above suspicion now that he had assured Beethoven would die?

In addition to prescribing wine for a man with liver disease, Malfatti made two other serious "errors in judgment." On January 24, Malfatti proclaimed that Beethoven's swelling abdomen was attributable to gas, while it was Wawruch who correctly diagnosed it as the retention of fluid. Unrelieved—as it would have been if Beethoven had been solely under Malfatti's care—it would have caused a rupture and immediate agonizing death. Earlier Malfatti had noted to Schindler that he thought Beethoven's nose-bleeds had come from his head, and wanted to know whether Beethoven had ever complained about headaches. Was Malfatti really unaware that it was his own "iced punch" that had given Beethoven a severe headache and other alarming symptoms? Gerhard von Breuning also noted that on either January 27 or 28 Malfatti had prescribed a steam bath for Beethoven. Writing as a physician many years later, Gerhard assumed that Malfatti had prescribed what then had been the normal remedy for someone in Beethoven's condition: a bath of birch leaves. The Conversation Book however indicate that Gerhard's assumption was wrong. Hayseeds had been used instead. Malfatti told those around Beethoven that he hoped with this remedy to achieve a sweating and dehydrating effect. In the book it was written "The bath with dry hayseed is supposed to make you sweat. Malfatti says we have to try it since the internal medicine is not having the desired effect." The bath Beethoven was given, however, had the opposite and disastrous results. His body swelled alarmingly, plunging him into a relapse that once again undermined his waning strength.

By now it was hardly necessary to give Beethoven any more poison as insurance that he would not recover. His remarkable strength was tapped out, and he was weakened to the point where recovery was impossible. He was reduced to "skin and bones." The cirrhosis that had started developing ten years before—most likely by similar toxins—was taking its toll by no longer allowing his liver and kidneys to remove any toxins—natural or otherwise—from his body. Infection caused by poor hygiene being observed during repeated operations set in. It is a testament to his incredible will to survive that Beethoven lasted through this repeated onslaught of "cures" for four months.

DEATH AND AUTOPSY

After a four-month struggle, Beethoven died around 5:45 in the evening of March 26, 1827. The next day an autopsy was performed by Dr. Johann Wagner and Dr. Karl Rokitansky. Beethoven's body would be examined two other times when his body was exhumed, but this post-mortem was the only one conducted without decomposition having taken its toll.

From the autopsy, which is presented in Appendix C, modern physicians have attempted to determined from what chronic illnesses Beethoven had suffered. "Irritable bowel syndrome" has been put forth as a possibility because Beethoven's chronic gastrointestinal complaints seemed to closely coincide with stressful periods in his life. Others have suggested that he was a victim of Crohn's disease because it can cause bleeding often mistakenly attributed to hemorrhoids, can be responsible for eye pain and sensitivity to light, and can cause kidney and gallstones, and even pains in the joints. However, there was no mention made of the telltale signs of definite inflammatory changes in either the large or small intestine which are usually associated with Crohn's disease. In fact, no abnormalities in that part of Beethoven's anatomy were reported at all. Dr. Burril Crohn who first described the disease in 1932, claimed that even outstanding pathologists—as Wagner was—did not always notice changes in the intestines. Neumayr, a proponent of the diagnosis of Crohn's disease, believed that Wagner may have overlooked this aspect, in favor of concentrating on his examination of Beethoven's ears. Indeed, the greatest emphasis of Beethoven's post-mortem did center around his organs of hearing. This was primarily a result of Beethoven himself requesting that his ears be thoroughly examined upon his death so that perhaps more might be learned about the cause of his deafness and subsequently help others similarly afflicted. However Dr. Wagner was a very gifted physician and pathologist and during his lifetime contributed significantly to developments in his field. He was known for drawing his conclusions about the nature of a disease from typical and distinctive organic changes and he ascribed particular importance to the correct interpretation of anatomical findings. It seems unlikely that someone with Wagner's credentials and professional thoroughness would have missed these irregularities, particularly since he did report on the state of Beethoven's intestines and stated that he found no abnormalities.

So how did Beethoven die? Officially, there is no doubt that he did have cirrhosis of the liver, but even here there is something of interest. The assumption usually has been that Beethoven's cirrhosis had been caused by his consumption of alcohol. Even Neumayr, who attempted to free Beethoven from the stigma of having been a heavy drinker, related his cirrhosis to alcohol, believing that he had a genetic defect that made even small amounts of alcohol harmful to him. However, other modern physicians, noting that the liver was covered with large nodules (macronodules) concluded that alcohol was not the cause of Beethoven's cirrhosis, which almost always results in micronodules. But if not alcohol, are there many alternatives? Hepatitis is one possibility. Toxins are another.

There is also little reason to doubt that Beethoven had developed pneumonia or suffered from the effects of other infections at the time of death. So perhaps our question cannot be, how did Beethoven die, but rather who or what brought him to the brink of death from which not even a man with the strength and indomitable will of a Beethoven could retreat? In my opinion, Beethoven's death had been insured by some person giving him regular but non-fatal doses of some toxin capable of seriously undermining his already fragile health, and with the cumulative effects necessary to insure that he would never recover.

And who might we suspect? The list has on it Malfatti, of course, but also contains a few interesting additions.

THE SUSPECTS OF 1827

Although presently I will give a more thorough review of each of our potential suspects, let me first list the possibilities. In each case we will examine only motives and opportunities, as the means—any number of poisons—were readily available to any one of them. Some of them might have had more knowledge of poisons, which might have helped them in carrying out their mission against Beethoven, but by and large it is motive and opportunity which will be of greatest importance. On our list we must include:

Johann van Beethoven, Ludwig's brother, who was a pharmacist in need of money.

Therese Obermayr van Beethoven, another of the composer's sisters-in-law with whom he had had some nasty interactions in the past, and may have still harbored ill feelings toward him. There were rumors of her having had an affair with Beethoven's nephew Karl.

Johanna van Beethoven, the other sister-in-law with whom we are already acquainted as a suspect of 1817-1818, who we recall had suffered a running battle with Beethoven over her son for the past 12 years.

Karl van Beethoven, Ludwig's nephew, now nearing adulthood, a young man heavily in debt, who would claim that he had attempted to take his life because his uncle had tortured him emotionally.

Karl Holz, supposedly Beethoven's friend, who pressed him to drink too much alcohol and who acted oddly as intermediary between Beethoven and Karl at the time of the latter's attempted suicide.

Anton Schindler, Beethoven's somewhat sycophantic friend and secretary who was extremely jealous of others' relationships with the composer, and who was not always well-treated by Beethoven.

And of course, Dr. Johann Malfatti, a man we now know still harbored a long-festering grudge against Beethoven and yet mysteriously changed his mind about coming to his aid.

Chapter 9
The Nephew: Karl van Beethoven

By and large, modern biographers have looked at the relationship between Karl and Ludwig van Beethoven in psychological terms, and it is usually the uncle who comes out the worst for it. He is blamed for being tyrannical, uncompromising, and domineering and having an obsessive and pathological love for the boy which threatened to smother him. Our modern times increasingly have declared "Poor Karl" at his uncle's expense. Thayer attempted to discern the truth which lay between these two people, but admitted that much had to be left to conjecture. But Thayer —writing several decades after Beethoven's death rather than a century and a half—concluded that in the case of Karl, his uncle did not deserve to shoulder the preponderance of the responsibility for the boy's behavior. It is my opinion that we give greater credence to a man writing with the same Victorian mind-set in which Karl himself lived than we do to psychoanalysts who often forget that their patients were citizens of the 19th century. The relationships between elders and youngsters, parents and children were very different then than they are today.

Conflicts were commonplace between the two, growing more frequent the older Karl became. Thayer did not hold Beethoven blameless in this, admitting that Beethoven's attitude toward his nephew so often vacillated between affection and accusation, pride and loathing, condemnation and forgiveness, that Karl probably was confused about his uncle's true feelings for him. Nevertheless, the times in which they lived demanded that a child give his elder unconditional respect. In this regard Thayer considered Karl's behavior "always disgraceful and in the end tragical" and Beethoven's love "almost idolatrous for one unworthy to receive it."

Thayer tells us that Karl had had a propensity for learning languages—so that his uncle thought he might become a professor in that field. Beethoven had high expectations for his nephew's behavior and education, but Karl often failed to live up to them. His enthusiasm for study quickly waned once he entered the University of Vienna. He increasingly spent his time in "idle amusements" such as billiards, dancing, and the theater. He borrowed money to cover debts incurred by gambling. He neglected his uncle in favor of those Thayer refers to as "low company and lewd women" and he adds "Of all this there can be no doubt." [1] Karl's teachers felt he had potential but lacked the motivation to be successful. To see ability wasted must have infuriated Beethoven who believed mankind was responsible for living as exemplary a life as possible, and being an asset to society. Even in his darkest days he said that "it seemed to me to be impossible to leave this world before I had brought forth all that I felt destined to bring forth. So I endured this miserable existence." (*Heiligenstadt Testament, 1802*) And to his friend Franz Wegeler, he reiterated this sentiment again in 1810: "If I had not read somewhere that a man should not voluntarily quit this life so long as he can still perform a good deed, I would have left this earth a long time ago." For Karl to have been young, healthy, and intelligent, and be wasteful of that health and intelligence, must have rankled Beethoven greatly.

As Beethoven's nephew Karl grew into adulthood, there was increasing tension between the two Beethovens. They agreed on very little. Beethoven the uncle was strict with the young man, feeling the need to counteract the negative effects of the boy's mother during his formative years. Karl craved freedom and independence as most people his age do. Yet when Ludwig was Karl's age he was virtually on his own, responsible for his family but with no parental authority against which to rebel. Perhaps at the time he had wished for a more responsible father and, remembering his own past, was determined to be that for Karl whether the young man wanted him to be or not. But even if Thayer does not exonerate Beethoven entirely, he felt Beethoven's love for him was genuine. By the time Karl was nineteen, he made his home away from his uncle by boarding with Matthias Schlemmer, a Viennese official. At that time he entered the Polytechnic Institute intent upon a career in business. In a letter to Schlemmer, Beethoven voiced the suspicion that Karl mingled with bad company in the evenings. His distrust was not entirely unwarranted. Karl did run with an unruly crowd, and he repeatedly associated with his mother behind his uncle's back. In 1825, Beethoven wrote to his nephew:

> Until now it was only conjecture although someone assured me that there were secret dealings between you and your mother—

---

[1]Thayer III, 251

Am I to experience once again the most abominable ingratitude? No, if this bond is to be broken, so be it, but you will be despised by all impartial men who hear of this ingratitude.... Shall I get involved again in all the vulgarities? No, never again—[2]

However angry Beethoven seems in this letter, he ends it by giving his nephew the benefit of the doubt, and asking Karl to come to see him along with a person he calls "the old woman." Thayer presumed this to be his housekeeper who he repeatedly referred to as "the old witch" and "the old beast" and her helper as "the wench" and "Satanas."

From the time he first sought full custody of Karl, Beethoven worried constantly about the influence Johanna would have over her son, and this concern never waivered, regardless how old Karl became. Perhaps Beethoven's concern was exaggerated; on the other hand, Johanna hardly led an exemplary life. Adultery, bribery, larceny, lying—such unethical behavior surely was imparted by her to her son. Beethoven's increasing concern over Karl's life in Vienna is indicated in discussions he had about these matters with his friends. He frequently asked for their aid and advice. On June 10 he wrote to Bernard asking him to see something of Karl since he was worried about his behavior and feared that he was becoming involved again with his mother.

One can sympathize with Beethoven, although the situation could not have been easy for Karl. However loose her morals, Johanna was still his mother and he loved her as a child almost always loves a parent, even if that parent is undeserving. Even though Johanna did not abuse Karl, she certainly neglected him at times when her own desires were in conflict with his needs.

Beethoven also may have been trying to force Karl into a mold into which he did not, by temperament, fit, although this is not unusual for a parent to do. Most of us with children hope that they will embrace and uphold the values that we ourselves have. Perhaps Beethoven could not understand the youthful inclinations of his nephew because he himself had been robbed of so much of his own childhood. He had a strong work ethic; from his early teens he had worked to help support his family. His mother died when he was just 17, and at that point he had been thrust into the role of family patriarch, taking on full responsibility for his brothers and his father as well. His father, Johann, whose drinking grew worse after his wife's death, was totally unreliable as head of the family. Ludwig had to work hard to rise above the shadow that his father's reputation for drinking had cast over the Beethoven name. (In fact, when his father died, someone

---

[2]Anderson,#1377, III, 1200-1201

made the unkind remark that the town's economy would suffer because it could no longer be able collect his tax on liquor.) It fell to Ludwig to carry the burden of family responsibility. Perhaps his own early thrust into maturity made him believe Karl should exhibit more maturity than the boy was capable of showing. Beethoven had high moral standards, he had never played at games of chance or spent his time playing billiards. All these factors may have made it difficult for him to understand why Karl did not have his diligence, his sense of responsibility, his drive to succeed. In a Conversation Book entry Karl showed the strain he was feeling from the demands made on him both by his uncle and by his studies, but his uncle seems not to have understood it. Maybe he simply could not.

Beethoven's friend, Karl Holz, took it upon himself to check up on the young man, perhaps to reassure Beethoven that his worries were exaggerated. He reported in a Conversation book: "He has gotten the love of money from your brother." Holz also told Beethoven that he had lured Karl into a beerhouse to observe his drinking habits, but in his opinion Karl did not regularly drink much. However, Holz reminded Beethoven in the conversation book that his brother Johann had said that Karl knew every strumpet in Vienna and Holz told Beethoven that when he had investigated the charge, he had found it to be true. Maybe Holz was simply telling Beethoven what he expected to hear. It is unlikely that the young man actually was acquainted with "every strumpet in Vienna," but no doubt—probably thanks to his mother—he associated with people that someone like Beethoven, accustomed as he was to socializing with the upper classes and aristocracy, would not have approved of as suitable companions. That is not to suggest that Beethoven was a social snob, however, his companions tended to be cultured, discussing politics, philosophy and poetry rather than local gossip, and frequenting theaters and concerts halls rather than billiard parlors.

Karl repeatedly asked his uncle for money causing Beethoven to become suspicious about how Karl spent the money he was given. Beethoven asked to see receipts for his nephew's expenditures, not an entirely unreasonable request since it was he who was doling out the money Karl was spending. Although Karl was not completely wrong in expecting to have a bit more autonomy at his age, we must remember that in Beethoven's day a person was not recognized as an adult until he was 24 years of age, and a person Karl's age was legally required to have decisions made for him by a guardian. Karl did not confess to his uncle how the money had been spent, stalling by indicating that they had been misplaced. He wrote in his uncle's conversation book: "It (a receipt for 80 florins that were to have been paid to Schlemmer) will show up all right." He added "When I go walking and have a drink and the like. I don't have any other expenses." This last statement from Karl must have been in answer to his uncle's question about how he used his money. Although Beethoven seems demanding and suspicious—and thus his nephew rightfully indignant—his questions must be seen in light of a statement made by Schlemmer in the Conversation Books, which was later corroborated by Breuning, that the principal reason that circumstances had become intolerable for Karl was that he was heavily in debt because he had acquired a delight in gambling. Beethoven became enraged when he learned that Karl had borrowed money from his servants. Beethoven felt —not unjustified—that his nephew's only interest in him was money, writing "The money-bag Herr L. v. B—n is here only for this purpose." Altercations usually sent Karl running to his mother, whom Beethoven still detested as much as ever and continued to believe was an immoral influence on her son.

Letters written during this time alternate between fatherly love and reproaches and bitter disappointment. They show Beethoven in despair, fraught with worry, and depressed.

> I wish that you would stop such selfishness at my expense. It does as little credit to me as it does towards setting you on the right and proper course. Continue this way and you will rue the day! Not that I shall die sooner, however much this may be your desire... The worse part is the results that will come to you because of your behavior. Who will believe or trust you after hearing what has happened and how you have inflicted mortal wounds upon me and wounded me daily? I hope at least to receive a letter from you tomorrow. Do not make me fear. O, think of my sufferings! By good right I ought to have no cares of this kind; what have I not experienced! God is my witness, I dreamed only of being rid of you and of this miserable brother and the hideous family which he foisted upon me. God hear my prayer for I can *never* trust you again. Unfortunately your father or better not your Father.[3]

Always when he wrote such angry letters, Beethoven would regret his harsh words and he would become afraid of alienating his nephew completely. The letter quoted above, so angry and full of hurt was followed by a plea from Beethoven for Karl to come to him: he was willing to forgive him.

---

[3]Anderson,#1379, III, 1202

> My precious son: Go no further—Come but to my arms, not a harsh word shall you hear. You shall be received lovingly as ever.... Come to the faithful heart of the father.[4]

At times, there were violent scenes between uncle and nephew, further embittering Beethoven. One particularly disturbing scene erupted following a quarrel over Karl's apparent mishandling of some funds—10 florins. Sometime in June 1826, Beethoven wrote to Karl Holz: "I only ask in great haste how you are—K[arl], however, appears to do wrong; one would have to presume that he gave S[chlemmer] 10 florins less the first time." Apparently, on Sunday June 25, 1826, Beethoven and his nephew Karl got into a heated argument over receipts for Karl's laundry charges, and whether those charges were paid in advance or after the service was rendered, and how the spending of this money affected the paying of Karl's room rent at Schlemmer's. Judging from a remark made by Holz in the Conversation Book, Karl had raised his hand against his uncle and threatened him with physical violence. Holz wrote "I came in just as he took you by the breast.... At the door as he was coming out." In addition to this disturbing incident, there may have been other altercations between them, for there are conciliatory notes from Beethoven, such as one in which he wrote:

> ...all is forgiven and forgotten; more today by word of mouth, very quietly.... Do not take a step which might make you unhappy and shorten my life. I embrace you cordially and am convinced that soon you will no longer *misjudge* me; I thus judge your conduct yesterday—... We shall be alone, for I shall not permit H[olz] to come—the more so since I do not wish anything about yesterday to be known. Do come—do not permit my poor heart to *bleed any longer*.[5]

Johann, Ludwig's brother, attempted to smooth things over between them, particularly when Karl complained to him about Ludwig's behavior. Johann's sympathy and empathy is easy to understand, since he himself had had difficulties with his older brother over the years. We have one example of Johann's intervention in a letter he wrote to Karl on June 10, 1825: "I have lodged a complaint with him on your behalf, although I believe that you should often go out to him [i.e. in Baden] on Sundays. It is true that he is somewhat difficult to be with; however, if you but consider what your uncle has already done for you: indeed he has already spent more than 10,000 florins on your behalf, and yet what pain and torment you have

---

[4]Anderson, #1445, III, 1258

[5]Anderson, #1489, III, 1289

already caused him. ... I beg you to do what you can to lend him a helping hand, for you owe him a great deal..."[6]

In addition to resisting Beethoven's invitations to come to him in Baden on Sundays, Karl also refused his uncle's requests that he come to visit him in the evenings after Beethoven had resumed his residence in town. Karl no doubt had more entertaining occupations at hand. Thayer, writing from the standpoint of a Victorian to whom filial allegiance was seen as Beethoven's due as Karl's elder, wondered "Was it merely work in the evening that detained him?"

Karl refused to tell his uncle how he spent his time, and with whom, giving him only the most cursory and vague answers that increased Beethoven's anxieties. As his nephew did nothing to allay his fears, it was natural that Beethoven should feel suspicious of the company Karl kept and worry about his desire to gamble. He constantly heard negative reports about the boy, from his friends and from Karl's teachers. Schindler wrote that he had seen Karl in coffeehouses in the company of "common people with whom he deals with dishonestly in games." Schindler was not fond of Karl, so his observation cannot be taken without question. However, this is well corroborated by observations by both Johann who, as noted before, had reported on Karl's association with "Viennese strumpets," by Stephen von Breuning—whose integrity was never questioned—and by Schlemmer. The latter two both had told Beethoven that Karl was deeply in debt. Thayer himself believed that Karl had led a "dissolute life" and gambled incessantly, sometimes cheating at these games. A Conversation Book tells us also of Karl selling some books which he had stolen from Beethoven. Even though Beethoven was his uncle, the act was still theft and constituted a penal offense; naturally, Beethoven did not press charges against the young man. In fact, he feared the police finding out about the theft as well as perhaps uncovering some other crime of which he was unaware that might have been still worse. Because of these things, Thayer conjectured that a bad conscience along with fear of punishment could have eventually driven Karl to attempt suicide.

Through the last years of Beethoven's life, Karl became increasingly sullen and angry. Although some of his behavior may be understandable given the pressure he was under to live up to his uncle's high expectations and standards, his unkind and ungrateful feelings toward the uncle who loved him—however misguided some of his efforts to show that love were—are disturbing. Schindler wrote that once when Karl was admonished by his teachers to remember his duty to his uncle, Karl had

---

[6]Albrecht, #410, III, 102

replied, "My uncle! I can do with him what I want. Some flattery and friendly gestures make things all right again right away." Holz corroborated this with his own remark, that Karl had said he could wrap his uncle around his finger. And a note written by Karl to his friend, Niemetz, points to the fact that these two men were not mistaken about Karl's attitude toward Beethoven. Karl had written: "I had to write you in such a great hurry from fear and worry of being discovered by the old fool."

Against Beethoven's wishes Karl began seeing his mother regularly and usually secretly, and also spending more and more time with his friend, Niemetz—another whom his uncle considered a bad influence particularly because Niemetz who apparently associated a bit too closely with Karl's mother. No pleas or warnings on his uncle's part kept Karl away from either of them, especially Johanna. Beethoven wrote to Karl in May 1826:

> Till now only suspicions, although I have received assurances from one that there is again secret intercourse between you and your mother. Am I again to experience the most abominable ingratitude?[7]

Given Karl's unhappiness and the anger he felt toward his uncle, it would not be surprising if Karl and his mother began to consider ways in which to rid themselves of the irksome behavior of the man they both detested.

A SUICIDE ATTEMPT

It has long puzzled me why more people have not questioned Karl's suicide attempt, or seen it as more than a cry of anguish against the mistreatment he allegedly had suffered at the hands of a possessive and tyrannical uncle. Looking at the attempt in a logical way has led me to suspect that there was far more to it than has been suspected. Let me present here the scenario.

The first thing we learn is that Karl had confided to Schlemmer, at whose house he was lodging, that he intended to do himself harm. He even told Schlemmer the probable day he would make the attempt, a Sunday. At the time, Schlemmer confiscated a loaded pistol from Karl's room, but Thayer tells us that at a later date, Schlemmer found yet another pistol there! Why did Karl tell Schlemmer of his intentions in the first place, and second, why did he leave his pistols in plain sight so that

---

[7]Anderson, #1377, III, 1209

Schlemmer would be prompted to take them? Karl must have suspected that Schlemmer would report his intent to his uncle, which indeed he did. It also seems that he must have wanted Schlemmer to take the pistols perhaps as proof that he was serious in his threat. A first question thus arises is: was this Karl's cry for help? Did he want someone to recognize his pain, stop him from making a rash move and rectify his situation? Or was this simply a ploy by a young man intent upon punishing an uncle he found too strict for his liking?

Having been given this news, Schlemmer went immediately to Beethoven and wrote in his conversation book: "I learned today that your nephew intended to shoot himself before next Sunday at the latest. As to the cause I learned only this much, that it was on account of his debts, but not completely, only in part was he admitting that they were the consequences of former sins." Schlemmer admitted that Karl had paid him for the present month, but not for August. Looking through Karl's papers he answered Beethoven, "This is not his handwriting, yet everything is paid for till the end of July."

Holz immediately went to the Institute where Karl took classes intent upon bringing Karl back to Schlemmer's. When he found Karl, the boy gave Holz the excuse that he needed to retrieve some papers from a friend's house, and thus easily slipped away forcing Holz to return to Beethoven without his nephew. Beethoven rebuked Holz for his carelessness, although Holz defended himself by writing:

> He would have run away from you just the same. If he has made up his mind to injure himself no one can prevent him. ... He said to me today, "What good will it do you to detain me? If I do not escape today, I will at another time.

Abruptly the Conversation Book entries end; pages have been torn out. Thayer wondered whether Schindler had done it to preserve the integrity of his recollections about the event. Alternately, he suggested that Beethoven himself might have torn them out some weeks later when Holz advised him to look through his books and consider that the police magistrate might demand to examine them. Possibly he had warned Beethoven that they might contain references to affairs which Beethoven might not want to bring into public discussion.

After giving Holz the slip, and being deprived of his original weapons, Karl pawned his watch and at the pawn shop acquired two more pistols. One might ask, why two? (And why two in the first place?) I assume here that he received them as a set, probably a pair of dueling pistols. He also bought powder and shot. These he took to Baden (likely

Saturday, July 29) where he proceeded to write letters. He wrote two: one is to his friend, Niemetz, and in this one he enclosed the second letter, to his uncle. Where is his letter to his mother? Had he not written her one? No plea to her for her understanding or forgiveness? No one has ever mentioned such a letter, if indeed ever one was written. The contents of the letter written to Beethoven has not been disclosed, but it is easy to imagine wording that would wound as sharply and deeply as possible.

  The next morning—a Sunday, July 30—Karl climbed high up to the ruins of Rauhenstein, an old castle, in the lovely Helenenthal that Beethoven loved particularly well, where it was he had determined he would shoot himself. Once at the top he set to his task, but here there are two possibilities: either he picked up both pistols at the same time, or initially he picked up only one of them. Although this seems obvious, in either case there are oddities about which we must wonder. For example, if Karl had picked up both pistols simultaneously, why did he do that? Was he anticipating a miss? For the moment, let us assume he picked up only one of them. As most people of the time were or were forced to be right handed, again for the time being only we will assume that Karl was, too. So with the pistol in his right hand, he pointed it point blank at his right temple, fired... and missed. This all by itself is very odd. Although Thayer called him a "bungler with firearms," to miss a shot at point blank range seems incredible. But perhaps we may assume that, under extreme stress, Karl might have been shaking so hard that he missed. So then he picked up the second loaded pistol... but must have done so with his left hand because it was his left temple area that suffered the wound and it would have been odd and awkward for him to have picked up a pistol in his *right* hand and aim it at his *left* temple. Karl again fired, and this time only managed to graze himself, meaning that the muzzle of the gun could not have been pressed dead-on against his head, but held at an angle causing a wound that was far from fatal. And is not this fact strange? How is it possible for a person—a healthy young person, not an infirm elderly person—to fire twice at point blank range—with the target not even a few inches from the end of the pistol's muzzle—and miss both times? Maybe the firing was not quite so point blank... on purpose.

  Since the idea that a right-handed person would pick up a pistol in his left hand is so odd, perhaps we may deduce from this that Karl actually was left-handed. Because if Karl was right-handed, why did he not attempt to shoot himself the second time with his right hand? If he had missed with his first shot when, presumably, the first pistol had been in his dominant hand—where more accuracy could be assumed—then why had he imagined he could accomplish the deed better with his left hand?

Because this is somewhat confusing, let me list the possibilities:

1. Karl was right-handed but picked up both pistols simultaneously. He raised the right pistol, placed the muzzle against his temple... and missed. Then, instead of transferring the other pistol to his dominant hand, he tried again with his left hand... and missed. Or fired both pistols at opposite temples simultaneously... and missed.

2. Karl was *left*-handed, and initially picked up only one pistol. He aimed, fired, and missed. He then picked up the second pistol, aimed, fired, and missed again. As the second scenario is more plausible, let us consider whether Karl might have been left-handed.

DEXTRAL OR SINISTRAL?

While I may not be able to prove beyond all doubt that Karl was dextral (right-handed) rather than sinistral (left-handed), the evidence is strongly in favor of his right-handedness.

First, the natural incidence of left-handedness is very small. Less than ten percent, and more accurately about six percent, of the population is naturally sinistral. So simply random chance would be against Karl being left-handed.

Second, there is some evidence, though not conclusive, that left-handedness may be genetic and that a child who is sinistral probably has a blood relation who is also left-handed. In my own family, I am a sinistral, but I do not know if anyone in my immediate family was. (My mother and my maternal grandparents were all dextrals, but I have no data on my paternal family.) My husband is also a sinistral. He had a dextral mother and a sinistral father. And our own son is also sinistral. So from my own experience I would say that there is a good chance that being left-handed could have a genetic cause. It is not apparent that anyone in Karl's immediate family was sinistral; certainly none of the Beethoven brothers were, but we cannot say for certain that Johanna or her relatives were not.

Third, until the second half of the 20th century, most sinistral children were routinely "changed over" once they entered school. At one time, being left-handed was considered being related to the Devil himself, yet although the 19th century was somewhat more enlightened, switching students from being sinistral to being dextral was as much as matter of routine as teaching the alphabet and simple math. Not until 1850 or so did anyone wonder whether they should be attempting to make this change in students. Thus even if Karl had been born with sinistral tendencies, the likelihood is that once he started school he was switched over to dextrality.

Finally, there is a matter of Karl's handwriting, a sample of which is given below. I have noted that I happen to be a sinistral, and I admit here that it is difficult for anyone who is not a handwriting expert to look at my penmanship and tell that I am left-handed. My writing does not slant to the left, nor is it perpendicular. On the other hand, the writing implements of the 20th century are far kinder to sinistrals than those of Beethoven's day. A sinistral is a "pen pusher" not a "pen puller." Our pen nibs are smooth enough to glide along the page which was not the case in the 19th century when dip pens usually had sharp nibs. Further, as a sinistral's hand often rubs against what has been written, a person using liquid ink would be prone to making a mess. Looking at Karl's handwriting sample below we can see that it slants perfectly to the right and that it is devoid of any blots or smears or gouges by the pen's nib.

From these four points—statistics, genetics, education, and handwriting—I think we must conclude that Karl was a dextral. Thus he either used his non-dominant hand—his left—to shoot himself or used his right hand to shoot at his left temple. Neither case supports a serious suicide attempt.

CONTINUING WITH THE SUICIDE STORY

To this puzzle of the two missed point-blank shots, we must add another piece in the form of an interesting comment made by Holz to Beethoven: that Karl had been lucky that he had not taken the original pistols which Schlemmer had confiscated. Why? Because they had been more fully loaded ("charged with powder and ball to above the middle") than the other pistols from the pawn shop that he loaded later. Holz remarked that if Karl had used the original pistols, he surely would have been a dead man. We know that Karl must have loaded all four pistols himself because first, Schlemmer confiscated pistols, powder and shot, and second, Karl had bought additional powder and shot from the pawnbroker, so the second pair of pistols he bought must not have been loaded at the time of purchase. We must ask, if Karl was able to fully load the first two pistols, why could he not do the same with the second pair? He certainly had the time to load them properly. Does it not seem as if his half-loaded pistols were deliberately loaded inadequately so that they would be incapable of firing a fatal shot?

Now Thayer's story continues, noting that "a teamster came upon him lying among the ruins." But how is that possible? A man with a team of horses driving among ruins that Karl had to climb to reach? The road does not go through the ruins; they are perched on a hill overlooking the road. As he could not have been seen from the road if he had been sprawled on the ground at the top, Karl must have been in good enough condition to walk down from the ruins again to the road where he hailed the teamster. And then Thayer remarked that "at his (Karl's) request" the teamster took Karl to his mother's house. Not only was Karl well enough to climb back down from the ruins and hail a passing wagon, he was also well enough to give the teamster explicit directions to his mother's house!

A stunned and upset Beethoven soon arrived on the scene at Johanna's house. Thayer does not know how he learned where Karl was, but Johanna later wrote in the Conversation Book that the teamster had "just driven out to you," so someone might have asked the teamster to tell Beethoven where his nephew was. It is also possible that her house was simply one place where Beethoven logically would have looked for him, since this was the usual place where he went whenever he had run away in the past. Naturally the distraught uncle wanted details of the incident, but a very lucid Karl wrote to him, "It is done. Now only a surgeon who can hold his tongue. Smetana, if he is here. Do not plague me with reproaches and lamentations; it is past. Later all matters may be adjusted." To this Johanna added: "I beg of you to tell the surgeon not to make a report or they will take him away from here at once and we fear the worst." To me, this first encounter of a supposedly upset mother with her long-time nemesis and probable cause of her son's attempted suicide is surprisingly sedate. There was no "Do you see what you have done to my son?", no beating him upon the breast, no screams of outrage, no tears of anger, or any of that. She was concerned about police involvement, but otherwise she did not seem the least bit agitated, let alone angry. In fact, even after Karl pointedly accused his uncle of driving him to this desperate measure, she still showed no outrage toward Beethoven himself. It was only later when she had the police's ear that she showed a "lack of mercy'" (reported Holz to Beethoven) when she "denounced [to the police] the conduct of the guardian of her son." And of course, there is another extremely interesting comment she made to Karl in the hospital, overheard by Holz and reported to Beethoven: "If you have anything on your mind, tell your uncle now," Johanna told her son. "You see, this is the time; he is weak, and now he will surely do anything you want."

From all these oddities, does it not seem likely that this action had been nothing more than an attempt on Karl's part—and likely Johanna's as well—to break off all legal connections with Beethoven and perhaps punish him emotionally, rather than a genuine attempt to take his life? A man accused of driving his ward to such a desperate act would not have been seen by the courts as a suitable guardian, so perhaps the two hoped to discredit Beethoven. Or, they might have thought this blow would cause Beethoven such anguish—which it did—that he would willingly, even eagerly, relinquish Karl's guardianship. The only other thing that I have found odd about all this is that I have yet to read a biography that thought there was anything wrong or suspicious with this whole suicide scenario![8]

Attempted suicide was a crime in 19th century Austria. While it was not an offense against the government, it was against the Church, and legal judgments were passed and the offender was punished. Although the one who had made the attempt was not imprisoned per se, under the Austrian code guilty persons were confined and remanded to the care of priests who imparted religious instruction until they were satisfied that the person regretted his or her action and a statement to that effect was obtained and recorded.

One could never be sure how long a person might remain in custody, so Johanna's reluctance to report Karl's attempted suicide to the police is not surprising. However, not to report it would have been a crime also; there was little choice. Karl Holz made the report, acting as Beethoven's intermediary, supposedly so that he could be the one to break the news (which certainly would not be good) to Beethoven regarding the consequences of Karl's act. Was Holz's action altruistic? He seems to have taken some pleasure in being involved in the thick of things, and in reporting to Beethoven all the grim details. Karl's punishment for the time being, Holz reported, would consist of a severe reprimand and police surveillance until he was well enough to be moved. Holz also reported that Karl had said, "If only he (his uncle) would not show himself again," and

---

[8] George Marek in his biography *Beethoven: Portrait of a Genius* said that he read of some other biographer's doubts, but he did not cite his source.

that he had threatened to rip the bandages from his head if Beethoven's name were mentioned to him again. Was it necessary to wound Beethoven with such a cruel report? One wonders whose side Holz was on, anyway.

On August 7th, about a week after the shooting, Karl was removed from his mother's house by the police and taken to the general hospital. Thayer had located the date of Karl's admission in 1862 when he visited the hospital. Dr. F. Helm, Director of the Hospital, certified that the boy had been received, treated, and discharged but stated that no history of the case could be found in the records. Who took Karl's records, and why? It seems unlikely that anyone could do so unless they served in an official capacity—a doctor or an officer of the court—so we are left with yet another oddity, it seems.

There are a few other notes from Holz in the Conversation Book regarding Karl's actions. We can only guess at Beethoven's questions which prompted them. Holz's notes are as follow:

> The Magistrat [the court dealing with issues involving commoners] as a criminal court is now concerned with this [Karl's attempted suicide].
>
> The priest will be sent by the Magistrat, you need not concern yourself with this any more.
>
> He will not be released until he has passed a complete examination in religious instruction and has been completely converted, so that there is no longer fear of a relapse.
>
> But custody must not be as a punishment but as a means of security for himself.

The religious instruction was administered to Karl by a priest belonging to a sect called the Redemptionists. This group had been founded in 1732 by Alphonsus Liguori (later St. Alphonsus) and it was he who established guidelines for determining whether a course of conduct was morally permissible. Thayer tells us that Liguorian penances were considered quite strict. Because of that Holz was able to inspire the hope in Beethoven that Karl's secret, his reason for attempting suicide, eventually would be discovered by the priest. He remarked "These Liguorians are like leeches." As Holz had predicted, Karl finally did give his reason for his suicide attempt, and the police recorded in their report that he had suffered "weariness of imprisonment" by his uncle and that Beethoven had "tormented him too much" by expecting him to be what he was not, by setting standards he could not possibly reach. When Thayer was preparing his biography of Beethoven, he was able to interview Holz who told Thayer that Beethoven had kept too close a watch on Karl and had not allowed him the slightest extravagance. For that reason, Holz said, Karl had taken to borrowing money and that was one reason he had fallen so deeply into debt. Yet Johann had remarked that his brother had spent over 10,000 florins on Karl's behalf, and the pursestrings tightened only after Beethoven felt Karl could not be trusted with having a substantial amount of pocket money.

While Karl was in the hospital there was no delay in discussing plans for his future. Beethoven was eager to make some prompt decisions for he lived in terror of what legal consequences might befall his nephew on account of his act. Holz's reassurances notwithstanding, he was still afraid of the penal aspects of the case. His fears might have been caused by remembering a similar case of attempted suicide which involved Countess Maria Erdödy, a woman who we recall was very close to him, In 1820, Maria's daughter Mimi, then about 22 years of age, had tried to take her life by swallowing opium. Mimi had been sentenced to a term at the convent in St. Pöltens where she had remained incarcerated until 1823, when her mother—a Hungarian patriot often questioned by and harassed by the police—apparently had agreed to leave Vienna permanently in return for her child's release. Three years! Little wonder that Beethoven feared such a fate for his own nephew.

Breuning, Schindler and Holz all urged Beethoven to consider giving up his guardianship and also to approve their plan to place Karl in the army. Some time before, Karl himself had wanted to join the army, but Beethoven had initially opposed the idea. (Karl had then proposed a career in the mercantile business which Beethoven did approve, albeit reluctantly.) "A military life will be the best for one who cannot endure freedom; and it will teach him how to live on little," Breuning argued, and eventually Beethoven saw the logic of this move and agreed to it.

TO GNEIXENDORF

In addition to long-term plans for Karl's future, there also was the immediate question of where Karl would go once released from the hospital. Karl's inclination, of course, was to go to his mother, a move that everyone knew the court might have been inclined to approve. Not surprisingly, Beethoven opposed the idea. He visited Karl in order to talk him out of this decision, and in the course of his argument, he began to berate Johanna. Karl refused to hear any more such talk about his mother and wrote to his uncle, "I do not want to hear anything that is derogatory to her; it is not for me to be her judge. If I were to spend the little time I shall be here with her, it would be only a small return for all that she has suffered on my account." (Johanna apparently had convinced her son that she had been the victim in her custody battle with Beethoven over him.) Thayer tells us that Beethoven had spoken to his "advisers"—Breuning, Schindler, and Holz—about the possibility of Johanna being sent away, to Pressburg or Pesth, but there were no grounds by which this could have been accomplished. Karl told his uncle that he wanted to leave Vienna as soon as possible. Apparently the police were in agreement because they made it clear they also wanted Karl out of Vienna within a day after his release from the hospital.

While preparations were being made for Karl's admission to the army, a suitable place for him to stay still needed to be found. Beethoven still would not agree to let him stay with his mother. Conversely, Breuning did not think it advisable for Karl should stay alone with his uncle. He wrote "If he were here you would talk to him too much and that would cause new irritation; for he testified in the police court that the reason why he had taken the step was because you harassed him too much." To be accused of being the reason for Karl's attempted suicide must have been a bitter blow to Beethoven, yet Breuning was right. Alone together they would have become embroiled in more conflict which neither of them needed. However, the very thought that Karl would stay with his mother rankled Beethoven, and he urgently wrote to a magistrate named Czapka regarding the situation:

> It must not possibly be allowed that Karl] be near his mother, that utterly depraved person. My solicitude and my request are justified by her bad and wickedly malicious character, the belief that she often tempted Karl to lure money from me, the probability that she divided sums with him, and was also in the confidence of Karl's dissolute companion [Niemetz], the notice which she attracts with her illegitimate daughter, the father of whom is still being sought, [Had Hofbauer suddenly disappeared?] and the likelihood that at his m[other]'s home he would make the acquaintance of women who are anything but virtuous.[9]

While awaiting word from Czapka, an unexpected solution came about. Late in September, Ludwig's brother Johann arrived in Vienna and

---

[9]Anderson, #1502, III, 1297

offered Beethoven and Karl a temporary home with him in Gneixendorf. Johann owned 400 acres and his estate, Wasserhof, consisted of two large houses. Although Beethoven had vehemently refused when the offer had been made earlier, in August ("I will not come. Your brother??????!!!! Ludwig), this time he accepted, his desperate circumstances no doubt helping to change his mind. Karl was discharged from the priest's care on September 25th and he and his uncle left for Gneixendorf on the 28th. They were scheduled to stay a week, until Karl's military preparations were completed.

About this trip Johann Jenger would later write to Marie Koschak-Pachler (December 29, 1826):

> Because of many vexations and illnesses that his nephew Karl caused the great master, he set out with the nephew on a journey to Upper Austria, intending to visit Beethoven's brother, and remained away from here for over six weeks. Bad treatment at his brother's house in the country, where he had to pay four florins C.M. per day for terrible room and board to his brother—who had invited him to visit the country—and then the weather which had already been persistently terrible, cast him on his sickbed, where I found him about 10 days ago.[10]

This story was probably the result of Jenger having been influenced by "my friend Schindler" who did not like Beethoven's brother. The story about Johann forcing Ludwig to pay rent was a great exaggeration.

Beethoven and Karl arrived in Gneixendorf late on September 29th, but not too late for Beethoven to take a long walk with Johann and look at his property. The next day they walked to the vineyards on the hill and then to Imbach in the afternoon. Beethoven also accompanied his brother on various excursions by carriage to Langenfeld and Langenlois and to Krems. While in Gneixendorf he kept to his schedule of rising at 5:30 in the morning and starting work on his music, then taking a long walk until lunch at 12:30, then working again until 3:00 in the afternoon after which he would take yet another walk until sunset. He worked again after dinner until 10 o'clock and went to bed. All this activity is important to keep in mind since, at this time, some biographers have indicated that Beethoven was a seriously ill man. He seems to have engaged in a great deal of strenuous exercise and kept to a vigorous schedule for one so ill! Even Thayer had to admit that "There was little mention of Beethoven's illness."

---

[10]Albrecht, #451, 165-166

Although peaceful moments were had between uncle and nephew with the rest of the Beethoven clan there to help diffuse difficulties, Beethoven still had some skirmishes with Karl, as noted by Karl's comments, such as: "Yours is the right to command, and I must endure it all." Karl had found diversions to his liking in Gneixendorf: there were soldiers stationed there for him to visit and discuss his upcoming army career. Gneixendorf also had a theater and a troop of English circus riders in town, and, best of all to Karl's way of thinking, a billiard-room. Karl absented himself from his Uncle Johann's house at every opportunity, renewing his Uncle Ludwig's old suspicions about the desolate ways in which he spent his time.

At this time Beethoven began to complain about the food tasting badly—which is strange since Beethoven was no gourmet when it came to food. I offer the following as proof of Beethoven's indifference to poorly prepared food. In his mid-thirties, Beethoven decided to try his hand at cooking and prepared a dinner for a group of his friends. According to Ignaz Seyfried who was among the guests,

> The soup recalled those charitable leavings distributed to beggars in the taverns; the beef was but half done and calculated to gratify only an ostrich; the vegetables floated in a mixture of water and grease; and the roast seemed to have been smoked in a chimney.[11]

An incredulous Seyfried reports further that Beethoven ate this virtually inedible fare with great gusto and even had seconds. This shows us that if Beethoven had rejected the food at Johann's house as "bad," it must have been truly wretched for him to have noticed. Yet no one else, not even Karl who was unaccustomed to the fare at his uncle's house, had any complaint about it. Was only Ludwig's food tainted? Antimony in particular has a bitter taste which could have imparted a disagreeable flavor to Beethoven food. Further, it causes symptoms virtually identical to arsenic.

Johann noted that his brother's appetite declined and as a result began eating little except for soft-boiled eggs and some wine. Johann also reported that his brother started having diarrhea, and that his belly had become distended. Beethoven complained of thirst and abdominal pains. By now the reader is no doubt familiar with the symptoms of arsenical intoxication (the symptoms of which are shared with toxins in the same family). Note of Beethoven's morbid thirst is an important clue since the illnesses associated with him do not cause this particular symptom.

---

[11]Sonneck, 39

Karl was in no hurry to leave Gneixendorf, finding the life of ease in the country much to his liking. And, if he was systematically feeding his uncle poison, he certainly could not return to Vienna, which would also mean his going into the army without his task being completed. In order to remain in Gneixendorf longer than scheduled, Karl gave the excuse to his uncle that "I cannot go to the Field-Marshal until I am able to appear without any visible sign left of what happened to me, because he wants to overlook the whole affair." This may have been the truth or merely an excuse on Karl's part. If true, it is interesting that officials were willing to overlook the criminal aspect of his attempted suicide. He also told his uncle that "the longer we are here, the longer we shall be together" though it is very difficult to believe that Karl wished to stay in Gneixendorf simply because he could not bear to lose his Uncle Ludwig's company.

Schindler intimated to Beethoven that Karl had become intimate with his Aunt Therese though there is no indication that Beethoven believed it. Thayer likewise did not believe it, saying that no reference to any such thing could be found in the Conversation Books, though this would not be surprising. Karl did write that "talk about intrigues needs no refutation," but whether he was referring to his alleged affair with his aunt or some other undertaking is unknown. It might be an interesting speculation to wonder if a distraught nephew had joined forces with an aunt who happened to be the wife of a pharmacist and who likewise had bad feelings toward the uncle in order to rid themselves of a mutual nemesis. Of course we must note that Therese was not often in Gneixendorf at this time—preferring her townhouse in Vienna to the ill-heated house at Wasserhof—and had made every effort to be cordial to Beethoven, who attempted to put past animosities behind him and reciprocate her hospitality. Yet it is possible that Therese left Karl "in charge of things" while she was absent, and used her cordiality as a way to divert any suspicion from herself.

If any "intrigues" were afoot as Schindler suspected, sex probably had little to do with them. We must remember that Karl was only 19 and Therese already 40, not a couple likely to engage in a romantic affair. Nevertheless, a liaison based on other needs and desires—freedom from a domineering uncle, revenge on a menacing brother-in-law—is not impossible nor, perhaps, even far-fetched. Admittedly, though, there is no proof of it, and we must remember that the source of this story was Schindler, a man who rarely had a kind word to say about any of Beethoven's associates.

BACK TO VIENNA

In November 1826, Johann expressed his growing concerns to Ludwig about their nephew's lingering in Gneixendorf:

> I cannot possibly remain quiet any longer about the future destiny of Karl. He is getting completely away from all activity, and will become so accustomed to this life that he will be brought to work again only with the greatest difficulty, the longer he lives here so unproductively. ... You see from Breuning's letter that it is absolutely his intention that Karl shall hasten to his profession; the longer he is here, the more unfortunate for him, because work will come all the harder to him, and therefore we may experience something else bad. It is a thousand pities that this talented young man wastes his time so, and who but the both of us will be blamed for it, because he is still too young to guide himself. I see from his behavior that he would gladly remain with us, but then his future would be lost, so this is impossible, and the longer we hesitate, the harder it will be for him to go away. I therefore implore you to make a firm resolution and not to let Karl dissuade you from it.[12]

Ludwig must have taken Johann's advice to heart and told Karl that they were going to return to Vienna because Karl retorted: "I beg you once and for all to leave me alone. If you want to go [back to Vienna], good." Then he added, "I beg of you once more not to torment me as you are doing; you might regret it for I can endure much, but too much I cannot endure." Although Therese assured Beethoven that Karl just had his rash blood and that "It is you that he loves, to the point of veneration" his attitude does not sound very loving or respectful.

There was a stagecoach from Gneixendorf to Vienna, but if you wanted to go by postchaise, you first had to go to St. Pöltens or perhaps to Krems, either of which was about an hour's drive from Gneixendorf. To briefly recap Beethoven's statement to Wawruch, they had left Gneixendorf in a *Leiterwagen*, a rack vehicle or milk cart. Surprisingly, no statement from Karl on anything that transpired on this journey remains. The duo stopped half-way for the night and around midnight, Beethoven suffered an acute and violent onslaught of illness which included "fever," a chill, a dry cough, a burning thirst, and pain in his side. He became so weak that he had to be carried to the cart the next morning.

What was Beethoven's condition when he arrived at his home in the Schwartzspanierhaus? We do not know exactly. About three days later, he wrote to Holz indicating that he was "*unpässlich*" or indisposed

---
[12]Albrecht, #446, II, 155

indicating that he had made a recovery from the horribly violent episode he had suffered on the road. In his biography of the composer, Schindler accused Karl of neglecting his uncle and not getting a doctor for him immediately, but rather amusing himself with billiards and other pastimes while his uncle lay suffering. We do not know exactly what Karl had done in the meantime, although Dr. Wawruch had been summoned by Holz on December 5th, and apparently it had been Karl who had contacted Holz and asked him to attend to his uncle.

Having already covered Wawruch's report on Beethoven's last days in a previous chapter, for now I will finish with Karl and his eventual departure from Vienna and the bedside of his sick uncle.

As Beethoven lay on his sickbed, Breuning made the following observation to him:

> That you name Karl as heir, in the event, hopefully still far distant, that we all have to leave this life—your opinion is in keeping with what you have already done for him. But since Karl up to now has shown himself to be very irresponsible and since one does not know how his character will develop from his present life, I would be of the opinion that for his own good and for the security of his future you limit his authority to dispose of the capital either for his whole lifetime or at least for several more years until he has attained his majority of 24 years. ... the limitation would protect him against the consequences of irresponsible actions before he fully reaches maturity.[13]

This caution was issued by Breuning because on January 3rd, Beethoven had written to Dr. Bach that "Before my death I declare my beloved nephew my sole and universal heir of all the property which I possess in which is included chiefly seven bank shares and whatever money may be on hand."

Breuning worried that Karl was too frivolous with money and should not be given Beethoven's estate to do with as he wished without some restrictions being placed on the estate for his own protection. Beethoven was reluctant to heed Breuning's advice. Breuning's concern about Karl's inheritance and his proposal that Karl's access to it be limited takes on new meaning when we remember Breuning's fate following Beethoven's death. He was dead just six weeks later. Might he also have been considered an obstacle to be eliminated?

In mid-December, just two weeks before Malfatti changed his mind about becoming involved in Beethoven's treatment, Karl joined up

---

[13]Albrecht, #452, II, 168
[14]Albrecht, #455, II, 172

with his regiment and left Vienna. On January 13, 1827, he wrote to his uncle: "The method of your earlier doctor (or still the present one?) had also aroused some distrust on my part; hopefully it will now go very well."[14] How interesting that Karl would tell his uncle that he had distrusted Wawruch and placed more confidence in Malfatti. Why would he offer his support to Malfatti over Wawruch? He had seen Wawruch's dedicated attention paid to his uncle (sometimes visiting him three times a day), while he had no first-hand knowledge of how Malfatti was treating him. Perhaps he had been instructed to plant the seed of doubt in Beethoven's mind about Wawruch so that he would rely solely on Malfatti.

Karl again wrote to his uncle from his camp (March 4, 1827) thanking him for some boots Beethoven had sent him, and expressing his happiness that he had been "saved by a frozen punch" and was "feeling quite well." He also asked his uncle to remember to "place postage on your letters because I must pay much postage here and have difficulty stretching my money to make my bills." Albrecht speculated that Schindler, who did not like Karl, sent him Ludwig's letters postage due in order that Karl would have to pay for them. Karl's letter is signed *"Dein Dich liebender Sohn"* "Your you-loving son" the same way he signed his letter of January 13th. Can we trust the sincerity of this closing when we know Karl was writing this letter to his former tormentor, the man he had only just recently accused of driving him to the brink of death, an uncle he had once called "the old fool?"

KARL AFTER BEETHOVEN

Less than two weeks after Beethoven's death, Captain (Chevalier) Bruno de Montluisant wrote a note to Schindler regarding Karl.

> June 8, 1827: The guilt that he (Karl) brought on himself earlier through youthful imprudence is indeed, as you said, very great; but the punishment that now has resulted is even greater. Therefore, I believe that it is necessary, so as not to completely remove all support and lessen his confidence, to forget the past and to exert all effort in support of his resolution to do well. [15]

Why exactly Karl now felt guilt is not clear because we cannot question Karl and have none of his thoughts committed to paper. It could have been as de Montluisant said, that Karl regretted how his bad behavior had distressed his uncle and perhaps he felt that he had brought Beethoven to an early grave in that way. On the other hand, is it not just as likely that

---

[15]Albrecht, #484, II, 238

Karl had felt guilty about the active and definite role he played in his uncle's suffering and death?

Stephan Breuning's sudden and unexpected death seems to me to have effectively removed the only potential problem in the issue of Karl's guardianship and his inheritance of Beethoven's estate. Interestingly, it was not Karl's last remaining male blood relative, his Uncle Johann, who was appointed to succeed Breuning and Beethoven, but rather it was Jakob Hotschevar who became Karl's new guardian. As we recall, Hotschevar was the relation of Johanna van Beethoven's who had represented her during the bitter custody battle over Karl some years earlier. Karl certainly could not have been too unhappy about this turn in events for this appointment finally allowed Johanna to achieve control over her son.

On February 10, 1828, Hotschevar wrote a letter to Ignaz Moscheles who had served as the representative of the London Philharmonic Society that had sent Beethoven money —1000 florins (£100)— a few days before his death. In it, Hotschevar hoped to convince the LPS not to try to reclaim the money, but requested that they consider it part of Beethoven's estate which was inherited by Karl. In his appeal, Hotschevar wrote, "The young man (Karl) ... has conducted himself with the strictest propriety since he entered upon the military profession (a whole two months of exemplary behavior!) as a cadet in an Imperial infantry regiment." He added that Beethoven

> thought it his duty to provide for his support. Doubtless that is why he looked upon the seven shares of the Austrian National Bank not as his own property, but as that of his favored nephew for whose support he designated them in his will. It was a matter of religious feeling with him, and he adhered to it faithfully, that the burden of maintaining his poor nephew, for whom he would have sacrificed his own life, imposed such a duty upon him.[16]

As a result of Hotschevar's eloquent plea, and in deference to the memory of Beethoven whom they revered, the London Philharmonic did not press for return of the money sent to Beethoven. Hotschevar's praise of the composer, a man he had denigrated in the courts, whose reputation he attempted to shatter, is very hollow indeed.

KARL UNDER SUSPICION: A REVIEW

Let us do a quick review of Karl as a suspect in the death of his uncle.

---

[16]Albrecht, #490, 251-253

1. Karl was Beethoven's sole heir, inheriting seven bank shares worth the equivalent of $25,000 American, a lot of money in those days.

2. Karl was with Beethoven in Gneixendorf when Beethoven's symptoms reappeared. Beethoven had made no note of being seriously ill prior to this time and his activities when he first arrived in Gneixendorf do not reflect the health of someone who would be dead within four months.

3. Karl was well known to the police, first in connection with the custody suit over his guardianship waged between his uncle and his mother when his behavior was evaluated by Sedlnitzky; second when he attempted suicide. They thus might have had some "bargaining power" with the young man in terms of his future. Although the attempted suicide was considered a criminal offense, he was not severely punished (as in the case of Mimi Erdödy). In fact, he gained what he had always wanted: a commission in the army.

4. It was when Beethoven wanted to return to Vienna that Karl opposed him, and en route, Beethoven suffered an acute attack of illness, the symptoms of which suspiciously match those of various toxins (e.g. arsenic) when a large dose is administered.

5. Karl expressed his distrust of Wawruch and instead offered support to Malfatti whose treatments caused Beethoven additional suffering and who himself is a suspect, even though Karl had no first-hand knowledge of how Malfatti was treating his uncle, and had no reason to denigrate the capable and devoted Wawruch.

6. Karl expressed strong feelings of guilt after Beethoven's death, and his behavior changed remarkably, as if to atone for his involvement in his uncle's death.

7. Far from being a loving nephew, Karl harbored a great deal of resentment against his uncle, as seen in his deprecating remarks to friends, the violent altercations he had had with Beethoven, and the lies he had told him about his feelings of affection.

8. There is a strong possibility that Karl had been influenced by either his Aunt Therese or his mother, or even both, for both of them detested Beethoven for many years.

9. Stephen von Breuning, appointed Karl's guardian after Beethoven's death, died just six weeks later, putting Karl's guardianship and inheritance in the hands of Jakob Hotschevar and, thus, of his mother.

We find ourselves with many reasons to be suspicious of Karl in the final illness of his uncle. If we suppose that it had been Karl who had administered a large dose of arsenic to Beethoven en route to Vienna, perhaps as a last-ditch effort to keep him from leaving Gneixendorf, we might also suppose that he had been alarmed by the violent effect the poison had had on him. Previously, small doses had made his uncle ill, but not terribly so. This last dose caused a violent reaction in Beethoven. It is possible that Karl, not being well educated in the fine art of poisoning, had accidently given him too large a dose, and the shock of seeing what he had done to his uncle had caused him to back out of whatever arrangements he had made to undermine his health. Perhaps his conscience finally hit him with the gravity of his actions, and he refused to continue administering poison to his uncle. This may explain why Malfatti, who at first—and three times, no less—adamantly refused to visit Beethoven, but then finally relented. Someone had to take over the assignment to make sure that Beethoven did not recover from this final illness, now that he had already gone so far down the path to his grave.

Chapter 10
Johanna van Beethoven Revisited

We left Johanna van Beethoven in 1820, having lost the guardianship of her son when her brother-in-law, Ludwig, filed a petition with the Court of Appeal and had himself reappointed as guardian of Karl, along with Karl Peters. It was at this time that Johanna also became pregnant by her lover, Joseph Hofbauer. Blöchlinger, who owned the Blöchlinger Institute where Karl was sent to school in 1819, was one source of the news. In 1820 he wrote in Beethoven's Conversation Book:

> She is simply a *canaille*. I am simply convinced of it, and unfortunately the boy also appears to becoming one. The boy lies every time he opens his mouth. His laziness, for which naturally he must be punished strictly, leads him astray continually. Will you please speak to him? Perhaps if he could be taken to Salzburg or to some distant place, he could perhaps improve, removed from the influence of his mother....
>
> It has seemed to me of late that the Beethoven woman was expecting. I would be very glad to know for sure, one would have new evidence for saying to Karl that his mother was immoral...Karl must get a clear understanding as regards his mother... for if he depends on her, he is lost.

Blöchlinger also told Beethoven that Johanna's presence at his house caused him shame and asked Beethoven for power of attorney to call in the police if Karl should run away to his mother. Beethoven consulted his attorney, Johann Bach, on the matter. Bach advised that this was not practical and suggested that Blöchlinger tell Johanna that she must visit with her son only at his uncle's house. Johanna did not like this arrangement before, when Giannatasio attempted to enforce it; it is logical to assume she had not changed her mind.

When Karl learned of Johanna's pregnancy he immediately ran away from his uncle and back to his mother, perhaps in a desperate attempt to assure himself that he still had a place in her heart. The police quickly returned him to his uncle. Late in the year Johanna gave birth to a daughter and, in what seems a gesture of antagonism toward Beethoven, Johanna named the girl Ludovica, a feminine form of the name Ludwig. One can only imagine Karl's state of mind, seeing his uncle proven true about his mother's lack of morality and yet still having feelings of love for her as most children do. The fact that Johanna expressed the desire never to see her brother-in-law under any circumstances following his successful appeal surely added to the tension felt by all concerned, especially adolescent Karl.

Exactly why Beethoven himself made reconciliatory gestures toward Johanna in 1822 is unclear. Perhaps he finally recognized how the antagonism between him and Johanna was adversely affecting Karl. He made some overtures of peace toward her, and even repaid a debt she owed to the publisher Steiner. This loan Beethoven had acquired for her when his brother suffered his final illness, serving as guarantor for the loan. He wrote to Bernard, "I want to do everything I can for her insofar as it isn't against Karl's interest."

In a Conversation Book for February-March 1823, we read a note from Bernard: "Have you heard nothing concerning your sister-in-law? My housekeeper has told me that she is sick and things are going very badly with her. The doctor has told it to her himself. He said that she could not pay for the medicine." When he learned that Johanna had taken ill, Beethoven anonymously sent her small gifts of cash. He again wrote to Bernard, "I am sending her herewith 11 gulden... Please have it delivered to her through the doctor, and what is more, in such a way that she may not know where it has come from.... I am prepared to help in any way." He also restored to her the half of her pension which she had had to give up to her son in 1817. And yet again he wrote to Bernard:

> ...assure her at once... that from this month onwards she can enjoy her full pension as long as I live... As she is so ill and in such straitened circumstances, she must be helped at once. ...I shall make a point of persuading my pigheaded brother also to contribute something to help her.[1]

Karl, now nearly 17, apparently had not yet forgiven his mother for her "betrayal" in having another child—and an illegitimate one at that—or perhaps was greedy enough not to want to give up the money to

---

[1] Anderson, #1256, III, 1101

her. Whatever the reason, he vehemently protested Beethoven's decision regarding the pension. He began to malign her to Beethoven, seemingly to prevent any reconciliation between them, but at first Beethoven would not be swayed from his good intentions. As a result of his kind gesture, the animosity between them gradually dissolved and their outward amicability remained for a short time. On January 1, 1824, Johanna sent Beethoven a friendly New Year's greeting and in response, he wrote the her following letter:

> Our many occupations made it quite impossible for Karl and me to send you our best wishes on New Year's Day. But I know that even without this explanation you are fully assured of both my and Karl's sincerest wishes for your welfare —[2]

Yet Beethoven's innermost feelings about his sister-in-law seem not to have changed a great deal, despite his efforts to make peace with her. In a letter to Bernard written shortly after he sent wishes for "all possible happiness" to Johanna, he wrote

> She is supposed to receive from Hofbauer too 480 gulden V.C. Since Hofbauer, I understand, believes that he is the father of the child, he is probably right. And as she has become such a strumpet I consider that after all I should make Karl realize the guilt of her wicked behavior.[3]

Learning that the father of Johanna's illegitimate child was fulfilling his financial responsibility toward them, Beethoven had a change of heart about restoring her entire pension to her. If she had the father of her daughter supporting her, she hardly needed the money that legally was to go to her son's upkeep.

> Hence if these 480 gulden of Hofbauer's are really and truly being paid to her, I think that she ought not to be allowed to enjoy the whole remaining half of her pension. ... Let me add that I do not want to have anything to do with her personally.[4]

By 1824, Karl periodically and purposefully stayed away from Beethoven, spending more and more time with his friend, Niemetz who Beethoven complained was "lacking completely in decency and manners" and added, accusingly, "I suspect that his interests are more with the housekeeper than with me—" Karl would not be dissuaded from his

---

[2]Anderson #1257,III,1101

[3]Anderson, #1259, III, 1103

[4]IBID

friendship with Niemetz, responding defiantly, "I will not stop loving him as I would my brother, if I had one."[5] Although he no longer aroused his uncle's rage when he ran away, Beethoven worried incessantly about him. He suspected Karl of having sexual liaisons and to Tobias Haslinger, expressed his concern that "poisonous breath coming from dragons" might be enveloping Karl.[6] Karl, now 18, did not appreciate his uncle's concern, and they had many violent quarrels that so disturbed the neighbors that Beethoven sometimes was threatened with eviction.

There is very little information on Johanna's life after this time other than that which I have already related through Karl's story. We know only that Johanna died destitute in Baden in 1868, aged at least 87 years—possibly as old as 89—and that both she and her daughter, Ludovica, for the most part had led continuously desolate lives.

JOHANNA AS SUSPECT 1827

One might think that Beethoven's good-will gestures toward Johanna in later years would have removed her from suspicion, that she would have felt enough gratitude toward him to keep her from wanting to harm him. Yet we see that his feelings toward her had not changed, and his original intention to restore half her pension to her was revoked. In addition, she surely heard horror stories—true or not—from Karl about his mistreatment at Beethoven's hand, so that even if mother and son had suffered a period of estrangement, they no doubt were reunited once again in their hatred for brother-in-law and uncle.

Although Johanna was not with Beethoven in Gneixendorf, her son was. She also may have found a sympathetic ear in her sister-in-law Therese who knew first-hand how difficult it was to deal with a Beethoven, any Beethoven. So while she certainly was not the one to offer the poisoned goblet to Beethoven, she could easily have been the guiding force behind the one who did. Verdict: indirectly guilty; most likely a willing accomplice.

---

[5]Thayer-Forbes, 922
[6]Anderson, #1316, III, 1147

Chapter 11
The Brother:
Nicholas Johann van Beethoven

Nicholas Johann van Beethoven was six years younger than his composer brother, born on or around October 1, 1776. Although as a boy neighbors recalled him being somewhat stupid but good-natured, as an adult he was intelligent enough to earn a considerable amount of money as a pharmacist. In fact, he was rich enough to buy farm property, called Wasserhof, with two large houses in Gneixendorf, and also keep a winter home in Vienna. Occasionally, as in the spring of 1822, he lived in the house of his brother-in-law, a baker named Leopold Obermayr, and rented out his other property for additional income. At one time, brother Ludwig also rented out part of Obermayr's house. Johann's relationship to his famous brother made him noticable to Viennese society and thus his idiosyncrasies, habits and public behavior (as well as the deplorable conduct of his wife) made him a somewhat comical figure in Vienna. Gerhard von Breuning described him in a note to Thayer:

> His hair was blackish-brown; hat well brushed; clothing clean but suggesting that of a man who wishes to be elegantly clad on Sundays; somewhat old-fashioned and uncouth, an effect which was caused by his bone-structure, which was angular and unlovely. His waist was rather small; shoulders broad; if my memory serves me rightly, his shoulders were a trifle uneven, or it may have been his angular figure which made him look unsymmmetrical... His hands were broad and bony. He was not exactly tall of stature but much taller than Ludwig. His nose was large and rather long, the position of his eyes, crooked, the effect being as if he squinted a little with one eye. The mouth was crooked, one corner drawn upwards giving him the expression of a mocking smile. In his garb, he affected to be a well-to-do elegant, but the role did not suit his angular, bony figure. He did not in the least resemble his brother Ludwig.

Breuning later added in his own book that Johann was sometimes seen driving in the Prater in an old-fashioned phaeton—a lightweight carriage with a folding top—pulled by two or four horses, either handling the reins himself or lolling carelessly in the seat with two servants on the box. Beethoven's friends used to ridicule Johann, even to his face. In a Conversation Book of 1822-23 Count Moritz Lichnowsky wrote: "Everybody thinks him a fool; we call him only the Chevalier—all the world says of him that his only merit is that he bears your name." Thayer felt that there was a good deal of the *parvenu* in Johann's character, that is, a person who has suddenly acquired wealth or power but who, by virtue of his birth or social position is not fully accepted by the class into which he has risen. He was not an intellectual person nor did he have the poise which would have allowed him to fit into the place in society where he he thought he was entitled to be by virtue of his wealth and his relationship to one of the most famous men of his age. It was apparent that Johann was not the sort of man who could command the respect of others. Nevertheless, he did have a talent for business, a talent he did not always use in the most ethical way.

Thayer noted," That Johann van Beethoven was fond of money is indicated in his remarks in the Conversation Books when his advice to his brother is always dictated by financial considerations and, no doubt, by the thoughts of profits in which he hoped to share." Thayer, however, tended to defend Johann, saying that Schindler had often misrepresented him and that other writers had simply accepted what Schindler had written, often adding their own "unscrupulous imaginations" to the pot. That Johann's character had been unjustly maligned and falsified was, according to Thayer, "beyond doubt." However, Ludwig himself questioned his brother's integrity from time to time, commenting to Stumpff in September 1824 as Johann came into the room during Stumpff's visit: "That is my brother—have nothing to do with him—he is not an honest man. You will hear me accused of many wrong actions of which he has been guilty." On the other hand, Ludwig often deferred to Johann's business acumen and placed his financial transactions in Johann's hands, showing that he must have had some confidence in his brother's honesty and judgment—or at least in his ability to turn a profit and negotiate a good deal. Yet sometimes Johann exceeded his authority to act in his brother's name in respect to business negotiations, causing Moritz Lichnowsky to warn Beethoven in the Conversation Book: "You ought to forbid him doing business or carrying on correspondence without your signature. Perhaps he has already closed a contract in your name." It is difficult to get a completely accurate picture of Johann, although he does not overall seem a bad sort.

He ended to vacillate between generosity and greed depending on the winds of his fortune. When he invited Ludwig and Karl to stay with him, he first wrote, "You do not need money here" but then later had a change of heart and wrote "You will need only half of your pension" and still later "I will charge nothing for the first fortnight; I would do more if I were not so hardpressed with taxes."

Thayer attributed Johann's greed to his somewhat impovished upbringing—a start that he shared with two older brothers who were seemingly not as affected by the family's poverty as the youngest boy. He does at times come across as avaricious, although his character was not as bad as those who disliked him—such as Schindler and Ries—made him out to be. They accused him of being demanding when he needed his brother Ludwig to repay a loan in 1808, although it would have been disastous for him to delay the asking. As it was, when he asked for the repayment, he was in genuine financial need, having already sold off the iron grating of his windows as scrap metal. But then he showed his cunning in business when he discovered that the shelves in his recently purchased apothocary shop were made of tin—a commodity in great demand at the time because of the war with Napoleon—and was able to turn a profit. At the same time he contracted with the French troops (notwithstanding that they were the enemy) to supply them with medical supplies which ended up making him a moderate fortune. This was a technically legal activity, although brother Ludwig was never sure about the ethics of this arrangement, so while he did not openly condemn Johann's actions, neither did he praise his business acumen in this situation. At times Ludwig accused Johann of unscrupulous dealings with him, but it is difficult to know how justified he was in his feelings. Much might be attributable to misunderstanding; although Johann was more passive than either of his two older brothers, there was a certain amount of volatility in all the Beethovens.

Johann's greed was also evident in an anecdote related about his actions immediately following Beethoven's death. Stephan von Breuning, Anton Schindler, Johann van Beethoven and Karl Holz met in Beethoven's apartment to gather up the dead man's papers, and, in particular, to look for the seven bank shares which the composer's will had left to his nephew. In spite of a thorough search they were not immediately found and Johann, annoyed, insinuated that the search was a sham. (He may not have been entirely wrong in this, because Beethoven had told Holz of the secret drawer in his desk where, indeed, the bank shares later were found. Holz had even admitted to Otto Jahn that only he had been told of the secret compartment. Why then he allowed the search to continue while knowing all along where the notes where is puzzling. Perhaps he had not immediately remembered where they were.) According to Schindler, after the first search proved fruitless, Johann had cried out: "Breuning and Schindler must produce them!" This was corroborated by Gerhard von Breuning, Stephan's son, who said that Johann's accusation had so angered his father that he immediately stormed out of the house and refused to return until a long time later.

JOHANN AS SUSPECT

Although Beethoven's brother seems easily motivated by greed, and had both the opportunity and the means to harm Ludwig, he does not seem to me a viable suspect. For one, he did not stand to profit from Ludwig's death financially, since Ludwig had left everything he owned to his nephew (and, indeed, had urged Johann to do the same and make out *his* will in Karl's favor, as well). Johann enjoyed the fame and social standing that his brother's reputation gave him—even pretending to appreciate his brother's talent and music when he did not understand it at all—making Ludwig worth more to him alive than dead. Other than his somewhat unethical dealings with the French army many years before, he was a respectable citizen over whose head the police seemed not to have anything to hang. There is little reason to suspect Johann of having done his brother harm. Verdict: not guilty.

Chapter 14
Another Sister-in-Law: Therese Obermayr van Beethoven

Johann van Beethoven married Therese Obermayr in 1812 over his brother's objections. Many scholars have spoken about these objections as having been a violent overreaction on Ludwig's part, claiming that he tried to prevent the marriage by having Therese banished from Austria on moral grounds and taking his complaints against her to both the church officials and the police. The evidence does not bear this out. Even the reputable Thayer talks about evidence which he does not cite provided by "perfectly competent authorities" whom he fails to name. All he says about the subject is that in 1860, nearly a half century after the event in question, he received a note stating that Beethoven had taken "drastic steps"—including appeals to the police and church authorities to have Therese banished—in order to keep his brother from marrying an "unchaste girl." Beyond mention of this note, no written confirmation has been provided: no police records, church documents, or letters to civil authorities, not even the note itself or the name of its author. Inasmuch as Therese had an illegitimate daughter, Amalie, who was five years old when Johann married the mother, and there being an indication that Johann and Therese had shared a bed prior to their wedding, it is little wonder that a morally upright Ludwig would find her unsuitable as a wife and may have attempted to dissuade his brother from marrying her. Yet no major altercation is proven to have taken place at the time. In fact, Ludwig stayed as a guest in Johann's house for a full five weeks, from his arrival in Linz to two days past the wedding. It is hard to imagine Johann not throwing his elder brother out on the street if he had truly caused such an uproar in the town. In addition, Therese's brother, Leopold Obermayr, bore Ludwig no ill will and some years later even rented him an apartment in his house. Surely he would have remembered such a ghastly event and not acted cordially toward Beethoven. Letters from Ludwig to Johann indicate that the former did attempt, for a while at least, to accept his brother's choice of wife, however poorly he may have regarded her.

However, there is documentary evidence that Ludwig made a strong attempt to rid his brother his "objectionable" wife in 1823, rather than in 1812 as Thayer had been led to believe. It is unclear how the error occurred, but it is apparent from Beethoven's own letters that the first altercations between them happened ten years later than Thayer's mysterious correspondent claimed. In May of 1822, Ludwig first broached the subject of living closer to his brother, an idea that did not appeal to Therese. Because of her objections, it was soon after that the animosity between Ludwig and Therese began to escalate. Her reluctance to have Ludwig living so close to them, prompted Ludwig to write:

> I have nothing against your wife. I only hope that she will realize how much could be gained for you too by your living with me and all life's wretched trivialities need not cause any disturbances between us... I repeat that I have nothing against your wife, although her behavior to me on a few occasions has greatly shocked me.[1]

If Ludwig had tried to have Therese banished from Austria in 1812, would he have referred to this effort as a "triviality?" Under those circumstances, would Johann had believed Ludwig had nothing against his wife? Or would Ludwig have been shocked that Therese did not like him? Again, the troubles between them could not have been too severe in 1812. Up through mid-1822, Beethoven's letters to his brother always ended with him sending best regards to his family. But by 1823, Beethoven's feelings toward his sister-in-law had begun to deteriorate. It was then that Johann was taken ill and Ludwig heard stories about Therese's callous treatment of his brother while he lay in his sickbed.

Ludwig sent Schindler to visit Johann and Therese so that he could "report back" on her unscrupulous behavior. We find that it is at this point that Beethoven's truly caustic letters regarding this sister-in-law began. Thayer tells us that Johann's wife's conduct had reached "the extreme of reprehensibleness" when, in the summer of 1823 Johann became very sick. Thayer tells us that "The woman chose this time to receive her lover in her house and to make a shameless public parade of her moral laxness. The step-daughter was no less neglectful of her filial duties." When accounts of his sister-in-law's immoral conduct reached Beethoven's ears, he wasted no time in denouncing her to his brother. He also asked

---

[1]Anderson, #1078, II, 946

Schindler to present the matter before the police, but Schindler thought it best to postpone that step until Johann's health improved so as not to upset him. Schindler wrote Beethoven a lengthy report on July 3, 1823. He said he had visited Johann three to four times a day and thus had a good opportunity to observe both Therese and her daughter, Amalie, Johann's step-daughter. Schindler wrote:

> I can assure you on my honor that, despite your venerable name, they deserve to be shut up, the old one in prison, the young one in the house of correction.... These beasts would have let him rot if others had not taken pity on him. He might have died a hundred times without the one in the Prater or at Nussdorf the other at the baker's (Leopold Obermayr's, Therese's brother) deigning to give him a look.... He often wept over the conduct of his family and once he gave way completely to his grief and begged me to let you know how he is being treated so that you might come and give the two the beating they deserve.... It is most unnatural and more than barbarous if that woman, while her husband is lying ill, introduces her lover into his room, pinks herself like a sleigh horse in his presence and then goes driving with him, leaving the sick husband languishing at home. She did this very often. Your brother himself called my attention to it, and is a fool for tolerating it so long.

Angered by Schindler's report, Ludwig wrote to Johann shortly thereafter, "You will not be entirely neglected whatever those two *canailles,* that loutish fat woman and her bastard may do to you." Ludwig began to urge his brother to divorce her. His letter continued:

> You can not well be wholly unadvised as to what the two *canailles,* (French meaning a mob, rabble, a pack of dogs) Lump and Bastard, are doing to you, and you have had letters on the subject from me and Karl, for, little as you deserve it I shall never forget that you are my brother, and a good angel will yet come to rid you of these two *canailles.* This former and present strumpet who received visits from her fellow no less than three times while you were ill, and who in addition to everything else has your money wholly in her hands. O infamous disgrace! Isn't there a spark of manhood in you?!!!... About coming to you I will write another time. Ought I so to degrade myself as to associate with such bad company?

As Thayer tells us, the main reason Beethoven was so reluctant to accept his brother's repeated invitations to visit him at Gneixendorf was

Therese's presence there. If he had tolerated her once, her conduct during his brother's illness now caused Ludwig to feel an intense hatred for her.

With Ludwig berating him for being spineless, Johann halfheartedly entertained the idea of divorcing Therese, but there was an obstacle: she had a marriage contract that gave her half of his property upon termination of the marriage. Though at one time she had told him she would be willing to surrender the contract she quickly changed her mind when she realized that if she did so she would be turned out into the world with neither a good reputation nor means of subsistence. For some reason Johann was reluctant to take any of the measures open to him—such as charging her with immoral conduct or adultery, both of which were grounds for divorce in those days. Much to his brother's annoyance, Johann decided to be complaisant: he needed a housekeeper, he told Ludwig, and for that she would serve well enough. "I go my way and let her go hers," he said. But brother Ludwig was relentless in his urgings, and finally Johann did take some action against his wife, though not enough to suit his brother.

In the Conversation book of 1824 is this very interesting exchange between the brothers:

> Johann: My wife has surrendered her marriage contract and entered into an obligation permitting me to drive her away without notice at the first new acquaintance which she makes.
>
> Ludwig (implied) Why do you not simply divorce her and be done with it?
>
> Johann: I cannot do that. I cannot know but that some misfortune might befall me.

Johann's response is shocking. Why was he afraid that any action taken against his wife might bring dire consequences to himself? Exactly what recourse did Therese have? What hold did she have over Johann? Unfortunately, there is nothing that gives us any indication of the answer, yet it does seem as if Johann was afraid of her and thought her capable of doing him harm. If a woman can inspire such fear in her husband, there surely was some reason for it.

One other interesting item to remember is Schindler's belief that Therese and Beethoven's nephew Karl had become lovers while Karl and Ludwig stayed with Johann and his family following Karl's suicide attempt. We know she took lovers, but would she have taken one so young?

Under these circumstances, with so much animosity between Ludwig and Therese, is it not difficult to imagine Therese agreeing to become the instrument of Ludwig's undoing. Such an undertaking might even appeal to her. Not only would she rid herself of a troublesome brother-in-law who was seeking her divorcement from his brother and thus threatening her means of financial support, but it is possible that a monetary reward could have been a further inducement. It is also possible that Therese acted out of sympathy for her sister-in-law, Johanna, and agreed to work in conjunction with her for the purpose of ridding themselves of a mutual problem.

Unfortunately her involvement in any poisoning of Beethoven must remain mere speculation. There are arguments both for and against her. In her behalf there is an indication from her remarks in the Conversation Books that she had tried to make amends with Ludwig. Her comments to him are cordial and respectful, and Ludwig's anger towards her seems to have cooled considerably. She tried to comfort Ludwig when Karl upset him, assuring him of Karl's love for him, and seems to have made an effort to make Ludwig's stay in Gneixendorf as pleasant as possible so long as she was still staying there. We also must recall that she was not in Gneixendorf when Ludwig became violently ill, which removes some suspicion from her, although, as also noted before, if Karl had been an accomplice, he could have continued administering the poison to his uncle in Therese's absence.

Evidence against her remains circumstantial, but weighty enough to consider. We must wonder whether her cordiality toward Ludwig was only for show, to keep herself above suspicion, or was it genuine? If she were the sort to harbor a long-standing grudge, she certainly would have had the motive. Was she Karl's lover? Did she at least feel sorry for him and his mother, too, for having also been "victims" of Ludwig van Beethoven? Might Karl have played upon her sympathy and her empathy as a fellow sufferer so that she became a willing participant to free all of them of the tyrant they all had been forced to endure? Therese not only had the opportunity, she also had the means and knowledge since her husband was a pharmacist. Further, she was acquainted with the police who were well aware of her immoral reputation and might have induced or encouraged her to undertake such a task. We should note that although a person could be banished from Austria under their morality laws, and Therese's reputation was far from sterling, nothing ever happened to her. Had the police offered her monetary reward for her services or agreed to overlook any charges of immorality which might have robbed her of her Austrian citizenship? Possibly, although there is no evidence for it; the police did not keep such records.

It is difficult to hand down a judgment on Therese without there being any definitive evidence against her. She certainly was in a position to gain peace of mind from Ludwig's death. Her weak husband was not likely to divorce her without his brother there to goad him. Yet unless she had been seduced into serving as an accomplice to some other suspect—Karl, Johanna, or the Court—it seems unlikely that this simple housekeeper would have taken the initiative to eliminate Beethoven on her own. My best verdict: possible accomplice.

Chapter 15
The Friends:
Anton Schindler and Karl Holz

ANTON SCHINDLER

When one looks at a photograph of Anton Schindler—he did indeed live to the age of photography—it is often difficult to imagine the grim, lined face as once having belonged to a young man. Yet it was precisely when Schindler was young, not yet 20, that he met Beethoven who was nearly 25 years his senior. Schindler was born in 1795, in Meddl (Moravia, a province in Czechoslovakia), the son of a local schoolmaster. In 1813, when he was just 18, he went to Vienna to study jurisprudence, although he was also trained in and quite accomplished on the violin.

Schindler the law student—who clerked for one of Beethoven's attorneys, Johann Baptist Bach—first met Beethoven in 1814 when a friend of his asked him to deliver a note to the composer from his teacher. Schindler noted that Beethoven had acted kindly toward him from the beginning; their relationship deepened later following Schindler's run-in with the Austrian police. In 1815, student rioting, particularly in Italy with the Carbonari, was of serious concern to the Austrian government. At that time, Schindler had accepted an itinerant teaching position in Brünn (now Brno, Moravia's chief city). When he arrived, the police immediately questioned him—as they typically did most faculty members. They wanted information about certain Italians, with whom Schindler was acquainted, believed to be in league with the Carbonari. They demanded to know what connections he had with the rioters at the University of Vienna, and then asked to see his papers. Unfortunately, his papers were not in order and their own paperwork—that listed where he was supposed to be lecturing and on what topics—also was incomplete. He was arrested and imprisoned until he could prove his innocence a few weeks later. Beethoven, who had no love for the Austrian government and its methods of governance, was sympathetic to Schindler's plight, and the latter's troubles helped forge the bond between them.

Schindler took and passed his law exams in 1819 and for a time was employed in the chancellery of Beethoven's patron, the Archduke Rudolph. But Schindler's heart was always in music and not law, so by the autumn of 1822, he quit the law and became leader of the violins at the Josephstadt-theater. Perhaps his closer association with Beethoven in 1820 helped him make this decision.

With the departure of Franz Oliva who had served for several years as a sort of secretary to Beethoven, Schindler was only too happy to take over as Beethoven's unpaid assistant, seemingly enjoying his self-imposed servitude to "the Master." He did everything from handling correspondence, to dealing with people seeking favors from Beethoven, to securing places for the composer to live, to doing the household shopping.

Schindler remained close to Beethoven for nearly four years when they had a falling out over receipts from a concert of the Ninth Symphony (et.al) which Beethoven hoped would clear him 2000 florins in profit. It was an artistic triumph and a financial failure and ended up netting only a disappointing few hundred florins. Beethoven accused Schindler of cheating him in his handling of the receipts, and although Beethoven recanted the accusation later, he and Schindler remained estranged for some two years, almost until Beethoven's death when Schindler once again attended him tirelessly and seemingly selflessly.

Of Schindler's relation to Beethoven Solomon wrote, "His attitude toward Beethoven himself was compounded of servility, worship and hatred in more or less equal parts, all of which alternate freely in his unreliable biographical studies of the composer." Since it is never wise to take Solomon's pronouncements at face value, it behooves us to consider carefully whether Schindler did, indeed, harbor a deep-seated hatred of Beethoven that vied with his adoration of him for dominance. It is true that Beethoven was not always kind to Schindler—though whether his reproaches were deserved is difficult to determine. Schindler sometimes took upon himself matters which he should not have and made decisions on Beethoven's behalf which were not his to make. For example, when Beethoven was incapacitated with eye problems, it was Schindler who assigned the dedication of the *Diabelli Variations* to Antonie Brentano against Beethoven's intentions. Beethoven had intended that the dedication should go to Frau Ries, and that a dedication to Frau Brentano was to be for the German-published edition only. The latter, Beethoven remarked, was done solely out of obligation and because he had nothing else at the moment available. Subsequently, because of Schindler, Beethoven had to apologize to Ries, for he had already informed him that the dedication was to be for his wife. Little wonder that Schindler often found himself outside Beethoven's good graces, despite perhaps his good intentions.

By nature Schindler was a serious fellow whose gloomy outlook on life Beethoven found depressing and at times intolerable. His habit of commenting on the terribleness of the moment and being predominantly cheerless sometimes caused Beethoven to "banish" him from his presence.

> ...I confess that your presence irritates me in so many ways. If you see me looking not very cheerful, you say "Nasty day again, isn't it?" For owing to your vulgar outlook how could you appreciate anything that is not vulgar?! ...it is impossible to have you beside me permanently because such an arrangement would upset my whole existence—[1]

Beethoven also ridiculed Schindler's habit of occasionally kissing his hand like a subject does a monarch[2] and often found Schindler's fawning behavior annoying.

Schindler found little of virtue in most of Beethoven's associates, whether family or friends. The only person who did not fare badly was Stephan von Breuning, a man whose character was so far above reproach that not even Schindler could find fault with him. Everyone else—and that included Beethoven's brothers, his nephew, his sisters-in-law, and many of his friends, especially the light-hearted Holz—were falsely portrayed as lowly creatures unworthy of Beethoven's time and trouble. Schindler's motivation in writing so scathingly about those who associated with Beethoven was probably jealousy. Thayer also believed Schindler wanted to drive a wedge between Beethoven and his brother Johann, his nephew Karl, and his friend Karl Holz, by bringing Beethoven sordid tales of their behavior which Beethoven, being rather naïve in such matters, was all too prone to believe. So, in this case, perhaps we can take Solomon's assessment—that Schindler sometimes harbored bad feelings for Beethoven—as somewhat accurate. Nevertheless, Schindler did remain steadfastly loyal to Beethoven, serving him without pay and little thanks, throughout the long, terrible months of his final illness.

Beethoven had many humorous nicknames for Schindler—as he did for all his closest friends—thus showing his affection for Schindler,

---

[1] Anderson, #1288, III, 1124
[2] Anderson, #1408, III, 1229-1230, letter to Johann van Beethoven

despite the fact that these good feelings sometimes waivered. Papageno, he would call him, or *Lumpenkerl* (ragamuffin) or even Chief Ragamuffin, or sometimes "Samothracian Ragamuffin!" On the other hand, he also called him "the biggest wretch on earth" and an arch-scoundrel (as he did during the *Diabelli Variations* dedication fiasco). To nephew Karl he wrote that Schindler had an "evil character which is prone to trickery." Beethoven occasionally accused him of dishonesty and even leveled a charge of theft upon him from his deathbed—although the agony of his illness could well explain Beethoven's irrationality in that regard. That Beethoven did not mean to act so unkindly is evident in the fact that when Schindler fell ill and was forced to be absent for a short time from Beethoven's bedside, the dying composer sent Schindler a meal and a kind note.

Thayer gave several examples of Schindler's deliberate doctoring of the Conversation Books. In 1977 two Beethoven scholars, Grita Herre and Dagmar Beck, using handwriting analysis, showed that he had, in fact, altered some 150 entries. He had reordered pages, added or changed dates, and made insertions or erased other passages, in short, often greatly changing their content. Thayer believed Schindler did so to cover up errors in his biography of Beethoven. Schindler's distortions and destruction of primary source material are unfortunate, not only because of our loss in terms of what we might have learned about Beethoven without them, but also because his own credibility has suffered so badly as a result. It is hard to know what is true in Schindler's writings and what is false.

After Beethoven's death, Schindler attempted to collaborate with Franz Wegeler on a biography of the composer—the composer's other choice, Rochlitz, having declined the task because of poor health. Wegeler suggested including Ries, but before collaboration could begin, Schindler had a falling out with Ries over what ought to be included or deleted. Ries insisted that the biography tell "the whole truth" as Beethoven had wanted. Schindler accused Ries of bearing a grudge against Beethoven and wanting to tarnish his memory by including things in the biography that were hurtful to his memory. (Nothing in Ries' eventual biography bears out this accusation.) Schindler eventually persuaded Wegeler to continue without Ries, but the collaboration did not work out. Wegeler announced to Schindler that his notes would be published without the latter's input in 1834, but the publication never happened. In 1838, Ries died suddenly and shortly thereafter, Wegeler published their collaborative effort, *Biographische Notizen über Ludwig van Beethoven*. Schindler's first effort appeared in 1840.

SCHINDLER AS SUSPECT

Although Schindler may have had hard feelings toward Beethoven from time to time, they hardly seem serious enough to saddle him with an accusation of having deliberately harmed the composer. It is true that Beethoven was periodically ill during the time of his association with Schindler, and that one such attack came after Schindler had dinner with him. In April 1824, he wrote to Schindler that, "I am not coming, for the bad food we had yesterday has made me sick."[3] On the other hand, Schindler was not with Beethoven in Gneixendorf, so any involvement he might have had in poisoning Beethoven at that time would have to have come later, that is, after December 14th which is the first day he saw Beethoven after the composer had returned to Vienna. By then, Beethoven had already suffered three acute attacks of illness.

Schindler did encourage Beethoven's faith in Malfatti, and even admitted that it was he who finally had persuaded Malfatti to visit Beethoven after making four attempts. And it was Schindler who wrote that Malfatti had encouraged Beethoven to "drink all you want" of the iced punch that had such disastrous results in terms of Beethoven's health. Yet Schindler may have thought that Beethoven wanted to believe in a doctor's ability to cure him, especially if that doctor happened also to have been a friend from long ago, and simply encouraged that belief, thinking it was in Beethoven's best interest psychologically.

Schindler had nothing to gain from poisoning Beethoven. In fact, his self-importance revolved around serving the composer, of being able to present himself as Beethoven's close friend and confidante. If one basks in the glow of a star, one hardly would want to shoot that star out of the sky. For a while, Schindler was supplanted by Karl Holz, and by a leap of the imag-ination one might suggest a "revenge factor" had driven Schindler to eliminate Beethoven. However, Schindler's animosity was directed at Holz, not Beethoven, and at the end, it was to Schindler whom Beethoven again turned for help, Holz being too involved in his new bride to attend his friend to any extent. While it is possible that Schindler had contrived to make Beethoven so ill that the latter would *have* to rely upon him, it is doubtful that Schindler (who we recall did not encounter Beethoven until mid-December) would have made an already seriously ill man worse.

An unsubstantiated rumor had it that after Beethoven's death, Schindler took to wearing one of the composer's dressing gowns when at home. If true, it is a testimony to his undying, if somewhat bizarre, hero worship.

---

[3] Anderson, #1276, III, 1119

Fatal Links

After Beethoven's death, Vienna held little appeal for Schindler and for almost two years he lived with his sister in Pesth. One might speculate from this that Schindler left Vienna to avoid falling under suspicion or that the government had requested him to leave, but that is all it is: mere speculation. He returned to Vienna in 1829 as a teacher—a profession for which he is said to have had a real talent—and writer, then left again in 1831 to take the position of *Musikverein* in Münster. In June 1835, he moved to Aachen to become that city's music director. His accomplishments are modest and probably were not achieved because the Austrian government "owed" him a favor—and anyway, his positions were outside the Hapsburg empire. He was almost as adept at making enemies as Beethoven had been, causing him to leave Aachen just five years later. His primary undertaking in Aachen had been the writing of his first Beethoven biography which was published in Münster in 1840. He then spent some time in Paris where he wrote a second edition of his biography.

Schindler claimed he had acquired little of real value—except in sentimental terms—from Beethoven, although he did sell off many documents and memorabilia he had been given (or appropriated) to the King of Prussia in exchange for a lifetime annuity. He did this, apparently, because by 1845 he had only a modest job as a private tutor—again in Aachen—and sold off his collection to supplement his income.

He continued to live life quietly and unextravagantly without any obvious compensation from a grateful government. He achieved no great honors—except for his fame as a Beethoven biographer—or any substantial increase in his bankroll. From Aachen he again moved to Münster, then to Frankfurt-am-Main in 1848. In 1856 he moved into his last home in Bockenheim, near Frankfurt. From then until his death he worked on the rewriting of his *Biographie*, but since he had sold or given away his collection of Beethoven memorabilia, he had to write almost completely from memory. Schindler died alone, having never married, in 1864 at the age of 69.

In my opinion, Schindler had far more to lose from Beethoven's death than he had to gain from it. Admittedly some of his actions may seem suspicious and there are a few coincidences—such as the "bad food" Beethoven experienced in his presence—to give one pause, and perhaps these were enough for author Harke de Roos, the biographer from the Netherlands to make Anton Schindler his prime suspect. Of course, as I cannot read Dutch, I do not know de Roos's arguments, and he may have uncovered far more substantial evidence than I have seen. However, unless something presently unknown comes to light, I cannot place blame for Beethoven's death upon Schindler's shoulders. Verdict: probably not guilty.

KARL HOLZ

In the midst of the more obvious suspects, we see Karl Holz about whom only bits and pieces appear in the Beethoven literature. Holz was a violinist who was 28 years Beethoven's junior—thus chronologically Schindler's peer. He had occupied a post in the States' Chancellery of Lower Austria, but had studied the violin with Glöggl and became so accomplished with the instrument that he became part of Schuppanzigh's Quartet in 1823. He met Beethoven in 1825 when he was scheduled to conduct a concert in the Ridotto Room of Beethoven's B-flat symphony, and requested a meeting with the composer so that he might be sure to get the *tempi* for the work. Holz often served as a conductor with the *Concerts spirituels* and eventually became the director of these affairs. Beethoven had received him cordially, and Thayer supposed that it was the warmth of their first meeting that had encouraged Holz to try to form a closer relationship with Beethoven. A friendship seems to have started around August of 1825, when Beethoven remarked in a letter to Karl that "It seems as if Holz might become a friend."

Holz was invaluable to Beethoven in that he was particularly good at figures, a skill the composer had never mastered. He was well-read, a clever talker, musically cultured, high-spirited and of a cheerful disposition, and he was also a man of strong opinions with the boldness to express them—much like the composer himself—so it is little wonder that Beethoven enjoyed his company, despite the disparity in their ages. At this time, Beethoven's relationship with Schindler was becoming strained, and Holz seems to have replaced Schindler—one reason why Schindler may have resented him. Although Thayer did not question Holz's sincere regard for Beethoven, Holz surely knew that he could learn from this great man, and he certainly must have taken pride in the fact that he could exhibit the great Beethoven to all the world as his confidential friend. In a short time, Holz had made himself indispensable to Beethoven and had acquired great influence over him. Holz assisted Beethoven in the copying of his works. He watched over Karl and reported on his activities to Beethoven. For instance, when Karl wanted to attend a carnival ball, it was Holz who served as chaperone. At first Beethoven himself wanted to accompany Karl, but Holz dissuaded him, saying he would be a spectacle there, and then offered to go himself. Holz advised Beethoven in answering correspondence and, at a time when Beethoven was interested in acquiring money so that he could leave a substantial inheritance to his nephew, helped him find ways to make additional income. Thayer notes that "In time, Beethoven came to entrust weighty matters to his decision, even the choice of publishers and his dealings with them."

In his *Biographie*, Schindler accused Holz of having lured Beethoven into activities in which he would not normally have engaged, such as frequenting taverns and excessive drinking. Thayer, in contrast, found Holz's actions admirable, in that he had "dragged him out of his isolation into cheerful company." Although Holz may have encouraged Beethoven to "go out drinking," it probably amounted more to socializing than it did "tavern-hopping," to being in the company of others, rather than simply drinking. Beethoven was aware of Holz's liking for alcohol, noting to Karl: "I have heard nothing from Holz—What a terrible misfortune if he has lost the manuscript. Between ourselves, he is a hard drinker." There is no evidence that Beethoven indulged as much or as often as has been believed besides a statement by Holz. He told Otto Jahn in an interview more than 25 years after Beethoven's death (1852) that "(Beethoven) drank a great deal of wine at table, but could stand a great deal, and in merry company he sometimes became tipsy." Holz and Beethoven once had tried to drink Sir George Smart under the table—Smart had heard Beethoven remark to Holz in jest, "We will try to see how much the Englishman can drink."—but Beethoven was unable to outdrink Smart, and that does not sound like something a "heavy drinker" could not accomplish. Besides, Beethoven knew very well that drinking too much interfered with his creativity, something he was reluctant to do. Despite the fact that even Beethoven himself occasionally expressed his doubts about Holz, noting to Karl in August 1825 that "Sometimes I wonder whether he is to be trusted," that was not unusual for Beethoven. Holz seems to have kept Beethoven's trust more often than not. Thayer, in contrast to Schindler, thought that "there can be no doubt of his reverence for Beethoven."

I must agree with Thayer here, that Holz did Beethoven more good than harm by bringing him once again into company—where Beethoven had always thrived—and that what Schindler actually objected to was Holz and not the activities in which he and the composer engaged. Schindler had little first-hand knowledge of Beethoven's relationship with Holz; as he himself admitted, he had lost touch with Beethoven during this time. Further, Schindler's statement that Beethoven's new habits had cost him old friendship was untrue and shows us how ignorant Schindler was about Beethoven's activities during this period of time: it was at this point that Beethoven resumed one of his oldest friendships, with Stephen von Breuning.

It was Karl Holz who also maintained, in that same interview with Jahn, that Beethoven had once been a Freemason. How Holz had come to this conclusion is unknown, but given the closeness of their relationship, and the fact that Beethoven thought Holz would eventually write his biography, it may have simply been one of many things Beethoven had told him about himself.

Holz was the one who wrote to the publisher Artaria and relayed to Beethoven that they wanted him to write a new finale for his *B-flat Quartet*, a piece which neither Schindler nor Holz truly appreciated, but they kept their opinions to themselves. It has puzzled biographers why this normally stubborn composer had agreed to make the change. Holz also seemingly had little trouble in persuading Beethoven to allow him to do a four-hand arrangement of his *Grosse Fugue*. He broached the subject in a Conversation Book (Solomon proposed that he did so flatteringly and falsely though the claim is unsubstantiated), writing "There have been already many requests for a four-hand arrangement of the Fugue. do you permit that I publish it in that form?—Score, the parts, the *Fugue á 4 mains* arranged by you, to be published simultaneously." These instances are merely indicative of the trust which Beethoven placed in Holz mainly because Holz had dealt with his affairs openly, never exceeded his authority, and asked Beethoven's permission before proceeding with any endeavor. There does not seem to be any evidence that Beethoven's trust ever was misplaced.

In the summer before his death, Beethoven wrote and signed the following:

> With pleasure I give my friend, Karl Holz, the assurance which has been asked of me, that I consider him competent to write my eventual biography, assuming that such a thing should be desired, and I repose in him the fullest confidence that he will give to the world without distortion all that I have communicated to him for this purpose. Vienna, August 30, 1826
> Ludwig van Beethoven

Although Schindler stated that Beethoven later changed his mind, there is no evidence for it. He stated also that Beethoven did not have the courage to request the document back, but that hardly sounds like Beethoven! Holz never made use of this permission and in 1843, relinquished it to a Dr. Gassner, of Carlsruhe, with his promise to give Gassner all the notes

Beethoven had left him "so that the errors in the faulty biographies which have appeared up to the present time may be corrected." This was an obvious stab at Schindler's book and on November 1, 1845 Holz made the statement (found among Thayer's papers) that Gassner's book would "not derive its dates from *fictitious* or *stolen* conversation books, and *unsophisticated* evidence will also give more intimate information about Mr. Schindler." For unknown reasons, Gassner's biography never appeared. It is a shame that it did not, for it would have been interesting to learn what "intimate information" Holz wanted the world to know about Schindler. Twice Schindler attacked Holz in the *Kölnische Zeitung* (Cologne Newspaper) in 1845, and it is possible that Holz responded once, but anonymously. Holz died on November 9, 1858 at the age of 60.

Is Karl Holz a viable suspect? It does not seem to me that he is, and I have included him mainly to appease those of my acquaintance who have long felt there was something "not quite right" about Holz's relationship with Beethoven. On one hand, he may have been somewhat sycophantic and self-serving, using his association with Beethoven to augment his own social and professional standing, yet he seems not to have become a man of either wealth or fame. Like Schindler, he stood to lose by Beethoven's death, not profit from it. Holz was not in Gneixendorf, and so could not have been responsible for Beethoven's sudden illness which overtook him on the road to Vienna. He did not see Beethoven until December 5th, and it was he who summoned the excellent Dr. Wawruch to help the composer. In addition, he was absent a great deal of the time during Beethoven's last illness. Karl Holz seems to have had neither the motive nor the opportunity to do Beethoven harm. Verdict: not guilty.

Chapter 14
The Duke of Reichstadt
(1811-1832)

Before returning to Malfatti's involvement in the case, it is essential that I present yet another link between Beethoven and the Imperial family. This link comes in the person of Emperor Franz's grandson. Francis Charles Joseph Bonaparte, the future Duke of Reichstadt was born in 1811, the product of a political marriage between Napoleon Bonaparte, then emperor of the French, and the Archduchess Marie-Louise, daughter of Emperor Franz I. He is important to our inquiry into the death of Beethoven not only because of his obvious connection to his famous father whom the composer admired, but because he and Beethoven share another, possibly fatal link: Dr. Johann Malfatti.

The Duke's mother, Marie-Louise, was Napoleon's second wife following his divorce of his beloved Empress Josephine who had failed to give Bonaparte an heir. The marriage had been arranged by Clemens Metternich. Napoleon had a low opinion of Metternich, remarking "Monsieur de Metternich is admirably fitted to become a statesman, he is such a good liar." Nevertheless, Napoleon was willing to accept Metternich's suggestion that he marry Emperor Franz's daughter. Metternich disliked and mistrusted Napoleon who had repeatedly humiliated Austria. However, he hoped eventually to make Austria the supreme influence in Italy and making an Austrian archduchess empress of France was one step toward this end. Marie-Louise wrote in regard to her proposed marriage to Napoleon: "Papa is too kind to force me to act against my wishes in a matter of such importance." But "Papa" did not find it in himself to oppose Metternich. The latter was probably not far wrong when he wrote to Napoleon:

> Sire, the Emperor of Austria takes nothing but the good of his empire into consideration, and will act in its interests without paying any attention to his daughter's fate. He is first and

foremost a sovereign and will not hesitate to sacrifice his family for his empire's good.

Marie-Louise's marriage by proxy was accompanied by many tears, but she did not remain inconsolable for long, for Napoleon plied her with expensive gifts and seemed genuinely fond of her. He treated her with respect and affection and she found her lot not nearly so bad as she had imagined.

The only son of Napoleon and Marie-Louise was christened Francis Charles Joseph, and was destined to be named Napoleon II after his father. He was nicknamed *l'Aiglon,* the eaglet, son of the eagle, *l'Aigle,* and bore the title "King of Rome" until his father fell from power. Although her early letters to Napoleon declared her undying love for and devotion to the French leader, the fickle Marie-Louise left him quickly enough when his fortunes soured. Conflicts between France and Austria arose once again despite their marital connections. In 1812, at a time when he was marching across Europe, and about to descend upon Austrian territory once again with the hope of making Austria part of his French empire. Napoleon believed that "Papa Francis" might be able to stand up to Metternich, who as he well knew, wanted his downfall, and no oppose him, but that was not to happen. "The Emperor Francis is strangely deluded," remarked Napoleon, "if he imagines that in France of all places a broken throne can offer protection to his daughter and grandson. Ah, Metternich, how much did England pay you to make you turn against me like this?" Napoleon wrote to his wife in 1813: "Do not take your father's behavior too much to heart. He has been led astray by Metternich. I want you to be brave."

Four years after their son was born Marie Louise moved back to Austria and thereafter repeatedly gave her husband excuses as to why she could not return to him. Eventually, Napoleon believed that Austria was holding his wife and son hostage, though that was not quite the case as Marie-Louise did not protest too much when she was prevented from rejoining her husband. Once back in Austria, the grandson of Emperor Franz was renamed Franz Karl Josef and denoted by the Emperor as the "son of our dearly beloved daughter, Madame Marie Louise, Archduchess of Austria and of a father unknown."

From the time Franz Karl was a small child, the European heads of state worried about his future. It was evident that Napoleon continued to entertain the idea that Franz Karl would eventually succeed him as Emperor of France, despite the fact that he now lived in Austria. This was not a pleasant prospect for the crowned heads of Europe who already had quite enough of dealing with one upstart in the form of the father, and thus were eager to prevent the rise of another one in the guise of the son. Talleyrand, attending the Congress of Vienna in 1815, proposed giving Marie Louise Parma, Guastalla, and Piacenza through the Treaty of Fontainebleu, and also suggested that she be given Lucca and fiefs in Bohemia so that it would "keep the Archduchess's son out of the way and deprive him of all expectations of ever reigning." This idea was fully supported by Metternich and on May 31, 1815, Metternich, Tsar Alexander I of Russia, and the King of Prussia signed a secret treaty to this effect. The Acts of Congress signed on June 9, 1817, omit any reference to this treaty. A day later, the allies signed a contract which disinherited the Napoleon's son altogether so that after the death of his mother, Parma would revert back to the Spanish Bourbons. Talleyrand wrote to Louis XVIII of France on January 19, 1815: "I must say that I consider this of the highest importance because by this means the name of Bonaparte could be struck off the list of sovereigns for the present and the future." As a substitute for her husband, Emperor Franz provided Marie-Louise with the one-eyed officer, Gustav Neipperg—with whom she was already fascinated—as an escort and he soon became her lover, much to everyone's approval. It was Neipperg who persuaded Marie-Louise to "sacrifice herself for the good of her child," by giving up the title of Empress of France, accepting the Duchy of Parma, being persuaded to "oversee" her new duchy, and leaving her son in the hands of the Austrian government.

That the Archduchess had an adulterous liaison and even two illegitimate children as a result of it, bothered no one in the Imperial family. Méneval remarked in a letter to his wife, "They are ready to tolerate anything provided she forgets her husband and even her son." This she seems to have done readily enough, for after his fourth birthday, the boy rarely saw his mother. Although Marie-Louise wrote to Dietrichstein that "I do believe I should have died of grief if I had not the hope of seeing him again in a few months," repeated excuses stretched those "few" months into twenty-seven! The boy saw her only four times in his life: once three years later in 1818, then once again in the summer of 1820. Then he did not see her again until 1828, and finally one last time in 1832 shortly before his death.

It was determined that the boy would be raised totally Austrian, completely isolated from French influence. Emperor Franz wrote to his daughter, "There is only one other thing I would ask you to see to if he is entrusted to the care of men, and that is to forbid his entourage ever to speak to him about his former situation." Frederick Gentz wrote that

Fatal Links

> ...little Napoleon is an object of fear and terror for most of the Cabinets of Europe... The Emperor... wants there to be nothing that may remind the Prince one day of the state of grandeur into which he was born. He must see no more members of his suite or others who took a share in his early upbringing. They even want to detach him completely from the French tongue and leave him with no other language than German... If the House of Austria had entered into a solemn engagement, not only to fight Napoleon's dynasty, but also to appease anyone in Europe who might take fright at his name or his shadow, it could not have adopted a more thorough system...[1]

The little boy's tutor, Mortiz von Dietrichstein echoed this sentiment in a letter he wrote to Marie-Louise on June 30, 1815:

> It is necessary to banish everything that might remind him of the life he has led until now. People retain clear enough memories of their childhood years... so that he may one day hanker after the life he might have led. Above all, care must be taken not to instill into him exaggerated ideas about the qualities of a people to whom he can no longer belong, for fear that these ideas might follow him into his years of maturity. It seems to me that the Prince... must be considered as of Austrian descent and brought up in the German fashion... Many of the ideas which have been implanted in his mind must be gradually eradicated.[2]

With his mother in Parma, the boy was soon taken from his mother's guardianship entirely, and he was not allowed to visit her. He was further deprived of his Bonapartist governess, Madame de Montesquiou, whom he loved dearly, and all of his other French attendants were released from service as well. Any reminders of his past life, anything that bore any of the Napoleonic emblems of the eagle or the bee, all his books and picture albums—even his French-made toys—were removed and burned. To Dietrichstein's chagrin, a little present accidently made its way to the little boy: a miniature carriage from Queen Caroline of Naples that had once pulled him around the Tulleries in Paris harnessed to a pair of sheep. Dietrichstein wrote with despair: "This apparition revived, as if by magic, all those memories of Paris and the imperial splendor of the court which had been somewhat dimmed since October."

The little Duke's language was switched from French to German, and he was never taught another word of French. The Hapsburgs had no

---

[1]Castelot, 192
[2]Castelot, 180

plans for him to ever occupy the Bourbon throne, as had been Napoleon's intent. As such, great effort was expended in trying to keep knowledge of his famous father from the boy. But despite his German education, the little boy declared when he was just four and a half, "I want to be French!" Dietrichstein admitted, "It is no easy task when speaking to him about filial sentiments, which ought to be consistently fostered in his mind, to pass skillfully over his father without his noticing." When he was just five years old, little Franz asked to read a book called *The Glorious History of the French People,* and one of his tutors obligingly opened the book cabinet for him saying, "You may choose whichever book you wish." Of course, the book was not there, having been purged from the library along with everything else French. "I see that someone has been silly enough to take the book away," the child observed. He was not fooled by this ruse, even then. As he grew older, he asked questions about the father he barely remembered, and answers were vague. One of his uncles, the Archduke Ranier wrote a niece: "It is a curious phenomenon that a child of that age should know so much about the past and about his father and that, far from talking about it, he should keep that knowledge such a closely guarded secret."

It also was imperative that a title be given him, and many suggestions were made and rejected including Duke of Mödling—but that was already taken and its owner did not wish to give it up. His mother thought the names associated with various Bavarian provinces (Tachlowitz, Kron-Porzitschen, Plosskowitz and Trnowan) were too unpronounceable to be suitable. After much deliberation, the boy became the "Duke of Reichstadt," a virtually meaningless title. The son of Napoleon had been successfully transformed into a royal bastard deprived of his surname. Despite that, Castelot noted,"They would find it impossible to kill the little Napoleon in him."

In 1818, when his mother was scheduled to come for a visit—the boy was only seven—he demanded to know from his grandfather, "My mother's coming, why isn't my father coming too?" Emperor Franz told him harshly, "I'll tell you why! It's because your father was wicked, so he was put into prison, and if you are wicked too, then you'll be put into prison as well." Of course, the little boy did not remember his father that way, nor could he be persuaded that Napoleon had been wicked. While playing, he was overheard saying, "When I'm big I shall take a sword and go and free my Papa whom *they* are keeping in prison!" Napoleon had been an attentive and loving father who played with his little son and those tender moments were never erased from the Duke's mind, however hard the court tried to do so. More easily put off when he was very young, by the time he reached his teen years, the boy's curiosity would not be denied, and he began to learn of his father's life through clever and vicarious ways, mainly by befriending in secret those military men who had known and served with his father.

By May 5, 1821, Napoleon Bonaparte was dead, murdered by the hand of a poisoner. He had been weakened with arsenic and then fed a deadly concoction of orgeat, a drink made with bitter almonds, and calomel, a purgative also known as mercury chloride. Separately they are harmless. Mixed together in his stomach, they formed mercury cyanide, a deadly poison. His last thoughts were of his ten-year-old son. As a final codicil to his will he wrote "As soon as my son has attained the age of reason, my mother, my brothers and my sisters must write to him, and make contact with him, whatever obstacles the House of Austria may put in their way.... They must urge my son to resume the name of Napoleon as soon as he has attained the age of reason and can conveniently do so." When Metternich learned of Napoleon's death on July 13, 1821 he said, "This event puts an end to a good many hopes and criminal conspiracies. It has no other interest for the world." In France, Napoleon's death had the effect of centering Napoleonic enthusiasm around the Duke of Reichstadt, and furthering the imperial cause. The memory of the "little king" held prisoner in Vienna served Bonapartist propaganda well. Major uprisings in 1817 (is it merely a coincidence that this was the year of Beethoven's worsening health?) and 1820 were spurred on by such groups as "Bonaparte's Vultures," the "Knights of the Dagger," and "The Black Pin" that worked to overthrow Louis XVIII and restore Napoleon's heir to the throne. It was not be a good time for someone—and by now the reader knows all too well that Beethoven was one of these—to speak against the Austrian government and in support of the ideals of the French revolution.

The French ambassador to Vienna was assured that the Minister of Police, Sedlnitzky, had the former King of Rome watched "with religious conscientiousness." But still he wondered what would happen when the young man came to realize the part he was expected to play by his father's supporters. "I fear there will come a time when the position of this young man will become increasingly embarrassing."

In the fateful Beethovenian year of 1826 the Austrian Duke began to rapidly disappear in favor of the French Prince. In the autumn of that year, the Duke wrote to his mother, "I am determined to keep my promises and prove myself a man under all circumstances." Despite Austria's greatest efforts, he had decided to become a soldier and an officer like his father. Dietrichstein complained to Marie-Louise, "You have no idea what the prince picks up at the table, after dinner and at the theater in his conversations, and now with Prince Leopold of Salerno, or how skillfully he questions the latter and gets everything he wants to know out of him." One can only imagine how much Beethoven might have been willing to share with the young man, had he been around as the court composer. Little wonder he was denied the position. Despite his isolation, the Duke managed to acquire the eight volumes of Las Cases's *Memoirs of St. Helena* written in 1823, Montholon's *Memoirs*, likewise penned in 1823, a 1822 book called *Napoleon in Exile* and Dr. Antommarchi's *Memoirs* written in 1825 that contained the text of his father's will. In this he learned that his father had written, "I beg her (Marie-Louise) to take care to protect my son from the dangers which still threaten him," and saw that his father had bequeathed to him his swords and pistols, his saber, his hunting knife, his gold dressing case, his field glasses, his uniforms, his washstand, his watches, his saddles and bridles, his entire library, everything he owned which was of any value to him—all left to the son who, thanks to the efforts of the Austrian government, would never receive them. From his readings, Napoleon became for him "the greatest man of all time" and the Duke was indignant over any attacks on his father's person.

The poet and ardent Bonapartist, Barthélemy, arrived in Vienna on New Year's Day 1829, hoping to present the Duke with a copy of his epic poem *Napoleon in Egypt*. Dietrichstein welcomed him on January 3 at which time Barthélemy presented him with two copies, one inscribed. According to Barthélemy, Dietrichstein's face "took on an expression, I will not say of annoyance, but of uneasiness and constraint." Considering the instructions which we know Dietrichstein had been given, he could hardly have brought his pupil into contact with an ardent Bonapartist whose poems were fired with a spirit which was bound to be considered dangerous. Barthélemy did not accept Dietrichstein's excuse of fear of assassination, and said, "You are afraid that too free a conversation with strangers might reveal certain secrets to him or inspire him with the desire to make certain dangerous experiments. But with all your power, you surely cannot prevent someone from openly or secretly handing him a letter, a petition, or a note, when he is out walking, or at the theater, or somewhere else." To this Barthélemy said that Dietrichstein replied, "You must understand this—that the prince hears, sees, and reads only what we want him to hear, see and read." In July of that year, Barthélemy was arrested and imprisoned for attempting to urge the Duke to return to Paris as a king. Interestingly, it was at this time that Duke began to lose weight, began to cough a great deal, and suffer what was called "chronic colds and chills."

By 1830, the Duke of Reichstadt began to feel he had a good chance of gaining the throne of France, and was "convinced that the Bourbons are doomed." He received a great deal of outside encouragement. The court was warned that a Colonel Deschamps, a former officer of the Imperial Guard, had advertised his intention of going to Austria to ask for the Eaglet's cage to be opened. The Emperor's representative told the informant, "I know no son of Napoleon, only the son of Marie-Louise." Deschamps was not the only one who supported the idea of the Duke inheriting the French throne. Belliard, Marshal Maison, and all the colonels of the Napoleonic regiments were working to "bring the Duke of Reichstadt back to Paris in triumph," Metternich noted bitterly. The Duke of Reichstadt even received a letter from Napoleone Camerata, daughter of Prince Bacciocchi and Elisa Bonaparte, the Duke's aunt. It was her plan to abduct the Duke and return him to France, but her letter to the Duke was intercepted by Dietrichstein, who dutifully handed it over to Sedlnitzky, the chief of police.

At the beginning of April the Duke had a dry cough every morning and was hoarse the entire day. Doctor's prescribed some "white powders" which easily could have concealed another "white powder"—arsenic—slipped into the legitimate medicine by someone intending the Duke harm. The Duke resisted taking these medicines, believing, and perhaps rightly so, that they were exaggerating his illness and that the intent of giving them to him was to keep him a prisoner in his bedroom.

Brook-Shepherd noted that "the real damage to the system came from outside. As Metternich had always realized, unrest could only be contained within the Monarchy if it was suppressed in continental Europe as a whole." If there was any reason for Metternich to rid himself of Napoleon II, this was it. The young man's idealistic worship of his famous father might have caused him to lead another republican revolution in France were he to assume power there. In fact, this came to pass without him: July 27-20, 1830 saw the Bourbons toppled from the French throne by latter-day Bonapartists. Although they managed to reclaim it, the Bourbons' position remained shaky. Had the Duke of Reichstadt been in a position to claim the French throne at the time, the Bourbons would have ruled no more.

Montholon, the man who presently stands accused of being responsible for the death Napoleon I by poison, applied for a passport to Vienna in 1831 under an assumed Swiss name in an effort to visit with the

Duke and discuss plans for his future. The political group to which he belonged intended to proclaim the Duke of Reichstadt Emperor of France, Napoleon II—but like everyone else, his attempt failed.

On January 4, 1831, upon hearing of unrest in Paris, the Emperor told his grandson,"If the French people asked for you, and if the Allies gave their consent, I would do nothing to prevent your mounting the throne of France." This was an easy promise to keep, as the Allies would never give their "consent" to any such move. The Emperor's brother, Archduke John, remarked, "The truth is that they do not want to emancipate him. In intelligence he far surpasses his entourage which is neither up to his level nor capable of securing his affection." It was becoming more and more obvious that eventually someone would succeed in setting the caged Eaglet free. The only way to prevent this was to make sure there was no Eaglet to be freed.

To accomplish this, all friends and allies had to be sent away so that there would be no suspicious people to interfere. Metternich gave Prokesch, the Duke's closest friend and source of encouragement, a diplomatic post to remove him from the Duke's sphere of influence. Metternich said to the Emperor, "Prokesch is a strange character who would fill the Prince's head with a lot of madcap plans. Between them they would turn the world upside down!!"

Metternich strongly reiterated Austria's position on the Bonaparte family to Marshal Maison: "We will have nothing to do with any plan which would favor that party which is trying to tie us to the Duke of Reichstadt. Here in Austria we are 'Philippists' from head to foot and nothing can divert us from the policy we have adopted."

Metternich detested Franz Karl more and more the stronger his personality became, and his dislike of the young man was not a secret among his intimates. As Gentz explained to Prokesch, "The very fact that (Metternich) has to occupy himself with (the Duke's) affairs makes him more odious in his sight."

As we continue with the last year of Franz Karl's life, our story must soon intertwine with that of Johann Malfatti. However, before we revisit the doctor, I must present another important link between the Duke of Reichstadt and Beethoven, the man the monarchy may have viewed as a potential "contaminant" of the young man. To look at this link in an already fatal chain, I give the reader Count Moritz Dietrichstein.

Chapter 15
Another Link: Count Moritz Dietrichstein

We will find in Count Moritz Dietrichstein-Prokau-Leslie (1774-1864) yet another fatal link in the chain which may eventually have bound Beethoven's fate. Dietrichstein was one of Beethoven's closest friends and ardent admirers and was generally very active in all musical and cultural activities in Vienna. He organized the church music for the Imperial Court and was Director of the Burgtheater from 1821 until 1826 when he was appointed Administrator of the Court Library. Dietrichstein also was a founding member of the *Gesellschaft der Musikfreunde* (Society of the Friends of Music) in the Austrian Imperial State. Dietrichstein was described as an extraordinary melomaniac, solemn, anxious, and humorless, an insufferable pedant who maintained a rigid code of behavior and who was a terrible bore. However, he was also noted to be honest and straightforward.

Dietrichstein's importance to the issue at hand lies in the fact that he was employed as tutor to the Duke of Reichstadt. Marie-Louise's lover, Neipperg, who was a great friend of Dietrichstein's, had persuaded the Duke's mother to accept Dietrichstein as her son's tutor, even though she herself did not like him. As a good friend of Beethoven's he thus becomes a link between the young duke and the composer. Dietrichstein and Beethoven also had a mutual friend in Count Moritz Lichnowsky, another prominent political figure and patron of the arts in Vienna.

It was Lichnowsky who took it upon himself to work out some way to bring Beethoven into the imperial court in the hope that, as Schindler tells us rather mysteriously, "once the first step had been accomplished with some success, further agreement and a full reconciliation might be reached." It is true that the Emperor did not like Beethoven and refused to attend concerts at which his music was to be performed. It is also true that Beethoven was very open in his negative feelings about the

Emperor. But exactly what sort of "reconciliation" Lichnowsky was hoping to accomplish is difficult to say. Perhaps he felt that if Beethoven prove himself of service to the Emperor, the latter might be more kindly disposed toward him and these feelings might manifest themselves in better financial prospects for the composer.

ANIMOSITY WITH A COURT ATTENDANT

Beethoven often found himself at odds with various theater directors who were also associated with the court. Most notable among them was Count Ferdinand Palffy.

Palffy, an advisor to Empress Maria Ludovica, was one of the directors of the court theaters, and became owner of the Theater an der Wien in 1813. Of interest is the fact that "His ownership of the Theater an der Wien all but ruined him, but he may be encountered in mid-century memoirs living in undiminished style and comfort at his country seat as though nothing had happened."[1] It is not difficult to imagine that his income had been supplemented from other services rendered. As Prince Ludwig Starhemberg, who was a leader of a group which opposed Metternich's government, corroborates: "Ferdinand Palffy is working for the secret police, Countess Esterházy-Roisin and Mlle. Chapius are the spies of old Princess Metternich... Prince Kaunitz, Franz Palffy {Ferdinand's brother}, Fritz Fürstenberg, and Ferdinand Palffy offered their services to the foreign monarchs, but they were turned down."[2]

The animosity between Beethoven and Palffy dates back to 1803 when Beethoven referred to him as a *Schwein* (pig) within his hearing. Palffy had rudely interrupted Beethoven's playing by laughing and carrying on conversation while the composer had been at the keyboard. Beethoven's letters between 1806 and 1809 complain about the treatment he received from the directors of the court theaters (there were seven more besides Palffy) although Palffy was singled out to receive the greatest share of Beethoven's wrath. Part of their troubles likely occurred because of Beethoven's intimate relationship with Countess Marie Erdödy, the wife—technically speaking, since it was in name only—of one of Palffy's relatives, Peter Erdödy. (Palffy's full name was Palffy von Erdöd.) Ludwig Spohr, who became acquainted with Beethoven in 1813, noted that "(Beethoven's) favorite topic of conversation at the time was severe criticism of Prince Lobkowitz and Count Palffy. He was sometimes too loud in his abuse of the latter when we were still in the theater, so that not

---

[1]Musulin, 94

[2]Musulin, 145-146

only the public, but also the Count in his office might have heard him." Evidence of their mutual hostility can be found up to 1824.

In 1809, Palffy convinced the Empress Marie Ludovica that Hungary was planning to join forces with Napoleon and rebel against the Austrian Hapsburg government. Convincing her probably was not difficult, as the Empress already hated and mistrusted Napoleon, and animosity between Hungarians and the Austrian monarchy had existed for many years. Hungarian noblemen and sympathizers were viewed as dangerous to the crown because they dared to wish independence, and a perceived alliance with the rebel Napoleon served to increase Austria's paranoia about the region and its peoples. Beethoven of course counted among his most intimate friends many prominent and patriotic Hungarians including the Brunswicks—Therese and Franz, and at one time, their sister Josephine—Countess Marie Erdödy (often persecuted for writing seditious petitions on behalf of the Hungarian cause), and *Hofrat* Nikolaus Zmeskall.

No doubt Beethoven's personal and political connections as well as his animosity toward a valued attendant at the court of the Emperor certainly contributed to the dislike the latter felt for him.

REFUSED A COURT POST

In November 1822, the court composer Anton Teyber died. Like other members of the Emperor's court, Teyber disliked Beethoven and often made his feelings known, but whether he truly disliked Beethoven as a person, harbored a form of professional jealousy toward him, or simply wanted to curry favor with a court already hostile toward the composer is not known. Schindler noted that "Teyber did not fail to take advantage of his opportunities to discredit the great master at court. An emperor's composer enjoyed far more prestige than a Beethoven, and could with high good humour ridicule and revile him."

When he learned of Teyber's death, Count Moritz Lichnowsky immediately thought Beethoven would be the ideal replacement and urged the composer to write directly to Dietrichstein about the vacant position and inquire as to the best way to approach the Emperor. It is surprising that Lichnowsky could have been so unaware of Beethoven's hostility toward the court and its toward him, and believed that such a scheme could work. Perhaps he thought that Beethoven could somehow work himself back into the court's good graces. Since the Emperor was a great lover of sacred music, the two counts proposed that Beethoven write him a Mass.

On January 1, 1823, Beethoven penned a letter to Dietrichstein about the position:

> I hear that the post of Imperial and Royal Chamber Music Composer, which Teyber held, is again to be filled, and I gladly apply for it, particularly if, as I fancy, one of the requirements is that I should occasionally provide a composition for the Imperial Court. Seeing that I have composed and am still composing, works in all branches of music, I do not consider that I can be accused of taking too great a liberty if I recommend myself to Your Excellency's favor.[3]

The issue of the court composer's position is an interesting one. On February 23, 1823, we find Dietrichstein writing to Lichnowsky that, "I can tell you confidently that the place of the deceased Teyber is not going to be filled. I would rather not write this information to Beethoven, for I do not want to adversely affect a man whom I honour so sincerely." However, nearly a month before, (January 30) Johann van Beethoven already had told his brother Ludwig that "It's a shame for you to write a mass specifically for the Court since Teyber's post will not be filled. Recently I have been with Count Dietrichstein twice, and the second time he told me that he now knew for sure that this post would not be filled. He told me that the last time I was with him." It is odd that Dietrichstein would appeal to Lichnowsky to break the news to Beethoven when he had already told the news to the composer's own brother a month earlier. How could he suppose that Beethoven did not already know? And, despite the fact that the post was not to be filled, on March 10, 1823, Dietrichstein sent Beethoven three texts for Graduals and a like number of Offertories from which to choose words to be used in the Emperor's mass, while Beethoven, in turn, seemed initially to be willing to compose such a work, writing to Dietrichstein in April, "I will... discuss with Your Excellency as soon as possible the graduale and the offertory in order to learn whether you approve of my ideas about them and of the way in which these ideas should be carried out."[4] In fact, he did begin sketching a mass, never completed, in C-sharp minor. However, if the main purpose of writing such music had been to secure Beethoven a post within the court, why were Dietrichstein and Beethoven still undertaking such a project when the expected reward was no longer available to him? Perhaps Dietrichstein, like Lichnowsky, was hoping to bring about a better relationship between the Emperor and Beethoven for the latter's benefit, and had convinced Beethoven that

---

[3] Anderson, #1121, III, 987
[4] Anderson, #1170, III, 1029

writing such a mass, even without the position available as a reward, would be beneficial to him, at least financially.

It is true that Teyber's post was never filled, although in 1828 Franz Schubert applied for a similar court position and was turned down with the same excuse: it was not going to be filled. My own feeling is that Teyber's position had to have been abolished in order to keep Beethoven out of the court and away from the proximity of the Duke of Reichstadt. After all, how could Beethoven, the finest composer in Vienna, not qualify for the position? How could they possibly turn him down? The only way to keep him from filling a position at court was to have no position available to fill. Dietrichstein, we recall, was the Duke of Reichstadt's primary tutor and companion. And though Beethoven was sometimes ambivalent about Napoleon, he was a staunch and vocal supporter of Napoleon's ideals. At the time Teyber died, the Duke was 11 and growing more and more interested in his famous father. He was full of questions about him which were answered either vaguely or negatively. The Court was determined that the boy be raised Austrian, with full Austrian allegiance, and with no connections to Napoleon whatsoever. They certainly did not want his head filled with ideas about republicanism and social equality. It would have been disastrous for him to come into contact with someone like Beethoven who, in the first place was distressingly outspoken and would have answered the boy's questions frankly, and second, who was supportive of the very revolutionary ideas that the court wished to suppress in the Duke. They could hardly risk any contact between Beethoven and the young Duke of Reichstadt, and the only way to accomplish that was to hold the Duke a virtual prisoner in the court and keep Beethoven out of it.

As for the Emperor's mass and any attempt to secure the favor of the Emperor and the Austrian court, Beethoven soon changed his mind about writing a "good will mass." A year later, in March of 1824, he wrote a short note to Dietrichstein about a concert, adding almost as an afterthought: "About the Mass for his Majesty I must still beg to be excused... I have an enormous amount to do."[5] And that was all that Beethoven said on the matter, but since so much time had already elapsed, it must have been apparent to all concerned that Beethoven had no intention of writing a Mass at all. He related—probably also to Lichnowsky as well as Dietrichstein—that he could not undertake such a project for the Emperor because of other tasks which required his immediate attention, that is,

---

[5] Anderson #1237, III, 1116-1117

correcting the subscription copies of the *Missa Solemnis*, finishing the oratorio promised to the *Gesellschaft der Musikfreunde* several years before, and completing a piano work for publisher Diabelli. Lichnowsky did not accept the composer's rather flimsy excuses and accused Beethoven of "old Dutch pigheadedness" Annoyed, he complained about Beethoven's refusal to write music for the Emperor to the Archduke Rudolph, a younger brother of the Emperor and a friend and patron of Beethoven's. Rudolph reproached Beethoven, who offered an apology, but he never did write the Emperor's mass for him. Schindler attributed Beethoven's refusal to "his deeply rooted aversion to the imperial court," a feeling that apparently was, and would remain, mutual.

Chapter 16
Malfatti Revisited, 1827

In May 1830, the Duke of Reichstadt's physician, Jakob Staudenheim, died and as in the case of others we have encountered so far, his death was unexpectedly sudden and violent. On May 26 Franz Karl wrote to his mother that "...Staudenheim... has died of a violent attack of colic. They have given me the doctor for pregnant women, Monsieur Malfatti..." Yes, Staudenheim was succeeded by none other than Beethoven's former doctor, Johann Malfatti, then fifty-five years of age. Having previously reviewed Malfatti's involvement in treating Beethoven at the end of his life, it will be interesting to compare this with his treatment of the Duke of Reichstadt. There are some surprising parallels. Exactly as he had done in Beethoven's cause with Wawruch's treatments, Malfatti immediately discarded former remedies and applied himself solely to curing a mild skin problem that troubled the Duke, which he proclaimed the prince had inherited from his father. As a matter of fact, the Duke had only begun suffering from skin problems in July 1830 a scant two months after Malfatti had taken over his care. As a brief aside, it is of note that 1) a rash is one symptom of arsenical intoxication, and 2) when his father had been Consul, he also had been troubled with a similar skin rash that the doctors diagnosed only as "the itch." Dr. Malfatti used this fact to support his contention that the problem with the Duke's skin was due to a hereditary constitutional defect because, in fact, both Napoleon and his sister Elisa had suffered with it. (We may recall that Elisa had been another unfortunate Bonaparte under Malfatti's care when she died.)

Reichstadt had been hoping to begin active service in the army in the autumn of 1830. Malfatti protested this idea in a memorandum which he addressed to the Emperor and, to the boy's despair, his entrance into a soldier's life was postponed for another six months. Naturally the young man could not have been allowed to find refuge in the safety of an army that would remove him from Vienna and from the ministrations of those who were plotting his death.

By the summer of 1831, the Duke enjoyed a remission in his ill health. This was attributed to the fact that he had been removed from the source of the cholera epidemic plaguing Europe at the time, but that is hardly likely. The Duke's medical problems did not include cholera. At that time, the Duke had a physical exam in preparation for entering the army. The examining doctor concluded, "His health is good and he is in a condition to withstand all trials." In the autumn of 1831, only a few weeks after being given a clean bill of health and feeling up to withstanding the rigors of army life, the Duke began to feel dull and heavy with sleep. It was noted that he became so hoarse he could barely talk.

Malfatti prepared a lengthy report (see Appendix D) on the Duke's condition in which he stated that he believed the duke "suffered from a liver complaint, similar to his father's case at St. Helena." Why he wrote this is puzzling for not only did Napoleon not have liver problems, but at the time it was believed he had died of cancer. The Duke's skin became yellowed with jaundice, and his liver became swollen and tender giving him pain in his right side. For that Malfatti recommended "muriatic baths" and Seltzer water and milk. Despite the Duke's coughing and weakness Malfatti told his superiors that there was far less danger from the boy's lungs than from his liver, again citing a matter of heredity. Aubry wrote that "Malfatti was all along obsessed by that preconception." We must recall that early in 1802, Napoleon had suffered from acute pain in his right side, along with conjunctivitis and a "cold." Likewise, similar eye problems, pain in the region of the liver, and "colds" had been recurrent ailments of Beethoven's. To anyone reading Malfatti's report today, it is obvious that at the time it was made the patient already was doomed by his doctor's refusal to recognize and treat his true symptoms. Masson goes so far as to say that even a hundred years ago one could hardly have been blind to all that it implied. However, there are two types of blindness: that which occurs because of ignorance and that which occurs deliberately . Masson further suspected Metternich "of realizing already in 1830 that the days of Napoleon's son were numbered and that there could be no hope of saving his life, but merely prolonging it for a little." It seems far more likely however that Malfatti and Metternich were determined *not* to prolong it.

THE DUKE'S LAST DAYS: 1832

On New Year's Day, 1832, the Duke fell gravely ill, and by January 20, 1832 began suffering intermittent sensation of fever, just as his father had some twelve years earlier (December 20, 1820). In a March 17, 1832 letter to his mother, the Duke complained of a painfully swollen liver, sensitive trachea, bad appetite and stomach trouble. His appetite continued to decrease and he began to lose weight. Dark rings appeared around his eyes. He was troubled with a terrible cough, nervous muscular spasms, difficulty in breathing and his feet swelled. His hearing deteriorated until he was nearly deaf. Occasionally he would spit blood and had pain in his right side.

Malfatti's treatment consisted primarily of ordering him to keep indoors. Even if it would have been difficult to recognize arsenic at work on the young man, his symptoms—long and violent spasms of coughing, spitting up blood, intermittent sensations of fever—would have caused a legitimate doctor to diagnose some illness involving the congestion of the lungs. Instead, Malfatti gave him another treatment for his liver and suggested sending him to Ischl to take the waters there as soon as the weather would permit.[1] Because the Duke hated being confined, Malfatti consented to him engaging in such activities as drives in a carriage, but later, in his defense, asserted that he allowed these thing "only in moderation."

Aubry found Malfatti "Guilty not only of a false diagnosis, of a misapprehension of the seriousness of the patient's condition and also of negligence towards him," and it was perhaps for this reason that Malfatti proclaimed: "It would seem as though there were working in that unfortunate young man some active force that was driving him to suicide. Our best wisdom, all our precautions come to naught in the face of that engrossing fatality." An interesting turn: if you cannot cure your patient, simply attribute your inability to the patient's desire to die! Despite Malfatti's gloomy outlook, to many members of the royal family he remained optimistic. "Malfatti's bulletins," wrote Marie-Louise on May 14th, "all say that he guarantees a cure."[2] In fact, Malfatti claimed that his colleagues "warmly congratulated him on affecting a palpable improvement in the state of his patient's liver"—a liver that had nothing wrong with it, as the autopsy would later clearly show. Malfatti admitted that he was somewhat concerned about the Duke's lungs and his coughing fits, but he assured the Duke's family that the condition was due to "changes in body temperature and the patient's excessive activity," and was nothing serious. Malfatti also complained that the Duke's health problems resulted from him not limiting his "strenuous activities" such as horseback riding,

---

[1] *Correspondance de Marie-Louise*, p. 298
[2] *IBID*, p. 301

although he himself had advised him to "live a normal life," and had not forbidden any activity other than resuming his military duties.

In the meantime, while Malfatti was patting himself on the back for restoring the young man's already-healthy liver to good health, Reichstadt's appetite began to decline alarmingly—at times he could not swallow solid food—and he was prone to flying into sudden rages. He suffered abdominal cramping. At times talking was beyond his strength. He would improve only to suddenly grow worse without apparent cause. He continued to suffer spasms of coughing now followed by hemorrhages, and his legs began to swell. His face was flushed red. How very similar these symptoms are to Beethoven's, who likewise had a decrease in appetite, and who, upon swallowing Malfatti's "remedy" of frozen punch suffered from a burning in his throat, and an inability to speak. The coughing, the swelling of the extremities, blood spitting, abdominal pain, a "flushed" or "burning" face, moodiness and bursts of unprovoked temper. Who could tell from these symptoms to which man one was referring?

When Prince Metternich questioned Malfatti at length about the Duke's condition, he came away convinced the Duke would soon die. "He was less useful than dangerous," Metternich commented, "the son of Napoleon was now free to join his father." The Duke's mother and other family members likewise remained optimistic based on Malfatti's reports to Marie-Louise that her son was recovering despite the obvious fact that the Duke was growing steadily worse. Aubry found it "remarkable that... Dr. Malfatti still cherished illusions of the young man's recovery which he confided to Count Hartman." Remarkable, indeed, since, as I just noted, Malfatti reported to Metternich that Reichstadt's death was imminent. It is probable that despite his grimly realistic reports to Metternich, Malfatti had been advised or perhaps ordered, to hold out hope—in effect, lie—to the Duke's family in order to keep them from considering calling in any other physician to attend him until it was too late for them to do him any good.

Finally, barely a month before the Duke's death (June 7, 1832), Metternich broke the news to the Emperor. As Masson wrote, "Metternich could not feign ignorance. He had that report in his hands and it was he who afterwards caused it to be published." To the Emperor, Metternich reported: "The condition of the Duke of Reichstadt unfortunately corresponds to the disease from which he is suffering... I see not the slightest hope of recovery." And at the same time he wrote to Count Apponyi in

Paris: "I consider the Duke of Reichstadt as marked for an early death... He has the characteristic symptoms of pulmonary phthisis and if that disease if implacable at all ages, it kills at twenty-one. I beg you to call King Louis-Philippe's attention to the person who will succeed the Duke." (It is odd that Metternich, himself not a doctor, proclaimed the Duke's problem to be with his lungs, while the Duke's own physician, Malfatti, still publicly maintained that it was the Duke's liver that was in jeopardy!)

Other doctors were called in, presumably because Malfatti was suffering from gout and could not attend him. As we recall, Malfatti used this same excuse to absent himself from Beethoven's bedside during the last stages of the composer's fatal illness. A change for the worst in the Duke's condition occurred on June 14 and was attributed by the new doctors in attendance to a rupture of an abscess in his lungs. Despite all other opinions, when he finally returned to the Duke's side, Malfatti still maintained the Duke suffered from a serious liver ailment!

THE DEATH OF REICHSTADT

Among his last ministrations to the Duke, Malfatti ordered fomentations (medicated lotions) and blisters (vesicatories) applied to his patient. It is interesting to note that the Duke's last words were "Poltices! Blisters!" Had he too late realized what was happening to him, making an important connection between his treatment and his illness? Or had he simply been crying out his realization that they were applied in vain? (I might recall for the reader that "poltices" were one means that poisons could be introduced into a victim's body since most are readily absorbed by the skin. Another method of introduction is through enemas. We might recall, also, that these common treatments had likewise been applied to both Napoleon and to Beethoven.)

During his illness, the Duke wrote frequently to his mother. On February 4 he told her, "The somewhat violent fever has completely abated, but the shivering fits which tire me more than any fatigue I can remember *return without fail every evening*." Interesting that the Duke suffered these relapses every night, presumably after dinner. The young man went on to tell his absent mother that he felt utterly exhausted, that he shivered and sweated and suffered bouts of melancholia. Malfatti, he said, was treating him with "mixtures so acid and bitter that rhubarb is sugary by comparison." He had no appetite and was extremely weak. Shortly thereafter, he added another complaint to his list of ills: he was totally deaf in his left ear. In a subsequent letter to Marie-Louise, on March 17, the

Fatal Links

Duke complained yet again of a painfully swollen liver, sensitive trachea, and stomach trouble. He still was plagued with a cough, with nervous muscular spasms, difficulty in breathing, and continued to lose weight. His feet were swollen. Occasionally he would spit blood and suffer pain in his right side.

By July 22, 1832, coinciding with the Duchess of Berry's efforts to have her son gain the throne of France as Henry V, the young duke, barely 21 years old, was dead. More than ten years before, Napoleon had remarked to one of his entourage, Las Cases, at St. Helena, in response to Las Cases' observation that Austria might one day want to make use of his son:

> Yes, as an instrument of intimidation, perhaps, but never as a means of doing good; they would be too much afraid of him. The King of Rome would be a man for the people; he will be the man for the Italian people; and so Austria will kill him.[3]

His father's fatalistic prophesy had come true.

After the duke's death Dr. Malfatti still maintained that it was the liver and hemorrhoids—a truly remarkable suggestion as a cause of death!—which had first and most seriously worried him, and offered his "regrets" that the Prince's chest trouble was late in being recognized—not recognized despite the fact that he had a persistent cough that he himself pointedly ignored! Weider noted that "A young man of 20 does not normally suffer from piles, at any rate not dangerous ones which might cause a doctor anxiety, and they are highly unlikely as a cause of death. Arsenic could have been introduced via an enema, causing the bowel to become irritated."

On the day after the Duke's death, the physicians performed the autopsy. They determined that the King of Rome had died of tuberculosis, convinced it had been inherited from his mother. although there is no evidence that Marie-Louise had tuberculosis and, in fact, she lived to be 56 years of age and died of pleuracy. It was decided that "intelligent care" probably would have cured him, but that he had been treated negligently. Malfatti had stuck to his diagnosis of liver disease down to the very moment of the autopsy, and Wiehrer supported him. Foresti wrote to Dietrichstein on August 2nd: "It is a lamentable spectacle to see two of the best physicians in Vienna doggedly insisting on the presence of a disease which did not exist while just as doggedly denying the real one of which the symptoms were perfectly evident."[4] Aubry concluded that "The

---

[3] Castelot, 205
[4] Oettingen-Wallerstein Archives

Duke's Austrian family certainly did not procure his death, but it acted with a carelessness that roused and still arouses suspicion." Perhaps his family did not procure it, but there were members of the Court who most likely did. The Emperor wrote to Apponyi on August 4th, "I regard the Duke's death as a blessing for him. I do not know whether it is a blessing or the reverse from the viewpoint of Europe. As for myself, I shall always regret the loss of my grandson." That was perhaps his sincere conviction. He mourned the loss of a grandchild and yet could not help regarding the Duke's death as a deliverance from a politically shaky situation. In death Franz Karl had ceased to be a political embarrassment.

SUSPICIONS, EVEN THEN

At the time of the Duke's death, suspicions arose, particularly among his friends. The rumor mill busily cranked out story after story. With no facts available, fabrication abounded. At first, the scapegoat of choice in Reichstadt's death was Metternich. "French and German papers speak with becoming regret of the early decease of the only legitimate child of Napoleon," ran the short notice in *The Times*, August 3, 1832, in London. "His illness has long given rise to rumours which the accounts of his death will be adduced to conform— namely that he has been carried off by poison." This was true. The Bonapartists rumored that Metternich himself had sent Reichstadt a poisoned melon. *The Times'* editor countered this suggestion by reminding the public that the late Queen of England had also (falsely) been said to have been poisoned. The newspaper noted also that "Austria had everything to gain by possession of this young man, who had value as a lever in international affairs." *The Times* added that "Metternich knew only too well what an admirable hostage they held in the person of Napoleon's son for any enterprise they wished to embark upon against France."

But was that true? According to historian Victor von Kubinyi, "The King of Rome was well beloved by everyone though it will be hard to believe this of Count Dietrichstein. Only Metternich hated him. The Duke was far more dangerous as a political pawn than he was valuable as a "hostage." Metternich had dangled the Duke before the eyes of Louis-Philippe, King of France, as a potential competitor for Louis-Philippe's throne, thus compelling the king's endorsement of the Austrian policy of conservation. But now that the French monarchy had chosen to "behave" and no longer were championing the cause of European liberty, and now that rebels and rebellions were quieting down, the Duke was no longer necessary to Metternich. The Duke's interest in following in his father's ambitions, and others' desires to place him upon the throne of France—thus upsetting the Bourbons' applecart which would have been disastrous for most if not all of the European monarchs—alarmed those who desired keeping the status quo. Unwittingly, perhaps, the young man threatened the very existence of the crowned heads of Europe and the positions of those who—like Metternich—both served them and profited from their service.

The death notices appearing in newspapers across Europe were of a similar opinion: "It was better that Napoleon's son had died—better for himself—better for the Royalists—better for the future peace of the world which great daily more troubled." All over France the news created a tremendous sensation, though it would have been politically incorrect to even mention the Duke's death. The Austrian Ambassador in France claimed that the death of the Duke of Reichstadt actually had made little impression in Paris though that seems unlikely with the Bonapartists making their vehement and very vocal claim that Metternich had served the Duke a poisoned melon!

By September, the King of Bavaria still was hearing rumors causing him to wonder if there were not perhaps a grain of truth in them. He spoke of them to an astonished Austrian ambassador, asking, "Tell me, did the Duke of Reichstadt die a natural death?"

On the Continent, rumors contiunued to fly about so thickly that Monsieur Count de Montbel—the personal representative in Vienna of King Charles X, a deposed royal but still a Bourbon power—was commissioned by Metternich to give the world a more "authentic" memoir than the Englishman Mr. W. H. Ireland had, in which he, too, had hinted about the possibility of poison. Montbel's book was intended to silence the critics and he appended to his text the report of the post-mortem that had been done at Schönbrunn on July 23, 1832 and also all of Malfatti's notes. Montbel's book had the opposite effect: its cold medical details were interpreted as evidence that the Duke indeed had been poisoned and that contrived medical"evidence" was being used to cover up that fact. Metternich's role in the publication of this book further destroyed its credibility. Oddie wrote,"To a public ignorant of the pathology of tuberculosis and inclined to mix it up with other diseases, Malfatti's notes suggested not a brief for the defense but for the prosecution. The fact that phthisis was given as the actual cause of death was of little account in 1832 when the general view was that consumption was one of the sequelae of riotous living." Unfortunately, Oddie overlooked the fact that, in the absence of sophisticated medical testing,the symptoms induced by various toxins were often mistaken for tuberculosis or other natural diseases. Many poisons mimic diseases.

The uncovering of a diary written by Baron Obenaus, one of the Duke's tutors under Dietrichstein, shows an entry which reads "The Prince died on July 22nd at 4:30 a.m., at Schönbrunn of consumption, the result of ____ _____ _____ as Obenaus frequently prophesied ___ ___ _." The blanks that Obenaus inserted were thought to suggest that the Duke's illness stemmed from "riotous living." That they might have been used to cover up a personal opinion of Malfatti's skill, which would have been even more impolitic and perhaps dangerous to lay out in black and white, was not considered at all.

Rumors of the Duke's murder by poison continued to be circulated even years after his death. In 1842 the Duke's friend, Count Prokesch-Osten, continued to bravely espouse the view that the son of Napoleon had been murdered. "Nobody will ever convince me that nothing further could have been done for the Prince," he declared. His assertions were dismissed as ludicrous.

Oddie wrote "If Prokesch-Osten was able to express doubts about the efficacy of Malfatti's medical treatment, there were others equally interested in the Prince who were ready to believe that the young man's death had been caused by deliberate neglect." Madame de Montesquiou, who had been nursemaid and governess to the Duke until she was dismissed for being "too French," as well as Ménéval and others who had been close to the Duke, all hinted at something unnatural in the death of Napoleon's son at such an early age. Ménéval wrote to his wife: "This is a fresh plot of the Coalition which adds to the execration with which posterity will regard it. I believe in his mother's despair, but I do not believe her to be inconsolable."

In his 1897 article, *Révélations sur la Mort du Duc de Reichstadt*, published in Paris, Philibert Audebrand also took the view that Austria, in the guise of Metternich and Malfatti, had intentionally brought about the Duke's death. His view and his article quickly were discredited by those journalists who undoubtedly were on the Court's payroll.

Weider concluded that

> It is probable that several persons in a position to observe the Duke of Reichstadt's illness suspected that the prince had been poisoned... His quick recoveries after days of very severe illness, his many 'relapses,' and his sudden fatal illness were accompanied by many symptoms that ought to have suggested poisoning. At that time it was one thing, however, to suspect poisoning, and quite another to show the courage or imprudence

to say so. Poisoning can so easily spread into an epidemic fatal to those who do not know the merits of silence.[5]

This may be cause to wonder about the case of Dr. Bertolini, his sudden attack of "cholera," and the subsequent burning of his notes.

Based on the Duke's post-mortem, Oddie concluded that the Duke of Reichstadt's untimely death had been the result of ignorance.

> Obviously tubercular, the Duke of Reichstadt suffered from dyspepsia, a marked susceptibility to catarrh, and a chronic skin condition described by his doctors in 1832 as herpetic, which was probably a tubercular manifestation. Treated as Malfatti treated the Duke of Reichstadt, a fatal result was inevitable.[6]

Oddie wrote his remarks in 1932, when it had been assumed that the death of Napoleon Bonaparte, the Duke's father, had been brought about by cancer. He no doubt wished to exonerate the Duke from the stigma of having caused his own premature death because of "loose living" and the contraction of syphilis. (It is of interest that scholars long had tried to pin that particular disease on Beethoven as well, although he manifested none of the symptoms.) Oddie wrote that "It may be noted here that 100 years ago the pathology of tuberculosis and of syphilis were rather apt to get confused." He was right, but failed to point out that there were other, far more logical reasons for the Duke's death, and that disease and poisons also were apt to be confused. He dismissed the accusations and suspicions of the Duke's friends and contemporaries too easily.

Oddie continued:

> It is now definitely established that Napoleon's son died of advanced phthisis wrongly diagnosed in its early stages. He died a victim of the medical ignorance of the time, and in this he shared to a certain extent his father's fate. Napoleon was treated by Antommarchi for a disease of the liver from which he did not suffer, the cancer which killed him being overlooked in its early stages.

We know now, however, that cancer had *not* killed the Duke of Reichstadt's father; scientific tests by the United States' Federal Bureau of Investigation showed without a doubt that Napoleon Bonaparte had indeed been poisoned. Oddie was right on one point, however: there is little doubt that the Duke of Reichstadt had shared his fate.

---

[5]Weider, 438-439
[6]Oddie, 235

MALFATTI AS SUSPECT: A REVIEW

Causing the death of a political target would be easy for a man of medicine. Not only would he have an extensive understanding of poisons, but his medicine bag was filled with potentially deadly concoctions which would make it all too easy to increase a dosage and commit a murder. Of course, being a medical doctor was not required to be a successful poisoner, but it would not hurt, either.

Although Malfatti was not with Beethoven when he suffered his first attacks of illness, subsequent episodes coincide with the administration of his treatments: the iced punch had a disastrous result, as did the steam bath he had prescribed. Malfatti readily supplied his own wine to Beethoven—wine, to a man with a liver disease!—and discouraged him from drinking anything else. His treatment of Beethoven paralleled that of the Duke's: eliminating a predecessor's treatments and supplying only his own; suggesting drinks, poultices, and enemas, all of which are convenient means to administer poisons; insuring the presence of other doctors so as to avoid suspicion. Malfatti also was implicated in Beethoven's severe bouts of illness between 1816 and 1818, when Beethoven also had been under Malfatti's care. Beethoven's health improved somewhat after he dismissed Malfatti on the grounds that he was "dishonest," but from then on, his damaged immune system made him even more susceptible to illness than he had been before

Bertolini, Malfatti's assistant, burned notes pertaining to Beethoven when he thought he was dying of cholera. The assumption had always been that the notes contained something of a delicate medical condition, such as syphilis, but as we now know Beethoven did not suffer from that venereal disease, that cannot have been the reason for Bertolini having disposed of his notes. What better reason than a political one?

As for motive, we have seen that Malfatti enjoyed great importance as a doctor even though his skills were often questioned by his colleagues. His financial situation never waivered even when the Austrian economy suffered, and he was made a member of the nobility despite glaring "errors" in diagnoses and treatments. Doctors who had skills far superior to Malfatti's were not so rewarded. He was a freiend of Metternich's who hated the Duke, and well thought of by the Imperial family who had hated Beethoven. Malfatti may have agreed to eliminate these two men in order to preserve his exalted status at court. Monetary gain, rise in professional and social status, and even the idea that he was being a "patriot" by eliminating those who were nuisances or considered dangerous to the welfare of the state—any of these could have been powerful motivators. The same motives easily applied to the Duke of Reichstadt's situation.

Although Malfatti could simply have been a person who had been in the wrong place at the wrong time and a victim of "coincidence," Malfatti was actually in three wrong places at the wrong time: with Beethoven prior to 1818, with Beethoven at his death in 1827, and with the Duke of Reichstadt at his death in 1832. As I noted in my introduction, when coincidences keep repeating themselves, one must consider that perhaps the events are not so coincidental after all. Malfatti's name must—for the reasons outlined above—rise high on our list of potential suspects. Verdict: most likely, in the cases of both Beethoven and the Duke of Reichstadt: guilty.

❖ Conclusion ❖

No doubt you, the reader, have already drawn your own conclusion about whether Beethoven had been the victim of a poisoner's hand. Unfortunately, unless you take the trouble to write me your thoughts on the matter, I cannot know whether I have convinced you that something was amiss. While I hope you agree that there is good reason to believe that Beethoven was the victim of foul play, I realize that possibly you have found the preceding 200 pages nothing more than an entertaining fairy tale. However—and without rewriting what I have already written—allow me to recap the most salient points of my argument. In case you already are inclined to agree with me, it may help firm your conviction. On the other hand, in case you believe the whole thing is a bunch of nonsense, it may reopen your mind to the possibility so that you will be receptive when new information shortly comes into play.

As I admitted at the outset, it has been difficult to create an ironclad case supporting the poisoning of Beethoven without the one essential element that I lack: raw scientific data resulting from the chemical analysis of Beethoven's hair. In lieu of that data, I have had to rely on historical documentation showing numerous similarities between Beethoven's medical history and that of Napoleon, who is known to have been poisoned. Repeatedly, the symptoms exhibited by Beethoven match those common to various toxins as well as having been manifested in the two Napoleons, one of whom had without a doubt ingested toxins and one of whom it is likely had ingested them. The old adage that reminds us "If it looks like a duck and quacks like a duck, etc. then it must be a duck," seems to apply here.

We have three levels of knowledge in this case:
1. those things that we know for certain,
2. those things which are very likely to be true based on the available evidence, and
3. those things we do not know and may never know.

ITEMS OF CERTAINTY

During Beethoven's lifetime and particularly during the last twelve years of his life or so, Austria was not a hospitable place for those with republican ideals to live. The government, headed by a Monarchy, was characterized by suspicion, intrigue, and rigidity. We have ample evidence that it hired spies and censors and watched everyone for subversive behavior. It attempted to control speech, action, and even thought. No one was immune, and acting in a manner contrary to the acceptable behavior established by the Court caused a person to be labeled as a danger to the state and to the status quo enjoyed by European monarchies.

That Beethoven was a staunch supporter of personal freedom, civil liberty, and equality is reflected time and again in his letters, journal, conversation books, and in recollections of acquaintances. He spoke out freely about each of these ideals and against the Monarchy that opposed them. Government records show that he was watched by Metternich's secret police, that he detested the Emperor, and that the feeling was mutual. Although Beethoven had some ambivalence about one of the most visible symbols of republicanism, Napoleon, overall his letters and the recollections of others show that he admired him and his ideals. Expressing support for a man like Napoleon was an unhealthy stance to take.

During this same time period, Beethoven was involved in a bitter court case involving the custody of his nephew Karl, contested by the boy's mother, Johanna. Court records and letters show that Beethoven spared no words in describing what he felt was her immoral and criminal behavior. The same records show that she did not hesitate to spread vicious rumors about him to the court and the community at large. Despite a few times when Beethoven seemed inclined to change his mind about her, it is safe to say that these two people tolerated each other in the best of times and hated each other in the worst. Conflicts between Beethoven and Johanna and between Beethoven and Karl lasted from 1815 until Beethoven's death.

We know that Dr. Johann Malfatti had at least three important people die under his care—Napoleon's sister, Napoleon's son, and Beethoven—and that his reputation as a doctor, as noted by his colleagues,

Conclusion

was shaky. Despite that, he was made a member of the nobility, was respected as a physician by laypersons if not by his colleagues, and lived life as a wealthy man even though the economy usually was in a deplorable state.

Beethoven's physical and mental health took a serious plunge beginning in early 1816. Somewhat improved by 1818, he endured periodic relapses from then until his death in March 1827. We know what symptoms he suffered, just as we know the symptoms of Napoleon and his son. We know that Beethoven died of cirrhosis of the liver complicated by pneumonia, and that the physical evidence provided by the autopsy shows that his cirrhotic condition was not consistent with that caused by the excessive consumption of alcohol. And we know that a high concentration of at least one toxin—lead—has been found in Beethoven's hair.

ITEMS OF LIKELIHOOD

Since Beethoven's cirrhosis was not caused by alcohol, we must at last exonerate him from the erroneous allegation that he was a heavy drinker. Two possibilities for the cause of his liver damage are viral hepatitis or the ingestion of toxins, or perhaps even both. It is of note that some of Beethoven's symptoms are not consistent with hepatitis B or C, the two forms that can lead to cirrhosis.

We have reason to suspect Dr. Malfatti of culpability in the case of Beethoven's serious illnesses and death because he was the composer's doctor at the times when he was most ill, his prescriptions worsened Beethoven's condition, his methods in treating Beethoven were virtually identical to those he used with the Duke of Reichstadt who also died under his care, and he was close to Metternich and the Imperial family.

We have reason to suspect Johanna van Beethoven as well. She had a long-term conflict with her brother-in-law, she seems to have gained the sympathies of Beethoven's servants, she was well-known to the police and the courts because of her behavior, the composer's illnesses seem to coincide with his attempts to have her son live with him, and money—in the form of her pension, part of which she was required to pay to Beethoven for her son's upkeep—was an issue.

Karl van Beethoven also cannot escape our notice. He had violent arguments with his uncle and despite his affirmations of respect and affection for Beethoven, in private he called him an "old fool," and ridiculed him. He ran with a rowdy crowd, gambled, stole books from Beethoven, and was heavily in debt. His suicide attempt is highly suspect, not only because of the oddities involved—such as missing two point-blank shots—but also because of an exchange between Karl and his mother in which they believed the incident had rendered Beethoven vulnerable to anything Karl wanted to demand of him. Karl also exhibited an inordinant amount of guilt following his uncle's death.

WHAT WE MAY NEVER KNOW

Unless a lock of Beethoven's hair from 1816-1818 becomes available for testing, we will never be able to know for certain whether he ingested any toxins during that period.

While it is already known that a concentration of lead was found in Beethoven's hair, and there exists the strong possibility that other toxins may be found as well, we will never know for certain—that is, beyond any doubt—exactly who the perpetrator was. At this point I will state that I believe no one person was culpable, but that at least three persons worked together for the purpose of eliminating a mutual nemesis. I will now conclude with what I believe is the most likely scenario.

THE CRIME OF THE (19TH) CENTURY

It is November 1815. Ludwig's brother, Caspar Carl, has just died. His survivors are his widow, Johanna and his son, Karl, aged nine. Caspar Carl's original intention was to give his brother sole legal guardianship of his son, although he wanted his wife to retain physical custody of Karl. On his deathbed, Caspar Carl was urged—if not coerced—to sign a codicil which granted joint guardianship to Ludwig and Johanna.

Ludwig, who saw Johanna with other men while his brother lay dying, who saw his sister-in-law neglect Caspar Carl during his last days, and even believed that she had hastened his brother's death with poison, is outraged by the situation and takes Johanna to court in order to keep her from morally corrupting the boy entrusted to his care. He is granted the boy's guardianship with only visitation rights being given the mother. She is ordered to pay half her pension to Ludwig for her son's upkeep.

The situation is tolerable for Johanna for a time because Karl lives at a boarding school where he is on "neutral territory." But eventually her unscheduled visits to Karl's school cause the headmaster to complain that these interruptions are detrimental to Karl's state of mind and the functioning of the school as a whole. Ludwig makes the decision to remove Karl from the boarding school and his mother's proximity. Alarmed that she might no longer have access to her son and that she might be forced to plead with her brother-in-law in order to see him, Johanna is upset and desperate

Conclusion

to find a way to prevent Karl from leaving his school. But she is at a loss as to what to do. At this point she is unaware that she—and her situation—has come to the attention of the Court.

Beethoven already had been an increasingly bothersome nuisance to the Monarchy for quite a few years. His popularity, especially among young people—a group that the government already feared for their revolutionary activities—made him a man of influence, and the Court became more and more concerned about the venomous remarks Beethoven made about the Imperial family. He was watched by the secret police and they knew he moved in seditious circles such as the Josephinists, that he was probably a Carbonari and Illuminati sympathizer and a Freemason, that he espoused the ideals of that upstart Napoleon (whose son who had only just come to live in Vienna), and that he was intimate with Hungarian subversives such as Countess Erdödy and other people of questionable character. Maddeningly, he was not a person easily dealt with. He could not be threatened with imprisonment because the people—who loved the somewhat eccentric composer—would not stand for his mistreatment. The Monarchy could not afford to create a martyr. He was not under the patronage and control of any aristocratic patron, such as his predecessors Mozart and Haydn had been. Even the majority of his publishers—such as Breitkopf und Härtel in Leipzig—were outside the Hapsburg empire and control. He was not predominantly dependent upon Austria for his livelihood. Although the Court attempted to use its intimates, such as Ferdinand Palffy who was close to the Empress, to censure him by making it difficult for him to give concerts for his benefit, and may have even tried to throw lucrative offers his way in an effort to tempt him to leave Vienna, their attempts to silence or remove him have been feeble at best. Beethoven has powerful friends among the aristocracy and they, in a countermove—spearheaded by none other than that troublesome Erdödy woman—band together to make it worth Beethoven's while to stay in Vienna by offering him a handsome contract.

In the midst of their dilemma about what to do with the problem of Beethoven, the Court becomes aware—probably through a member of the Landrecht—of the bitter altercation raging between the composer and his sister-in-law. And then another interesting fact comes to light: an intimate of the Emperor's right-hand man, Prince Metternich—who was in actuality the true power behind the throne—was none other than Beethoven's own doctor, Johann Malfatti. Malfatti has his own reasons to hold a grudge against Beethoven. For one, the composer had bitterly disappointed Malfatti's flighty, immature niece, Therese, by not responding to her flirtatious overtures and marrying her. And Beethoven was becoming more and more irritated with the doctor to the point of berating his professional ability in public. It was irrelevant that Beethoven's assessment of Malfatti probably was accurate; Malfatti could not afford to lose the patronage of important people in Vienna. The Congress had just begun, drawing heads of state from all over Europe. Malfatti's court connections had won him many new influential and wealthy patients and he could ill afford to lose any of them because of Beethoven. The idea of teaching his unruly patient a lesson appealed to him.

Someone connected to the Court, perhaps even Johanna's relative, Hotschevar, who worked in an official capacity, likewise approaches Johanna with a proposition: would she consider helping with a plan to eliminate Beethoven as a rival for her son? Having an accomplice who was in a position to see Beethoven periodically without arousing suspicion was preferable to having Malfatti—who might only see Beethoven periodically—work alone. Why was Johanna selected for this task? Beyond her obvious connection to Beethoven which provided a substantial motive, the police knew her reputation. She was a somewhat unsavory character without many scruples. She was expendable. And she could be easily controlled with bribes or threats of incarceration. After all, Austria had a Morality Law that could have been used against her to banish her from the Empire had they chosen to invoke it. Johanna's initial reaction to the proposition is unknown. While she may have balked at the idea of killing her brother-in-law, the idea of incapacitating him appealed to her. Malfatti already knew that Beethoven's health was fragile. If it could be further undermined with poison, it was likely that the composer would succumb to a natural illness and solve everyone's problem. There was no need to murder him outright, they assured Johanna. Simply bring him to the point of death and then let Nature take its course.

Discouraged by repeatedly losing her appeals to the court to regain the guardianship of her son, feeling more and more desperate because of Beethoven's threats to take her son to live with him, and being deprived of half her pension, Johanna is in the perfect mental state to find the idea appealing, and she finally agrees. Malfatti will supply the means—and perhaps administer a dose or more himself through his medical "treatments"—and Johanna will find the opportunity, either personally or through Beethoven's servants whom she had already won over to her side. (How could a man want to rip a child from his mother's bosom? It was unthinkable! Of course they would help her.)

Conclusion

For a while the plan works well. Beethoven becomes seriously ill and must abandon his first attempt to bring Karl to live with him. He physical and mental health deteriorates alarmingly. He is bedridden for weeks on end with violent headaches and severe colics, with fever and vomiting and weakness. Mentally he is confused and rumors surface about him going mad. These attacks on his health continue for well over a year. All concerned held their collective breaths, believing he might soon succumb to his various ailments. But they had not counted on his indomitable will. A second attempt to bring Karl to live with him is not thwarted regardless of his ill health, and Beethoven stubbornly clings to life.

All of a sudden, interference comes from an unexpected quarter. Malfatti's assistant, Bertolini, somehow stumbles upon the truth, or at least finds cause to be suspicious, and gives Beethoven a warning about Malfatti. Bertolini does not tell Beethoven the complete truth, but gives him enough reason to make him wary. To the conspirators' chagrin, Beethoven immediately breaks off his relations with Malfatti and with Bertolini as well, in order to protect his friend from falling under suspicion of having warned him that something was amiss.

With access to his victim denied, Malfatti is forced to abandon his role in the task, leaving Johanna to carry on alone. But she is haphazard in her administrations and despite the few periodic relapses she is able to cause, Beethoven's health slowly began to improve. The effects of toxins are cumulative and slow to dissipate from a person's system, and the damage done to Beethoven over a year's time is enough to make him susceptible to natural disease. By now his immune system is so impaired that he is no longer able to fight off assaults on his health from pollutants, viruses, or bacteria. In addition, his liver has sustained irreparable scarring that will worsen with repeated attacks.

By 1823, Beethoven begins to surprise Johanna with kind overtures toward her. He offers to return her pension to her, loans her money, repays a debt she owned since her husband had died, and sends her cordial letters. He still does not like or trust his sister-in-law, but for his nephew's sake, he attempts to make amends with her. At this point Johanna abandons all thoughts of causing Beethoven further harm as it would not have been to her advantage to eliminate this unexpected source of support.

By 1825, two new factors enter into the picture, both in the guise of young men. One of these is Beethoven's own nephew, Karl, now nineteen; the second is the fourteen-year-old Duke of Reichstadt, son of Napoleon. Karl's conflicts with his uncle have escalated to the point of violence. Karl wants to join the army but his uncle is determined to make him a gentleman and a scholar. Karl dislikes his studies and is frustrated by them, and begins to spend more and more of his time gambling and running around with friends of questionable character. He runs up enormous debts, steals money or begs it from Beethoven's servants, and robs his "old fool" of an uncle of some books which he sells. His quarrels with his uncle over his behavior continue and often come to blows. As a result, Beethoven becomes more and more strict with the young man. The two find themselves trapped in a vicious circle.

The adolescent Duke, shielded from his fourth birthday from any knowledge of his revolutionary father, is becoming increasingly determined to find out about his infamous parent. He cleverly questions people who had known Napoleon, finds ways to procure books and soldiers' memoirs that talk about his father's ideals and campaigns, and dreams of one day following in Napoleon's footsteps as leader of the French. The Eaglet had grown wings; those around him know they must be clipped or he would fly.

At this time, court composer Anton Teyber dies leaving his post vacant. Both Count Dietrichstein—who also happens to be the Duke of Reichstadt's tutor—and Prince Lichnowsky urge their mutual friend Beethoven to apply for the position. How either of them imagined that Beethoven would be welcomed into a position at Court is a puzzle. The last person the Court wanted the adolescent Duke to meet and spend time was Beethoven, with his revolutionary ideas and his strong positive opinions of the boy's father. Dietrichstein is appraised of this folly and quickly relates to Beethoven's brother and to Lichnowsky that Teyber's position is not going to be filled. Indeed the post was abolished, but not for the financial reasons given. They could hardly have denied Beethoven the post; how could he possibly have been unqualified for it? To keep him out of the position there simply could be no position.

Just prior to this, Beethoven had once again made his revolutionary noises in public with the premier of his Ninth Symphony with the "Ode to Joy" in its finale, a rousing entreaty for freedom, equality, and brotherhood. The first concert was a rousing success, even though the Emperor, Empress, and the rest of the Imperial family purposefully stayed away. Their absence was no doubt noted by the public who perhaps thought it unwise to attend the repeat performance. It was not a good idea to support something which had incurred the Emperor's disfavor.

With the Duke of Reichstadt growing ever more curious about his father, and the Court unsure whether Beethoven might produce another

Conclusion

work equally subversive, the situation clearly would soon be intolerable. Once again the question of "what to do with Beethoven" presents itself without a solution readily apparent.

Then Providence strikes again. Beethoven's nephew—who has come to find his uncle as intolerable as the court and perhaps more so—comes to their attention in a surprising way. He recently made an attempt on his life. This ploy was concocted by Karl and his mother Johanna to rid themselves of Beethoven's control. They had decided that if they could make Beethoven distraught enough he would willingly relinquish control of Karl's guardianship. Not only having his nephew attempt suicide, but hearing from the young man that he himself was the cause of it, surely would leave him guilt-ridden and emotionally vulnerable. As Johanna told her son following the shooting, "Now is the time to ask for what you want. He is weak and will not refuse you."

As soon as the news is reported to the Court, a new plan begins to be concocted. As suicide is a police matter, Karl is visited by officers of the court who quickly ascertain that they all have a mutual nemesis in Beethoven. The officers propose that if they cooperated with one another, it could be of benefit to all of them: Karl is promised immunity from prosecution and the commission in the army which he has long desired; Johanna will have her son taken from Beethoven's control and placed under the guardian of her choice, and she will also retain all of her pension; and the Court will no longer have to worry about Beethoven influencing the Duke of Reichstadt or any other young Austrian, or making any more disparaging remarks about the Emperor or the Court itself.

The police make it clear that once sufficiently recovered Karl must leave Vienna immediately. At Johann van Beethoven's fortuitous invitation, Beethoven and Karl leave for Gneixendorf; Karl is entrusted with the task of feeding his uncle enough poison to sicken and weaken him. Although Beethoven's health was not bad when he left Vienna, he soon begins experiencing the same symptoms that are now so familiar to us: headaches, colics, pains in his eyes, "rheumatism," fever, weight-loss. After some weeks, his failing health begins to concern him, and he is eager to return to Vienna. Beethoven's sudden decision alarms Karl. Not only has he not completed his task, but Karl has found himself enjoying the pleasant pursuits available to him in Gneixendorf. In desperation, Karl feeds his uncle a larger dose of the poison than he should have. As it takes several hours for the effects to be felt, it is not until they stop for the night at a wretched depot that Beethoven begins to suffer a violent reaction to the toxins he has been administered: he is weak to the point of fainting, he feels feverish, his thirst is morbid, he vomits and spits up blood, his head aches unmercifully, he suffers incapacitating bouts of diarrhea and his stomach pains are so severe he cannot sleep. Not only has Karl not prevented their departure from Gneixendorf, he virtually has stranded himself on the road with a violently ill man.

It has been impressed upon Karl that a physician must be in attendance at the time of his uncle's death to avert suspicion, so upon their arrival back in Vienna, Karl asks Holz to procure a doctor for his uncle. Based on Beethoven's severe reaction, the conspirators suspect that the composer might soon die; he disappoints them. In fact, he rallies, and the doctor who has been summoned, Andreas Wawruch, is encouraged by his patient's amazing improvement. Beethoven's recovery has the opposite effect on Karl and his mother. Afraid that he might lose his army commission as promised and that all their other plans would go awry, Karl is persuaded to dose his uncle once again. The too-large dosage might have been unwitting, but the reaction this time is more terrible than the one Beethoven endured on the road to Vienna.

Karl was unruly and ungrateful perhaps, but he was no murderer, and seeing his uncle's horrible suffering stabs him with guilt. His conscience will not allow him to continue torturing his uncle. He refuses to give Beethoven any more poison. But the conspirators have come too far to turn back now. As Karl readies himself to join his army regiment in mid-December, Dr. Malfatti is prepared to return to the picture. It is unknown how he came to be called. Thayer tells us that it became Beethoven's "ardent wish.... that Malfatti undertake his case," but how the composer came to think of a man he had not seen in ten years and with whom he had bitterly parted company is unclear. Had Karl suggested him? Or Schindler? At the end of the year, the Conversation Book has the following entry from Schindler: "Yesterday I urged your brother earnestly to hold a medical council of men who have known your constitution longer. Staudenheim, Braunhofer and Malfatti, three capable men whose judgment is not to be rejected." Why did Schindler suggest Malfatti? Was it an innocent coincidence or an idea planted in his head by another?

On January 2nd, Karl leaves for Iglau and will never see his uncle again. By January 11th, Malfatti is on the case. In barely a month, Malfatti has gone from flatly and coldly refusing to have anything to do with Beethoven—giving the excuse that his colleagues would disapprove—to taking over Beethoven's treatment by eliminating all of Wawruch's prescriptions and providing only his own. Malfatti is closely linked to the Court, after all, particularly to Metternich, who surely urged him to attend

Conclusion

Beethoven and take whatever steps were necessary to bring closure to the situation. At his first visit he finds a desperately ill Beethoven, yet he knows that Beethoven's constitution and will to live are remarkably strong. After eliminating all of Wawruch's medicines—but still insisting on Wawruch's attendance—he prescribes an iced "punch," an alcoholic beverage. To ward off any suspicions on Wawruch's part, he "confides" to the latter that Beethoven has always been inclined to be a heavy drinker and to change his habit at a time when he was so ill was unwise. At first, Malfatti carefully prescribes only a few teaspoons so that the alcohol will lessen Beethoven's pain and act as a sedative, allowing him to rest. He gradually increases the dosage, finally telling his patient—without Wawruch's knowledge—to drink all he wants. As soon as Beethoven comes to depend upon the beverage for relief, Malfatti laces the punch with poison. Beethoven's reaction is violent and immediate, but the poison fails to kill him. An alarmed Wawruch blames Beethoven's reaction on his "abuse of the prescription" and—no doubt to Malfatti's dismay—forbids him to drink any more alcohol. Malfatti is forced to resort to other means to deliver toxins into Beethoven's system: enemas, poltices, and a "sweat bath," that, like his other "treatments" causes an alarming, life-threatening reaction. He attempts to steer Wawruch away from removing excess fluid from Beethoven's abdomen by insisting that the bloating is due to gas. Luckily Wawruch follows his own instincts and performs a series of "tappings" that eliminate the excess fluid, prevents rupture, and provides Beethoven with temporary relief. Yet despite Wawruch's ministrations, Beethoven's strength begins to wane. Knowing he has accomplished his task by bringing Beethoven as far to the brink of his grave as he dares, Malfatti begs off the case by claiming he is ill himself. Sapped of every ounce of his reserve strength, Beethoven develops pneumonia, and finally succumbs on March 26, 1827.

After Beethoven's death, Stephan von Breuning becomes Karl's guardian, but he dies too, unexpectedly, just six weeks later. Thus Jakob Hotschevar—distantly related only by marriage—and not Johann van Beethoven the surviving blood uncle, becomes guardian.

Karl, overcome with guilt, lives out the remainder of his life as a model citizen. He marries, has five children, and even names his only son Ludwig, after his "beloved" uncle. His mother, Johanna, and his half-sister Ludovica, live out their lives in absolute poverty. Karl never offers assistance to either one of them. Perhaps he blamed her for the role she played in his uncle's death, and the way she had involved him in a situation which would plague him with guilt his life long. The surviving Beethovens appear to have paid for their involvement in Beethoven's death.

Dr. Malfatti continues to enjoy a lucrative career, treating members of the royal family. Then, in 1831, the year when the Duke of Reichstadt turned 20 and began his campaign to be a soldier and follow in his father's footsteps, he is called in to serve as the boy's physician (Dr. Staudenheim having met an untimely death himself). The Duke could not be allowed to live and fulfill his dreams and thus damage the status quo enjoyed by the European monarchies. Just six weeks after being given a clean bill of health and being told that he was fit for army duty, the Duke comes under Malfatti's care—presumably for a skin condition—and becomes increasingly ill. Periods of good health are interrupted more and more frequently with bouts of serious illnesses. His symptoms—fevers, colics, increasing deafness, vomiting, spitting up blood, a dry cough, a morbid thirst—mirror those of his father and of Beethoven. Malfatti repeatedly insists that the boy's liver is affected—and that he is successfully affecting a cure—while his puzzled colleagues who believe the Duke's lungs are the source of his problems, shake their heads over Malfatti's diagnosis but say nothing to contradict him. Malfatti continually reassures the Imperial family, and particularly Marie-Louise the Duke's mother, that the boy is steadily improving, while secretly informing Metternich that the young man's death is imminent. He prescribes bitter medicines—perhaps laced with antimony—and poltices—as he had done in the case of Beethoven—which gradually break down the boy's already frail health. The Duke dies in 1832 at the age of 21. Official cause of death: pneumonia.

Meanwhile, Malfatti's old assistant, Dr. Anton Bertolini, learning of the Duke's death and realizing how closely the circumstances around it resemble Beethoven's, unwisely intimates that he suspects foul play. He lets it be known that he has damning evidence on Beethoven and Malfatti's role in his illnesses, and perhaps he even threatens to expose the culprits publicly. But he is playing a dangerous game with experts he cannot hope to match. As Weider pointed out, poisoning has a way of becoming epidemic. Bertolini suddenly falls ill and realizes that he cannot hope to win justice against such formidable opponents. Their message is all too clear. To save his own life and perhaps that of his family, Bertolini is forced to burn all his notes regarding Beethoven's mistreatment at the hands of Malfatti. Later he would only say that they were of a "sensitive nature" and that he had been afraid they might fall into unscrupulous hands. The myth of Beethoven's "syphilitic condition" is born.

Conclusion

Malfatti went on to receive a title from the Court in 1837 in grateful appreciation of his services, and died a wealthy and well-respected physician in 1859 at the advanced age of 84. Although suspicions surrounded him concerning the death of the Duke of Reichstadt, he never suffered from any serious accusations, either as a doctor or as a private citizen. Although one might make a good case for the proposition that Malfatti had acted in the best interests of his sovereign and country, and that therefore he should be exonerated of wrong-doing, in my opinion he simply was one of those rare persons in history who has gotten away with murder.

Appendix A
Some Common Medicines of the 18th and 19th Centuries

SUBSTANCE	USES, CAUTIONS
amatanthus caudatus	dysentary, haematemesis, haematuria
borage (borago officinalis)	cardiac stimulant; toxic in high doses
castor oil (ricinus communis)	purgative, stimulate hair growth, now known to be toxic
chicory (cichorium intybus)	urine and liver disorders, abcesses
cochicum (alkaloid derived from lily family)	treatment for gout; highly toxic
cod liver oil	general tonic; non-toxic
costmary (impatiens balsamina)	cleansing wounds
cowslip (primula officinalis) (primrose family)	gout, paralysis, coughing, jaundice non-toxic
crosswort gentian (gentiana cruciata)	"cure all" but primarily used for gastrointestinal disturbances; non-toxic
devilsbit scabious (succisa pratensis)	variety of uses
Donovan's Solution (liquor arseni et hydrargyri iodidi)	made from equal parts arsenious iodide and mercuric iodide, used for syphilitic skin lesions, lymphadenitis, chronic joint diseases; toxic
Egyptian fig-tree (ficus sycomorus)	purgative; semi-toxic
foxglove (digitalus)	cardiac stimulant; still in use today but dangerous if used incorrectly
ground-pine (ajuga chamepitys) club moss family	apoplexy, vertigo, gout, antitoxin
heath speedwell (veronica officinalis)	bladder disorders, bronchial catarrh semi-toxic

Fatal Links

hemlock (Conium maculatum)	used externally for cooling in cases of erysipelas (an infection of mucous membranes) sedative, treatment for ulcers; antispasmodic and analgesic (pain relief); highly toxic; can cause paralysis, convulsions and death.
herb robert (geranium robertianum)	haemostatic
hyoscyamus (derived from henbane and other plants of the nightshade family)	anti-spasmodic, sedative; highly toxic
marjoram (origanum vulgare)	gallbladder disease, dropsy; still used as a seasoning
oil of sassafras	syphillis, skin diseases. Ingestion causes severe diarrhea, vomiting, and circulatory collapse; toxic
Prussian blue (compound of potassium chlorate and sulfuric acid reacting to potassium ferrocyanide and ferrous sulfate)	using for laundry blueing, in cloth dyeing, manufacturing inks and paints. Also used for variety of medical complaints; highly toxic
sulfur	fever, infection; high doses cause headache, myalgia and drowsiness
tannic acid	astringent; used in both tanning leather and medicine; can produce severe gastroenteritis with abdominal pain and is toxic to the liver
Turkscap lily (lilium martagon)	haemorrhoids and bladder disorders
wall germander (teucrium chamaedrys)	variety of uses; non-toxic, related to mint
water forget-me-not (myosotis palustris)	used for problems with the eyes

Appendix B
Toxins and Diseases: Comparitive Symptoms

Symptom	Cirrhosis, Hepatitis, Tuberculosis	Toxic Reaction	Manifestation in Beethoven ca.1818Δ	1827
weakness/ fatigue	C, H, T	Yes	Yes	Yes
frequent headaches	T*	Yes	Yes	Yes
weight loss	C	Yes	No	Yes
loss of appetite	H	Yes	No	Yes
nausea/ vomiting	C, H	Yes	Yes	Yes
impotence	C, T	No	?	?
loss of body hair	C	No	No	No?
vomiting blood	C	Yes	No	Yes
jaundice	C, H	Yes	No	Yes
spider-like blood vessels on the skin	C, H	No	No	No
decreased urine output	C	Yes	No	Yes
overall swelling	C, H	Yes	No	No

Fatal Links

Symptom	Cirrhosis, Hepatitis, Tuberculosis	Toxic Reaction	Manifestation in Beethoven ca.1818	1827
swelling of feet and legs		Yes	No	Yes
pain in area of the liver	C, H	Yes	Yes	Yes
hearing impairment/deafness		Yes	Yes**	Yes**
nosebleed	C°	No	No	Yes
bleeding gums	C°	No	No	No
reddening of the skin, flushing		Yes	?	Yes
pimples, (mouth area)		Yes	No	No
constipation	C	Yes	Yes	Yes
breast development in males	C	No	No	No
abdominal pain	C, H, T*	Yes	Yes	Yes
itching		Yes	Yes	Yes
noticeable change in disposition		Yes	Yes	Yes
disturbance in sleep rhythms		Yes	?	?
indigestion/ gaseousness	C	Yes	Yes	Yes
clubbing of fingers/toes	C	No	No	No
bronzing of the skin		Yes	Yes***	Yes***
difficulty breathing	T	Yes	Yes	Yes

Appendix B

Symptom	Cirrhosis, Hepatitis, Tuberculosis	Toxic Reaction	Manifestation in Beethoven ca.1818	1827	
persistent cough (usually dry)	T	Yes	Yes	Yes
muscles of the calf subject to fatty degeneration		Yes	No	No
increase in weight, bloating, ascites or corpulence	C	Yes	No	Yes abdomen
increase in the size of the liver, subject to degeneration	C, H	Yes	No	Yes
sensitivity of eyes to light; conjunctivitis	H	Yes	Yes	Yes
tendency to pleurisy	H, T	Yes	?	Yes
sensation of fever without rise in body temperature	H, T	Yes	Yes†	Yes†
icy cold legs		Yes	No	No
sweating, often heavy	T	Yes	No	Yes
tachycardia (rapid heartbeat)		Yes	?	?
severe hoarseness		Yes	No	Yes
quick & irregular pulse		Yes	?	?
extreme thirst		Yes	Yes	Yes
severe diarrhea		Yes	Yes	Yes
severe pain throughout body/joints "rheumatism"	H, T	Yes	Yes	Yes

Fatal Links

It should be remembered that this list shows possible symptoms which *may* occur but this does not mean that all these symptoms *will* occur. Not everyone will exhibit all these symptoms, regardless of the cause of their pathology. For example, in rare cases of cirrhosis there are very few symptoms. Also the type and severity of symptoms noted in the Toxic Reaction column depend upon the dosage ingested by the person. One should also remember that stetoscopes were not invented until 1817 and were not regularly used even in 1827. Doctors had no means of determining blood pressure

Δ Beethoven did not suffer from cirrhosis in 1818.

* Tuberculosis can infect other organs besides the lungs. This symptom can occur in this event.

** Deafness caused by other factors may have masked this symptomwhich was evident in both Napoleon and his son.

*** Beethoven's dark complexion and tendency to tan may have masked this.

† We cannot know whether Beethoven actually suffered from fever or simply felt feverish; doctors did not regularly carry themometers.

° This symptom can manifest in advanced stages due to portal hypertension.

? The manifestation of this symptom was not noticed or reported by either Beethoven or his doctors. Where the symptom would have been obvious, such as enlarged mammary glands and yet were not noted, I have put "no." If the symptom was less obvious, as in the case of impotence, I have put a "?."

In the case of lost body hair, I have put a "No?" because there was one possible indication that Beethoven had sustained bodily hair loss. On the 28th of March, two days after Beethoven's death, J. Danhauser made a sketch and later an oil painting of Beethoven's hands clasping a cross. Although reports from earlier years tell us that Beethoven had black hair on the tops of his hands and on his knuckles, the sketch shows none at all. Possibly Danhauser did not think including hair on Beethoven's artistic hands was aesthetically pleasing; on the other hand (no Beethovenian pun intended) perhaps there was none there to sketch.

Appendix C
Post-Mortem on Ludwig van Beethoven
March 27, 1827

Note from Dr. Anton Neumayr:

> The original of the autopsy report was discovered among various documents removed from the Pathological-Anatomical Institute of the University of Vienna, and was reproduced for the first time in the Beethoven pathological study published in 1987 by Bankl and Jesserer. ... now we know with certainty that Dr. Johann Wagner, who performed the autopsy and dictated his report to a secretary, did not provide any synoptic diagnosis at the conclusion of his report. Instead, the report ends with *Sectio privata die 27 Martii MCCMXXVII Doktor Joh. Wagner, Assistent beym pathologischen Musäum.* Translation: "Private autopsy, the 27th of March, 1827, Doctor Johann Wagner, Assistant in the Pathological Museum."
>
> This is a final rebuff to all the writers and biographers who thought there must have been a concluding diagnostic statement and looked on its absence as evidence of possible deception and cover-up and thus grounds for suspecting that Beethoven might have had a venereal disease."[1]

It is still curious to me why there was no concluding diagnosis. Could there still have been a cover-up? Could Wagner have been directed not to report any evidence or suspicions to the effect that Beethoven had been poisoned? Or was the cause of death so obvious that the doctor found such a statement unnecessary? Since doctors report even on something as obvious as a fata gunshot wound, this seems unlikely. The findings of the autopsy are provided on the next page.

---

[1]Neumayr, 306

Fatal Links

Beethoven's Post-Mortem
March 27, 1827
(excluding report on Beethoven's ears)
Reported by specific body area, is as follows:

The entire body was emasciated, especially the arms and legs and covered with petechiae (minute red spots of blood just under the skin).

The lower abdomen was inflated and tense with an abnormal accumulation of serous fluid. Four quarts of cloudy greyish-brown liquid were spread throughout the abdominal cavity.

The liver was shrunken to half its volume; hard as leather, greenish-blue in color, infested with pea-sized nodules (macronodules) on its bumpy surface as well as inside the organ itself. All the blood vessels were narrow, thickened, and devoid of blood. [The large nodules contradicts the suggestion that Beethoven's cirrhotic condition was alcohol-induced.]

The gall-bladder contained a dark-brown liquid and numerous gritty gallstones.

The spleen was enlarged to twice the normal size and was black and rough.

The pancreas likewise was enlarged, similar to the spleen, its excretory duct the size of a quill.

The stomach and intestines were found to be inflated with air. [No other pathology was noted, which contradicts the suggestion that Beethoven suffered from Crohn's Disease.]

The kidneys were encased in an inch-thick capsule completely soaked by a cloudy brown liquid; their tissues were pale red and breaking up. Each kidney had a wart-sized chalky stone about the size of a split pea.

The rib cage and organs showed no significant abnormalities. [This is interesting since a severe cough was a long-time symptom of Beethoven's. A lack of fluid in the lungs contradicts the suggestion that he suffered from pneumonia.]

Appendix D
Malfatti's Report on the State of Health of the Duke of Reichstadt

(As reprinted in *Napoleon II: King of Rome*, by E. M. Oddie, 1932)

From the past sufferings, the medical treatment, and the observsations I have made, it appears:

I. That by reason of his extremely rapid growth and a remarkable unevenness in development, the Prince was in a state of general weakness which gave us some anxiety, particularly as to the state of his chest.

II. In consequence of the weakness of the chest, His Highness was easily affected by catarrhal troubles, and subject to an irritable cough, principally based in the trachea and bronchial tubes. The frequency of the local sufferings has, not without grave reason, alarmed the previous doctors. It is on this account that His Highness has been ordered to drink Seltzer water[1] and milk.

III. Besides the retarded development of the organs of the chest, I must also enter into the cause of his malady a discrasia of the cutaneous system. I have in fact found on different parts of the body, and particularly at the base of the skull the skin in such a condition as to suggest the beginning of a herpetic eruption. Even the hands of His Highness showed these anomalies, which one cannot attribute to simple chilblains. Suitable and frequent baths would react favourably on the discrasia.

---

[1] Unlike the seltzer with which the modern world is familiar, in the 19th century this water was obtained from the springs at Neider-Seltzers, Germany which had a high carbon dioxide content in its water. It was reputed to have curative value in treating various diseases and was very popular in the 19th century.

Such constitution of the exterior skin which could spread so easily to the internal membranes and particularly to the trachea and bronchial tubes might also, in the case of His Highness, account for the local disease in these organs. In all probability the discrasia of the skin is hereditary on the paternal side. At the present time, the anomalies in the development of the Duke of Reichstadt might lead one to hope for a change for the better and that the herpetic discrasia will clear up, little by little, as I hope it will, with the use of baths. Although as long as the Prince's development is not completed we must not lose sight of one or other cause as an accessory malady which might intervene during the epoch of growth, which would be very significant and dangerous both at present and in the future—which would to be feared because the prince has no exanthematic condition of the skin such as measles or scarlatina.

The Prince must avoid all great exertions and principally vocal ones and must be guarded against heat and cold and particularly against inclement weather, and must observe a strict regime.The vigilance cannot be too great if the Prince is to be saved those unpleasant symptoms, when we bear in mind his lively and impetuous temperament, so difficult to moderate.

I shall take, in consequence, the greatest care of the Prince and observe him, particularly in the Autumn when those symptoms might reappear easily, and shall direct his treatment and regime according to circumstances.

❦ **Appendix E** ❦
Excerpts from the Post Mortem Report
on the Dissection of the Corpse
of the Duke of Reichstadt

A. The body was emaciated. There were marks on his body showing that it had been rubbed with pomade émetique. On both arms were marks of blisters from poltices.

B. The blood vessels of the brain were full of dark blood. In the left ventricle, a half ounce of serous fluid was found and in the right ventricle, about one dram. At the base of the skull there was an additional ounce of serous fluid.

C. In the lungs there were innumerable sacs of matter which formed a scirruhs base carcinoma, containing ichorous fluid matter of a most foul odor. On the left lung was a large tubercule on the point of suppuration. The rest of the lung and the heart were normal. The thymus gland was enlarged, cartilaginous and hard, rough to the touch. The mucous membrane of the trachea was corroded on all sides, probably by the passage of the ichorous liquid leaving the lung.

D. The liver was enlarged but otherwise normal. The spleen likewise was enlarged, although the pancreas and gall bladder were healthy. The mesenteric glands were harder and larger than normal. Kidneys and bladder were healthy, although the left kidney was slightly enlarged.

The post mortem was signed by
Semlitsch, Royal and Imperial Court Physician
Johann Malfatti, Physician-in-Ordinary
Franz Wirer, M.D.
Joh. Fr. Edler von Hieber, Royal and Imperial Court Physician
Dr. Rinna, Royal and Imperial Court Physician
Dr. Zangerl, Royal and Imperial Physician to the Household and Actuary

Bibliography

Ackerknecht, Erwin, H., *A Short History of Medicine*, revised edition, 1982, Johns Hopkins University Press, Baltimore.

Anderson, Emily, *The Letters of Beethoven*, Vols I-III, St. Martin's Press, New York, 1961

Albrecht, Theodore, *Letters to Beethoven and Other Correspondence*, Vols I-III, University of Nebraska Press, 1997

Arena, Jay M., *Poisoning: Toxicology, Symptoms and Treatment*, Charles C. Thomas Publisher, Springfield, IL, 1970, revised 1996.

Aubry, Octave, *The King of Rome*, translated by Elizabeth Abbott, J.B. Lippincott, Co., 1932

Audebrand, Philibert, *Révélations sur la Mort du Duc de Reichstadt*, Paris, 1897

Bankl, and Jesserer, *Pathólogie Ludwig van Beethovens,* Vienna, 1970.

Barsley, Michael, *The Other Hand: an Investigation into the Sinister History of Left-Handedness,* Hawthorn Books, Inc., New York, 1967

Berkow, Robert, editor, *Merck Manual of Medical Information*, Merck Research Laboratories, Whitehouse Station, NJ, 1997.

Breuning, Gerhard von, *Memories of Beethoven: Aus der Schwartzspanierhaus,* (In the House of the Blackrobed Spaniards), edited by Maynard Solomon, Cambridge University Press, 1995

Brook-Shepherd, Gordon, *The Austrians: a Thousand-Year Odyssey,* Carroll & Graf Publishers, Inc., New York, 1996

Burns, Leigh Ann, Meade, B. Jean, and Munson, Albert E., "Toxic Responses of the Immune System," *Casarett and Doull's Toxicology,* McGraw-Hill, 1996, p. 355-377.

Emerson, Donald E., *Metternich and the Political Police: Security and Subversion in the Hapsburg Monarchy (1815-1830)* , Matinus Hijhoff, The Hague, 1968

Erickson, Raymond, "Vienna in Its European Context," *Schubert's Vienna,* Raymond Erickson, editor, Yale University Press, New Haven & London, 1997.

Fournier, Auguste, *Die Geheimpolizei auf dem Wiener Kongress,* Vienna, 1913.

Frodl, Gerbert, "Viennese Biedermeier Painting," *Schubert's Vienna,* Raymond Erickson, editor, Yale University Press, New Haven & London, 1997.

Goyer, Robert A., "Toxic Effects of Metals," *Casarett and Doull's Toxicology,* McGraw-Hill, 1996, p. 691-698.

Hanson, Alice M., "Vienna, City of Music," *Schubert's Vienna,* Raymond Erickson, editor, Yale University Press, New Haven & London, 1997.

Heindl, Waltraud, "People, Class Structure, and Society," *Schubert's Vienna,* Raymond Erickson, editor, Yale University Press, New Haven & London, 1997.

Bibliography

Hickel, Erika, "Das Kaiserliche Gesundheitsamt (Imperial Health Office) and the Chemical Industry in Germany During the Second Empire: Partners or Adversaries?" *Drugs and Narcotics in History,* edited by Roy Porter and Mikulás Teich, Cambridge University Press, 1995.

Hilmar, Ernst, "Vienna's Schubert," *Schubert's Vienna,* Raymond Erickson, editor, Yale University Press, New Haven & London, 1997.

Holloway, S.W.F., "The Regulation of the Supply of Drugs in Britain before 1868," *Drugs and Narcotics in History,* edited by Roy Porter and Mikulás Teich, Cambridge University Press, 1995.

Klaassen, Curtis, Amdur, Mary O, and Doull, John, *Casarett and Doull's Toxicology: the Basic Science of Poisons,* fifth edition, Mc-Graw-Hill Health Professions Division, New York, 1996.

Kohler, Karl-Heinz and Grita Herre, *Ludwig van Beethovens Konversationhefte,* Vols. 1-8, Leipzig:VEB Deutscher Verlag für Musik, 1972, usv.

Kraehe, Enno, "The Congress of Vienna," *Schubert's Vienna,* Raymond Erickson, editor, Yale University Press, New Haven & London, 1997.

Kubinyi, Victor von, *The King of Rome,* Knickerbocker Press, New York, 1907.

Maehle, Andreas-Holger, "Pharmacological Experimentation with Opium in the Eighteenth Century," *Drugs and Narcotics in History,* edited by Roy Porter and Mikulás Teich, Cambridge University Press, 1995.

Marek, George, *Beethoven: Biography of a Genius,* Funk & Wagnalls: New York, 1969.

Mez-Mangold, Lydia, *A History of Drugs,* F. Hoffmann-La Roche & Co. Ltd., Basle, Switzerland, 1971.

Moslen, Mary Treinen, "Toxic Responses of the Liver," *Casarett and Doull's Toxicology*, McGraw-Hill, 1996, p. 403-409.

Musulin, Stella, *Vienna in the Age of Metternich*, Westview Press: Boulder, Colorado, 1975

Nettl, Paul, *Beethoven Encyclopedia*, New York: Citadel Press, 1956, 1994

Neumayr, Anton, *Music and Medicine Vol. II: Hadyn, Mozart, Beethoven and Schubert*, Medi-Ed Press, Illinois, 1994

Oddie, E. M., *Napoleon II: King of Rome*, Low, Marston & Co, London, 1932

Palferman, T. G., "Beethoven: Medicine, Music, and Myths," *International Journal of Dermatology*, Vol. 33, No. 9, September, 1994, p. 664-671.

Plantinga, Leon, "'Classic' and 'Romantic,' Beethoven and Schubert," *Schubert's Vienna*, Raymond Erickson, editor, Yale University Press, New Haven & London, 1997.

Rice, Robert H., and Cohen, David E., "Toxic Responses of the Skin," *Casarett and Doull's Toxicology*, McGraw-Hill, 1996, p. 529-543

Scherman, Thomas K, and Biancolli, Louis, editors, The Beethoven Companion, Doubleday & Co., Garden City, NY, 1972.

Schindler, Anton, *Beethoven as I Knew Him*, edited by Donald McArdle, translated by Constance S. Jolly, The University of North Carolina Press, Chapel Hill, 1966.

Shearer, Patricia D., "The Deafness of Beethoven: an Audiologic and Medical Overview," *The American Journal of Otology*, Vol. 11, No. 2, September, 1990, p. 370-374.

Slinn, Judy, "Research and Development in the Pharmaceutical Industry from the Nineteenth Century to the 1960s," *Drugs and Narcotics in History*, edited by Roy Porter and Mikulás Teich, Cambridge University Press, 1995.

Bibliography

Solomon, Maynard, *Beethoven*, Harvard University Press: Cambridge, 1977, revised edition, 1998.

Sonneck, O.G., *Beethoven: Impressions by His Contemporaries*, New York: 1926, revised, 1967.

Thayer, Alexander Wheelock, *The Life of Beethoven Vols. I-III*, edited by Henry E. Krehbel, The Beethoven Association, New York, 1921.

Thayer, Alexander Wheelock, *The Life of Beethoven Vols. I-II*, edited by Elliot Forbes, Princeton: 1970.

Weider, Ben, *Assassination at St. Helena Revisited*, John Wiley & Sons, Inc., New York, 1995

Weisberger, R. William, *Speculative Freemasonry and the Enlightenment: a Study of the Craft in London, Paris, Prague and Vienna*, East European Monographs, Boulder CO, Distributed by Colombia University Press, 1993

Internet Sources: www.healthanswers.com/database: cirrhosis
www.pages.prodigy.com/hepc: diseases of the liver
www.fkmedical.com: liver cirrhosis

Index

Alexander I, Tsar of Russia, 58, 167
Allgemeine Zeitung, 51-52
Amenda, Karl, 50
antimony, 11-12, 204, 209-211
Apponyi, Count, 184-185
Aqua toffana, 13-14
arsenic, 7-10, 15-17, 22, 172, 186, 209-211
Austria, history. 27-44

Bacciochi, Elisa Bonaparte, 84, 172, 181, 194
Bach, Johann Baptist, 45-46, 136, 141, 155
Barthélemy, 171
Beethoven, Caspar Carl, 23, 69-73, 77-80, 196
Beethoven, Johann van, 5, 45, 60, 92, 99, 112, 120, 131-135, 137, 145-152, 157, 178, 201
Beethoven, Johanna Reiss, 5, 23, 68, 69-82, 83, 112, 117, 122, 125-127, 130-131, 137, 151-144, 153, 196, 198-199, 201, 203
Beethoven, Karl, 5, 23, 45, 48, 68, 72-79, 81-82, 92-93, 98-100, 102, 104, 112-113, 115-139, 141-144, 147-148, 152, 161-162, 195-199, 201-202
Beethoven, Ludwig, and the aristocracy, 52-54; drinking habits, 8-9, 95, 106-107, 112; friends, 56-60; and England, 50-51; hair, xiv-xv, 8 ;mental deterioration, 22-24; and Napoleon, 61-63; outspokenness, 47-50; post-mortem, 213-214; reading habits, 51-52; and secret societies, 54-56

Beethoven, Therese Obermayer5, 70, 99, 112, 134-135, 139, 145, 149-154, 158
Bernadotte, Johann, 58
Bernard, Joseph, 57-58, 142-143
Bertolini, Dr. Andreas, 24, 71, 86-89, 190-191, 199, 204
Bihler, Dr. Johann, 18, 24
Blöchlinger, 57, 141
Bonaparte, Jerome, 63
Bonaparte, King Louis, 59, 84
Bonaparte, Napoleon, xi-xiv, 2, 7-8, 15, 22, 25, 34, 37-40, 55, 58-63, 87, 90, 97, 100-102, 106-108, 147, 165-166, 169-170, 172, 179, 181-182, 190, 193-194, 197
Börnstein, Heinrich, 36-37
Bourbons, House of, 40, 65, 167-168, 172, 188
Branhofer, Dr Anton, 92, 202
Brauchle, Johann, 17
Brentano, Antonie, 60-61, 156
Brentano, Franz, 19, 91
Breuning, Gerhard von, 109-110, 145-146, 148
Breuning, Stephen von, 109, 118, 130-131, 135-137, 139, 147-148, 157, 203
Brinvillier, Marquise de, 14-15, 104-105
Brown, John, 3
Brunswick, Charlotte, 23
Brunswick, Franz, 53, 177
Brunswick, Josephine, 53, 177
Brunswick, Therese, 53, 177
Bursy, Dr. Karl von, 23

Camerata, Napoleone, 172
Carbonari, 34-35, 55, 155, 197
censorship, in Austria, 32-34, 42-43, 51, 59
Cherubini, Madame, 50
cholera epidemic of 1831, 88-89, 192
Christus am Ölmberg, 58
cirrhosis of the liver, xiii, 10-11, 95, 195, 209-211
Coffin, Albert I., 2
Congress of Vienna, 35, 39-40, 64, 84, 1948
Corolan Overture, 58
Crohn's Disease, 111
Czerny, Carl, 39, 61-62

Der Wanderer, 52
Deschamps, Colonel, 172
Diabelli Variations, 157-158
Dietrichstein, Moritz, 167-171, 173, 175-180, 186-187, 200

Erdödy, Marie (Nizcky) 16-17, 19, 23, 85, 85 n.3, 130, 176, 197
Erdödy, Marie the younger (Mimi), 85 n.3, 130, 138
Erdödy, Peter, 85, n.3, 176
Eroica Symphony, No. 3, 58, 61
Ertmann, Dorothea, 19

Fidelio, 60
Forshufvud, Sten, xi, xvi
Fouché, 38
Frank, Johann Peter, 84
Franz I, Emperor of Austria, xii, 31, 33, 37-38, 40, 47, 49-50, 53, 59, 66, 78, 90, 165-167, 169, 173, 175-180, 187, 197
Freemasonry, 34-35, 55-56, 67, 163

Galvani, Luigi, 84, 84 n.1
Gampf, Prussian Minister, 42
Gassner, Dr., 163-164
Gebauer, F. X., 56
Gentz, Frederick, 36, 39-40, 61, 167-168, 173
Giannatasio del Rio, 73-77, 79-80, 141
Gleichtenstein, Ignaz, 85-86
Goethe, Johann, 23, 58, 61, 65
Gougand, Gaspard, 109
Grillparzer, Franz, 33, 41-43, 57, 59-61, 68

Hager, Baron Franz, 30-31
Heiligenstadt Testament, 116
Henry Peter, Lord Brougham
hepatitis, 9, 112, 209-211
Hofbauer, Joseph, 70, 131, 141, 143
Holz, Karl, 57, 97, 100, 113, 118, 120-121, 123, 126-127, 129-131, 135, 147, 157, 159, 161-164, 202
Hotschevar, Jakob, 77-78, 137-138, 194, 203

Illuminati, 197

Jahn, Otto, 147, 162
Jenger, Johann, 105, 132
John, Archduke of Austria, 173
Joseph II, Emperor of Austria, 27-29, 34, 52, 54, 59
Josephinists, 54-55, 57, 67, 197

Kanka, Joseph, 19
Kant, Emmanuel, 65
Karlsbad Decrees, 41
König Ottokars Glück und Ende, 42-43
Koschak-Pachler, Marie, 105, 132
Kotzebue, August, 58

Index

Kyd, Alexander, 86-87

Landrecht, 72-74, 76-78, 197
Las Cases, Emmanuel, 109, 171, 186
lead, 11, 13, 195
Leber, Peter von, 72
Leopold II, Emperor of Austria, 28-29, 40
Lichnowsky, 53, 146, 175, 177, 179-180, 200
Liguorians, 129
liver disease, 9-11, 209-212
Lobkowitz, 176
London Philharmonic Society, 137-138
Louis XVIII, 40, 167, 170, 185, 187

Magistrat, 77-78, 129
Maison, Marshall, 172
Malfatti, Anna, 85-86
Malfatti, Johann, xii-xiii, 5, 20, 24, 66, 8390, 96, 102, 103-110, 111-112, 113, 146, 139, 159, 165, 173, 181-189, 191-192, 194-195, 197-199, 202-205, 215-217
Malfatti, Therese, 85-88, 197
Maria Ludovica, Empress of Austria, 176, 197
Maria Therese, Empress of Austria, 27
Marie-Louise, Archduchess of Austria, xii, 165-170, 172, 175, 183-186
medicines, 19th century, 1-5
Méneval, 167, 189
mercury, 11, 12
Metternich, Clemens, 23, 31, 39-43, 47, 51-52, 54, 60-61, 66, 83, 85, 90, 165-166, 170, 172-173, 182, 184-185, 187-189, 191, 195, 197, 202
Milder-Hauptman, Anna, 60
Missa Solemnis, 66, 179
Montbel, Count de, 188

Montesquiou, Madame de, 168, 189
Montholon, Count Charles de, 107, 171-172
Montluisant, Captain Bruno de, 127
Moscheles, Ignaz, 137
Mozart, Wolfgang, 13-14, 34, 53, 56, 197
Müller, W. C., 48-49

Neate, Charles, 19
Neipperg, Gustav, 167, 175
Niemetz, 122, 143
Ninth Symphony, 56, 65-66, 92, 200
Noverraz, 109

Obenaus, Baron, 189
Obermayr, Leopold, 145, 149
Obervormundschaft, 64
Ode to Joy, 56, 65-66, 200
Oliva, Franz, 57, 72

Palffy, Ferdinand, 176-177, 197
Palmer, Dr. William, 83
Pasqualati, Johann von, 72, 108
Pergen, Anton, 28-30, 33-34
Peters, Karl, 55, 78-79, 141
poisons, 1-5, 9-24, 71
Prokesch, 173, 189

Reichstadt, Duke of, xi-xiv, 2, 4-5, 22, 25, 63, 88-90, 97, 100, 102, 108, 165-173, 179, 181-195, 197, 199-200, 204-205, 215-217
Ries, Ferdinand, 91, 147, 157-158
Rochlitz, Friedrich, 48, 158
Rudolph, Archduke of Austria, 17-20, 53, 66, 91, 156, 180

Salieri, Antonio, 14
Sallaba, Matthias von, 14
Saurau, 34, 36
Schiller, Friedrich, 65-66
Schindler, Anton, 3, 43, 45-47, 49, 52, 54-57, 63-64, 66, 97, 103-106, 110, 113, 121, 123, 130, 132, 134-135, 137, 146-148, 150-151, 155-164, 175, 177, 202
Schlemmer, Matthias, 116, 118-120, 122-123, 126
Schnabel, George, 42
Schneider, Eulogius, 58-59
Schneller, Julius, 35-36, 59
Schubert, Franz, 27, 54, 179
Schutz, Edward, 50
Scott, Sir Walter, 39, 61
Secret Cipher Chancellery, 32-33
Secret Police, 28
Sedlnitzky, Joseph, 31, 34, 36, 41-42, 51-52, 78-79, 138, 170
Seyfried, Ignaz, 48, 52, 133
Shreyvogel, Joseph, 41, 59-60
Simrock, Nikolaus, 32, 50
Smart, Sir George, 162
Sonnenfels, Joseph, 57
Staudenheim, Jakob, 20, 91, 181, 202, 204
Streicher, Nanette, 19-21, 23-24, 80-82
Stumpff, Johann, 50, 146
Sturm, Christopf, 65

Tagebuch, Beethoven's
Talleyrand,
Teyber, Anton, 49, 177-179, 200
Tofana, Julia, 13
Trémont, Baron Louis-Philippe, 63
Trenck von Tonder, Moritz, 60-61
Tuscher, Matthias von, 78

Velox, see Schneller

Wagner, Dr. Johann, 111, 213
Waldstein, 62-63
Wawruch, Dr. Andreas, 95-103, 105-110, 135, 164, 181, 202-203
Wegeler, Franz, 56, 97, 116, 158
West, Thomas, see Schreyvogel
Wiener Kunst und Industrie Comptoir, 57, 60
Wiener Zeitung, 30, 52, 57
Wildmann, Anna, 73

Zelter, Karl, 23
Zmeskall, Nikolaus, 18, 20-21, 76, 81-82, 177

Also by
Gail S. Altman.....

Beethoven:
a Man of His Word
Undisclosed Evidence for His Immortal Beloved

In 1977 American musicologist Maynard Solomon claimed he had solved the riddle of Beethoven's mysterious "Immoral Beloved." Beethoven, Solomon claimed, had loved Antonie Brentano, the wife of a close friend.

This theory has long been accepted. It has been repeated as fact time and again, in encyclopedias, in textbooks, in college classrooms. Unfortunately, it is not true.

Unfortunately, too many theories do not get the scrutiny they deserve, and therefore are slipped into the realm of history where they do not rightfully belong.

Important documents have been overlooked or ignored. Information has been taken from its historical and literary context. And it has never been viewed with common sense.

Author Gail S. Altman examines this theory, and other myths revolving around Beethoven's life and love life, and shows that what is accepted very often is not the truth.

Available now from Amazon.com and Barnesandnoble.com or through your local bookstore.

Anubian Press
Auguste-Schöne Publishing
P.O. Box 12694 Centerville Station
Tallahassee, Florida 32317-2694